AF352675

Monsters on Maple Street

MONSTERS

ON

MAPLE STREET

The Twilight Zone
and the Postwar American Dream

DAVID J. BROKAW

Scholarly publisher for the Commonwealth,
serving Bellarmine University, Berea College, Centre
College of Kentucky, Eastern Kentucky University,
The Filson Historical Society, Georgetown College,
Kentucky Historical Society, Kentucky State University,
Morehead State University, Murray State University,
Northern Kentucky University, Spalding University,
Transylvania University, University of Kentucky,
University of Louisville, University of Pikeville, and
Western Kentucky University.

Editorial and Sales Offices: The University Press of Kentucky
663 South Limestone Street, Lexington, Kentucky 40508-4008
www.kentuckypress.com

Sections of the introduction, chapter 5 and chapter 6 were originally published in
History of Retailing and Consumption, 3:1, 38-52, as "The purchasing powerless:
postwar consumption in *The Twilight Zone*." Reprinted with permission by
Taylor & Francis Ltd, http://www.tandfonline.com.

Library of Congress Cataloging-in-Publication Data
Names: Brokaw, David J., author.
Title: Monsters on Maple Street : the Twilight Zone and the postwar
    American dream / David J. Brokaw.
Description: Lexington : The University Press of Kentucky, 2023. |
    Includes bibliographical references and index.
Identifiers: LCCN 2022060186 | ISBN 9780813197845 (hardcover) |
    ISBN 9780813197852 (pdf) | ISBN 9780813197869 (epub)
Subjects: LCSH: Twilight zone (Television program : 1959–1964) |
    Television programs—Social aspects—United States—History.
Classification: LCC PN1992.77.T87 B7625 2023 | DDC
    791.45/72—dc23/eng/20230203
LC record available at https://lccn.loc.gov/2022060186

For Janet, Andy, and Liz
Your love is always with me in and out of
The Twilight Zone

Contents

Introduction

The Twilight Zone, A Socially Critical Fantasy

The seventeenth episode of *The Twilight Zone,* "The Fever," tells the story of Franklin and Flora Gibbs, a married couple that has won an all-expenses-paid trip to Las Vegas, Nevada, for three days and two nights (S1, e17). As they become acquainted with the casino and hotel where they will be staying, Franklin is noticeably uncomfortable amid the extreme hedonism, greed, and gambling, decrying that a vacation spent in the casinos is "a miserable, terrible waste of time." Flora, however, is more than excited to be there and pleads: "Oh, Franklin, try to enjoy it, won't you?" After receiving some more admonishment from Franklin, she puts a nickel in one of the slot machines, to no avail. Feeling somewhat vindicated after his wife's gambling failure, Franklin tells her that he is going to head up to the room. But before he can get to the elevators, a drunk stranger grabs him and gives him a nickel. After some resistance, Franklin reluctantly places the coin in the machine, slowly pulls the lever, and immediately hears the clinking of coins—his very first attempt at gambling is a success. His initial excitement, however, is soon replaced by sober reflection, as he explains to his wife that unlike so many Vegas dupes, he knows when to stop, and the couple retires for the evening.

But Franklin cannot sleep. He lies on his back, his hands clasped behind his head, while he repeatedly hears his name, "Franklin," in a raspy tone mixed with the sound of tinkling coins—it is "the voice" of the slot machine beckoning him downstairs. He gets up from bed, returns to the slot machine, and becomes so infatuated with winning the jackpot that he pulls the lever again and again until the next morning. When Flora tries to gently suggest he get some sleep, he only becomes more incensed: "I'm concerned with this . . . this machine! It's inhuman the way it lets you win a little and then takes it all back. It teases you! It holds out promises and weasels you! It sucks you in. . . . This machine it mocks me. . . . It's got to pay off sooner or later. It's just got to,

"

Room service at this hour? Franklin opens the door to find the slot machine in the hallway, beckoning him to keep gambling. Still from "The Fever" (21:03)

I tell you!" The scant intermittent rewards, however, do not indicate any sense of mechanized morality or ethical fair play.

Finally, at eight o'clock in the morning, the machine jams. Franklin starts screaming at the silent, indifferent metal contraption to give him back his dollar. Sweaty, broke, and psychologically shattered, he charges the machine, knocking it onto the carpeted casino floor. After security escorts him up to his room, Franklin, still unable to sleep, anxiously explains to Flora how the machine actually broke down purposefully because it knew he was about to hit the jackpot: "It's not even a machine, Flora. It's an entity. It's a thing with a mind and a will of its own!" Immediately thereafter, the raspy slot machine once again calls out for Franklin, and Franklin darts around the room, screaming, "It's chasing me! It's following me! It's trying to get me, Flora!" His wife, in vain, admonishes him that nothing is, in fact, there. Completely over-come by his delusions, Franklin retreats backward and crashes out of his hotel room window to his death.

"The Fever" is a quintessential example of *The Twilight Zone*'s social drama and commentary on the pursuits of pleasure, comfort, and wealth that epitomized the postwar American Dream. A classic middle-class, white, midwestern American couple is given the chance to vacation in the ultimate geographical location and expression of American consumerism and abundance: Las Vegas. Deliberately setting the episode in a casino, which thrives on exploiting the wealth of tourists, speaks to postwar affluence and the anxieties that frequently came with it. Coming on the heels of the Great Depression, many Americans, accustomed to penny-pinching and saving like Franklin, were put off by what they saw as the excesses of consumerism, thrill-seeking, and loose-spending. Serling shows, however, that those same people could frequently be the most vulnerable to the deep and vast changes occurring in the postwar American economy, possibly bringing them to the point of addiction and even death. While Flora seems innocently curious and open to having some new experiences in this new world of consumerism, Franklin tries to resist the tide, only to drown underneath its irrepressible force.

This episode's third main character, the slot machine, also speaks to an increasingly pervasive phenomenon of postwar consumer culture—the spread of anthropomorphic consumer goods and technology. And just like actual humans, these goods could be a blessing or curse to the consumer, depending on who was using whom. Not surprisingly, marketers promised the wares they were selling, the experiences they were promising, and the technologies they were promoting were all more akin to benevolent angels freeing consumers from boredom, helping them achieve their deepest dreams and desires. As Ernest Dichter, the famed marketing researcher, articulated without any misgivings, "Things which surround us motivate us to a very large extent in our everyday behavior. They also motivate us as the goals of our life—the Cadillac that we are dreaming about, the swimming pool that we are working for, the kind of clothes, the kind of trips, and even the kind of people we want to meet from a social-status viewpoint are influencing factors. In the final analysis objects motivate our life probably at least as much as . . . childhood experiences." Dichter goes on to explain how humans are not only ones who have souls, but "all objects which surround us have souls of their own, have human qualities because they only exist in a human world. There are really . . . no raw inhuman objects."[1] The Vegas vacation, the slot machine seduction, and the addictive promises of a jackpot were all representations of Dichter's assessment that the objects that made up the consumer world of postwar America possessed souls all their own.

How their magnetic power should be wielded, however, was seemingly up for debate. While Dichter nonchalantly claimed that people who buy items to merely impress others are clearly being possessed by objects, rather than the possessors of them, he showed, albeit predictably, little thought over how one ought to overcome or escape such a consumeristic black hole.[2] While manufacturers and marketers were able to enjoy the luxury of indulgence more freely, eager consumers were to merely envy it. If consumers attempted to mirror the behaviors of major manufacturers and marketers, they would find themselves, like Franklin did, without any more nickels to play. This episode—which aired nearly three years before President John F. Kennedy outlined a consumer bill of rights and eight years before the Consumer Federation of America was founded—illustrates how Americans were still struggling to grasp how to handle such sweeping, profound influence on their lives as it related to manipulative mass marketing, specious product information, and the need for enhanced consumer protection.[3] Relatively uninitiated in the vast world of consumerism and luxury spending, many postwar Americans found themselves in the middle of a dreamlike scenario, only to see it quickly devolve into an inescapable nightmare.[4]

Rod Serling's *Twilight Zone* (1959–1964) emerged during a period of American history that has since become something of myth, legend, and lore. Popularly portrayed as a golden age when middle-class aspirations were within reach, suburban housing widely accessible, and the nuclear family perfectly contented, postwar America was more accurately characterized by profound cognitive and social dissonances. At a time when the Cold War was understood to be foremost a battle of ideas, psychological marketing promoted many different facets of the consumeristic American Dream. While market researchers plumbed the depths of American minds and explored their subconscious desires and insecurities to better promote goods, homes, and jobs, American consumers were generally not as well-acquainted with how psychological manipulations were affecting their rapidly changing world. Consequently, a fast-growing knowledge gap began to emerge between marketers and politicians on the one hand, and the consuming public on the other. *The Twilight Zone,* by focusing on the "dimension of mind," worked to raise viewers' awareness of how their minds represented fiercely contested ground for marketers and postwar policymakers alike. Rather than simply extolling the virtues of the consumeristic American Dream, *The Twilight Zone* sought to portray something very different—the American Nightmare. These nightmares, which covered a wide range of social topics, reveal a need to look more deeply into this relationship between social criticism, public intellectual thought, and the development, as well as the potential, of popular television content.

The Twilight Zone stood out as a unique program when compared to most television content at the time. By the late fifties, programming was mostly dominated by westerns, cop shows, family sitcoms, and game shows, making *The Twilight Zone* an exception in *TV Guide* lineups. The increasingly strained relations between the Soviets and Americans and the heightening of the Cold War pressured sponsors, networks, and writers alike to promote the American way of life rather than critique it. During this time, the Federal Communications Commission even changed its definition of *public interest* from one that included creative experimentation, minimal advertising, and inclusion of minority tastes to one that sought to legitimate the status quo and praise the values of capitalism.[5]

In this consumption-fueled age, nearly 90 percent of American homes had TV sets by the end of the 1950s, making television the premier medium for communicating with the widest possible audience. Throughout the decade, however, it remained far from clear how exactly the medium should be used. Early TV executives like Sylvester "Pat" Weaver, president of NBC from 1953 to 1955, desired television to not merely entertain and advertise but to offer viewers high-quality and enriching cultural experiences. He worked to ensure that NBC aired live performances of symphony orchestras, Italian operas, and Shakespearean dramas. At the same time, CBS, partially owing to the regulations set forth by the Fairness Doctrine of 1949, aired acclaimed news broadcasts featuring Edward R. Murrow, who frequently covered controversial subject matter. In his program *See It Now*, Murrow famously zeroed in on McCarthyism providing viewers the opportunity to more clearly understand how McCarthy manipulated popular fears for political gain while he destroyed the lives and careers of others in the process. In the television documentary *Harvest of Shame*, Murrow revealed the profoundly exploitative conditions agricultural laborers had to experience. Television audiences, in other words, were given opportunities to better understand the real conditions of the world in which they lived.

Networks sought to make early American television educational not only in its news broadcasts, live theater, and musical performances but in a lot of its creative dramatic content as well. From Reginald Rose's legal dramas, *Twelve Angry Men* and *The Defenders*, to the *US Steel Hour's* productions, such as *The Two Worlds of Charlie Gordon*, which dramatized the treatment of the mentally disabled, postwar television writers often tackled controversial social issues with gusto. Even Paddy Chayefsky's popular 1953 teleplay *Marty*, seemingly a simple love story, presented powerful social commentary, spurning commercialized ideals of glamour, beauty, and family life in its casting. In Chayefsky's own words, part of his motivation for writing a romance about a butcher who refers to himself as a "fat little man," and a woman whom the other characters called a "dog," was to challenge certain assumptions, including the notion that "love is simply a matter of physical attraction." The characters' far-from-idealistic appearances, occupations, and relationships with friends and family members struck a chord with audiences, as did the awkward, bumbling romance that developed between them. However, while letters flooded in from home viewers praising *Marty*, marketers had a clear interest in seeing that pedestrian romantic tales that showcased the "marvelous world of the ordinary," with no clear connection to the "magic" of consumerism, would be less frequently broadcast in the future.[6] As historian Andrew Falk has convincingly argued, "the very same institutional forces that initially welcomed controversial themes later restrained them" in order to promote "anticommunism, unfettered capitalism, and a national image of exceptionalism."[7] And while Chayefsky abandoned writing for TV and went on to harshly criticize the inner operations of television in his 1976 film *Network*, other writers, including Reginald Rose and Rod Serling, contributed to the medium into the sixties and beyond.

As anthology dramas dwindled, episodic series proliferated. Sitcoms, westerns, and cop shows with consistent characters and predictable storylines represented a safe "variation of an approved ritual" and soon became the preferred standard of sponsors. As name brands became that much more visible to home audiences, sponsors feared the consequences of alienating potential consumers—associating one's product with a controversial program represented a risk fewer and fewer seemed willing to make. Additionally, programming with clear, simple resolutions at the end helped to reinforce marketing that promised consumers their product would be the definite answer to their problems no matter how complex. As media historian Erik Barnouw has explained, "Most advertisers were selling magic. . . . In their commercials there was always a solution as clear-cut as the snap of a finger: the problem could be solved by a new pill, deodorant, toothpaste, shampoo, shaving lotion, hair tonic, car, girdle, coffee, muffin recipe, or floor wax. The solution always had finality."[8] Amid advertising that always had clear solutions, television content that featured easily resolved conflicts fit with ease.

Conflict arose between sponsors and creative writers, however, when television scripts dealt with real-life problems and made them appear complicated and not so easily resolvable. Concerned about this phenomenon, Serling noted in 1957, "We're developing a new citizenry. One that will be very selective about cereals and automobiles, but won't be able to think."[9] Complex, thought-provoking, socially conscious, and open-ended dramas epitomized by Serling's early teleplays and most episodes of *The Twilight Zone* made advertising content seem absurd or even fraudulent. Consequently, stories that offered nuanced, complex, or even just realistic depictions of anything from family life to foreign policy became increasingly endangered.[10] As Alan Nadel has explained, "That television omitted, ignored, or distorted just about everything in American life is less surprising than that it did so at the same time it touted itself as the definitive source of 'reality.'"[11] The truth was, television was actively divorcing Americans from reality. For the millions of Americans struggling to navigate the realities of postwar life, television programming seemed to mostly offer a variety of temporary escapes and invitations to consume more merchandise.

Another crucial component of 1950s television detaching Americans from their real world was the overwhelming whiteness and conspicuous lack of racial diversity on the screen. In many ways, postwar television exemplified Adilifu Nama's concept regarding science fiction, namely how the "structured absence" of nonwhite characters served as "the symbolic wish fulfillment of America's staunchest advocates of white supremacy."[12] Nonwhite performers would, by and large, be structurally absent from the vast majority of television programming throughout the postwar period, particularly in lead roles. Some short-lived exceptions to this dominant trend included *The Hazel Scott Show* (1950), *The Amos 'n' Andy Show* (1951–1953), and *The Nat King Cole Show* (1956–1957). Hazel Scott was the first African American to host a nationally syndicated television program. With a backing band that included Charles Mingus and Max Roach, Scott's show achieved considerable acclaim, airing three times per week because of its growing popularity. However, when Scott's name appeared in *Red Channels,* the notorious booklet that included the names of supposed Communist sympathizers, the popular series was canceled. Despite Scott's best efforts, including an appearance before HUAC to clear her name, the damage was already done, sealing her program's fate. Several years later, *The Amos 'n' Andy Show* led to civil rights protests and the NAACP calling for the show's cancellation due to its offensive and demeaning portrayal of African Americans. Ultimately, however, the show was cancelled because CBS also feared the ire of white viewers who objected to having any portrayal of Black Americans at all on TV. *The Nat King Cole Show* featured a host brimming with musical talent, much like Hazel Scott, as it also featured renowned stars such as Eartha Kitt, Ella Fitzgerald, and Tony Bennett, many of whom performed for little to no pay because of the show's lack of sponsorship. Eventually, without a national sponsor willing to fund a program hosted by an African American, which made it inherently controversial to many white viewers, the show was cancelled.

In the pursuit of "nonthreatening" material that supported the status quo of racialized consumerism and white supremacy, the mere appearance of a racial minority on television was consistently deemed too much controversy for sponsor, network, and audience. This structured absence of nonwhite Americans helped to guarantee the declaration of Ralph Ellison's protagonist would remain something of a cultural standard: "I am an invisible man . . . simply because people refuse to see me. . . . You wonder whether you aren't simply a phantom in other people's minds . . . a figure in a nightmare which the sleeper tries with all his strength to destroy."[13] In addition, merely alluding to how ethnic, racial, and sexual differences continually shaped larger social inequities would also be largely consigned to the realm of invisible realities. As Richard Dyer later explained, "white power secures its dominance by seeming not to be anything in particular."[14] Making "white" the default norm that everyone needed to relate back to, television content ensured that "whiteness" would be everywhere but would also be difficult to really *see* and, therefore, critique. The conspicuously limited presence and forced absence of many nonwhite Americans in participating in the American Dream led Malcolm X to conclude in 1964, "I don't see any American dream; I see an American nightmare."[15] This racially restrictive, nightmarish version of the American Dream did not just limit its participants, but it also denied potential cocreators. In this sense, the American Dream lacked creative refinement, redefinition, revision, and reshaping from nonwhite visionaries and dreamers, for it meant not just barring most nonwhite Americans from the consumeristic dream itself but excluding them from the essential process of defining and redefining the contents, meaning, and purpose of the American Dream. In this sense, the dream ensured its own haunting.

Rod Serling's *Twilight Zone* represented a compromise between a creative writer and the dominant trends of his day. In Serling's own career, the show was a marked shift from dramatic realism to fantasy, horror, and science fiction. Prior to creating *The Twilight Zone,* he was already a household name, garnering three Emmy Awards for his teleplays *Patterns* (1955), *Requiem for a Heavyweight* (1956), and *The Comedian* (1957). The three provided a critical, dramatic look at the worlds of big business, sports, and entertainment. However, as TV began to shift away from critical content, some of Serling's scripts exhibited the impact of censorship and "pre-censorship," when writers deliberately conceal or leave out certain details to avoid conflict with sponsors and networks.

In 1956, for example, Serling wrote a teleplay for the *Steel Hour* titled *Noon on Doomsday*, based on the vicious murder of Emmett Till, who had allegedly flirted with a white woman, and the subsequent mistrial that took place in the Mississippi of 1955. Not only were Till's killers, J. W. Milam and Roy Bryant, acquitted of their crimes, they later described the gruesome details of how they kidnapped and brutally murdered the visiting fourteen-year-old Chicago boy. In the January 24, 1956, issue of *Look* magazine, they recounted how after they kidnapped Till and threatened him, the young boy emphasized how he was just as good as they are and that he had "had" white women before, adding that his grandmother was also white. Till's frank, unapologetic discussion of miscegenation was too much to bear for Bryant and Milam, however. Milam recounted in the *Look* interview, "As long as I live and can do anything about it, n——s are gonna stay in their place. N——s ain't gonna vote where I live. . . . They ain't gonna go to school with my kids. And when a n—— gets close to mentioning sex with a white woman, he's tired o' livin.' I'm likely to kill him."[16] After repeatedly pistol-whipping Till, Bryant and Milam recounted how they then stole a seventy-four-pound cotton gin fan, even though they were slightly concerned they might get caught for doing so. They said nothing, however, about being worried that they might eventually be brought to justice for the murder. Their presumptive overconfidence was soon vindicated, however, after they shot Till in the head with a .45 handgun, then tied his dead body to the barbed wire gin fan and rolled it into the muddy waters of the Tallahatchie River. In 2007, Carolyn Bryant, the target of Till's alleged advances, explained in an interview that the story she told at the trial was not based on actual events but was instead filled with "Black Beast" rapist imagery, a trope all too familiar to every white man sitting on the jury. Regarding Till grabbing her around the waist and uttering sexually explicit language, she simply stated, "that part's not true." Bryant concluded, "Nothing that boy did could ever justify what happened to him."[17] And in 2022, an August 1955 warrant for the arrest of J. W. Milam as well as Roy and Carolyn Bryant was discovered in the basement of a Mississippi courthouse—it was never served.[18]

Television writers like Serling proved no match for this vast web of mass-marketed, popular racist imagery, false testimonies, and unified injustice. After Emmett Till's corpse was recovered from the river, his mother insisted on having an open casket funeral, back in Chicago, to display the horrifying condition of her son's body, hoping to raise the public's racial consciousness. ABC and US Steel, however, proved to have significantly less resolve amid growing pressure. Before Serling's teleplay aired, news of the upcoming program led to an outpouring of thousands of threatening letters from southern White Citizen Councils, raising public relations concerns for US Steel and ABC, both of which did not want to upset any viewers or potential consumers, including unapologetic white supremacists. Thirty editors went to work and changed the setting of the drama and removed from the script everything that might even suggest the South, including the word *lynch* and Coca-Cola products.[19] Serling later sardonically explained how the "locale was changed from the South to New England, and I'm convinced they would have gone up to Alaska or the North Pole using Eskimos . . . except I suppose the costume problem was of sufficient severity not to attempt it."[20] Serling later confessed how the script actually "suffered from its inception from the overall censorship imposed upon it long before the United States Steel Company got a look at it. . . . If we were to tell this story in black and white, it would have never been produced. And the terms of television censorship are such it would have been ridiculous to try."[21] The combined forces of Serling's self-censorship and the sponsors' forced revisions meant that commenting on real contemporary events and issues on television was a near impossibility.

After attempts to write socially conscious scripts like *Noon on Doomsday* fell short, Serling made a career move by concealing social criticism within fantasy and science fiction stories. He believed that dealing in fantasy would enable him to tackle social issues, albeit in a metaphorical and veiled manner, and at least partially uphold what he believed was the chief role of the writer: to "menace the public's conscience." He further emphasized, speaking before the Library of Congress in 1968, that writers "must see the arts as a vehicle of social criticism," and in doing so, endeavor to highlight the most vital issues of their time.[22] In this limited way, Serling sought to use television as a means to reframe popular portrayals of white Americans' wish-fulfillments as nightmares rather than aspirational dreams. And, in doing so, he attempted to raise critical thought at the exact time the medium generally worked to limit critical thinking and promote stereotyping. Amid programming and advertising that promoted the commodity-based American Dream and largely ignored social issues, Serling reminded Americans that a commodity-based existence was not only shallow but even perilous. Excessive dreaming without an occasional nightmare could be bad for the national psyche. His next stop was *The Twilight Zone*.

Serving as the executive producer for Cayuga Productions, Rod Serling personally authorized every episode of *The Twilight Zone* during its five-season run. He wrote 92 of the 156 episodes and approved the other 64 before they aired. Serling's exceptional production control ensured that the series as a whole, including episodes penned by other writers—such as Charles Beaumont, George Clayton Johnson, and Richard Matheson—lined up with his own creative vision. And even though Serling realized that explicitly dealing with race relations on television was off limits, his social commentary would remain racially inspired. Knowing that depictions of socially marginalized groups were sure to alert increasingly paranoid sponsors and networks, Serling instead focused on white American society and its collective preservation of bigotry, prejudice, and white supremacy. By injecting horror into suburbanization, space exploration, white-collar work, consumerism, war, and technology, Serling's *Twilight Zone* challenged the priorities and major investments of white mainstream society, which frequently necessitated greed, corruption, self-harm, waste, indifference, and violence. The collective addiction to racialized consumerism and white supremacy reflect what the American Society of Addiction Medicine has outlined in that those suffering from addiction "engage in behaviors that become compulsive and often continue despite harmful consequences."[23] Without question, the harmful consequences of the commodity-based American Dream, fueled by the reinforcing addictions of white supremacy and racialized consumerism, are legion.

As George Lipsitz has eloquently argued, Americans have been "encouraged to invest in whiteness, to remain true to an identity that provides them with resources, power, and opportunity." Despite the completely unscientific and fictional nature of racial difference, this collective "possessive investment in whiteness" has exerted an overwhelming amount of influence throughout American society. Like an addiction, Lipsitz argues that the "artificial construction of whiteness almost always comes to possess white people themselves . . . unless they disinvest and divest themselves of their attachments to white supremacy."[24] In many ways, Serling was attempting to create opportunities for viewers to disinvest in, or at least question, mainstream priorities disproportionately shaped by a consumer culture suffused with whiteness. By making the "whites only" American Dream deeply unsettling, viewers might question whether the dream was as good as the sales pitch. James Baldwin stated, "This is the crime of which I accuse my country and my countrymen . . . that they have destroyed and are destroying hundreds of thousands of lives and do not know it and do not want to know it."[25] Like other addictive behaviors, the pursuit of elusive satisfaction wreaks havoc, spreading inhumanity to the outside world and relationships. At the same time, the user is also suffering from a great deal of self-abuse and delusion, much like Franklin experienced in "The Fever." In this sense, criticizing the white consumeristic American Dream might be considered not simply a negation, a deconstruction, or an attack but an invitation for Americans to participate in something far greater: to create authentic, unique, and humane dreams for themselves, their families, and their communities. Because of the addictive investment in whiteness, many Americans fear what might lay beyond it. *The Twilight Zone* proposed an alternative possibility: "A journey into a wondrous land whose boundaries are that of imagination." The boundaries of the American imagination were too stifled, limited, claustrophobic, materialistic, and too racially homogenous. As Serling instructed at the beginning of each episode, "You unlock this door with a key of imagination." Americans struggling to find that key might just find it in *The Twilight Zone.*

In placing the racially homogenous consumeristic American Dream inside a nightmare, Serling attempted to raise critical thought as it related to manufactured desires, public policies, advertised products, and white utopian visions that predominated postwar life in the United States. And while millions of individual Americans had unprecedented access to a variety of comforts, Serling sought to remind them that this consumption-based existence could trample on the needs of others, divorce us from ourselves, and contaminate our social conditions to the point of toxicity. Responding to one particularly angry viewer, who wrote Serling a letter accusing him of aiding the Communist international conspiracy, he simply expressed that his work was based on a core belief, namely "that human beings must involve themselves in the anguish of other human beings."[26] In fact, viewers might find, the anguish is also their own.

While racialized forms of corporate capitalism exerted an increasingly hegemonic influence over postwar life and television content, they also sparked a wave of lively social commentary and criticism throughout popular print culture, profoundly shaping public intellectual life. Writers and intellectuals such as E. Franklin Frazier, Betty Friedan, Paul Goodman, Michael Harrington, C. Wright Mills, Vance Packard, David Riesman, William Whyte, and many others disseminated a wide array of insights, critiques, indictments, and proposals to a postwar society that was experiencing so many dramatic changes all at once. While most historical conceptions of television have taken the sweeping influence of consumer culture and marketing into account, fewer have deeply considered how a thriving popular print culture rife with critical thought also affected television's early development. Postwar television was not only influenced by social criticism throughout the public sphere, but it also meaningfully contributed to it as well. While most programs featured consumer-based images of the white American Dream, many television writers, such as Serling in his early teleplays and in *The Twilight Zone,* followed a critical path more in line with Packard, Riesman, and Friedan.

All too often the relationship between postwar television and print culture has been characterized by aloofness, antagonism, or detachment. This artificial and arbitrary separation has largely manifested itself in two ways—with an emphasis on the inherent differences of each medium's effect on audiences and on differences in content. The former differentiation is most closely associated historically with media scholar Marshall McLuhan who, most famously of all, explained how the "medium is the message" and that a society based around television was "retribalizing" mankind, whereas the printed word had worked over the centuries to individuate human beings. Although McLuhan argued that the content of television merely represented a "juicy piece of meat carried by the burglar to distract the watchdog of the mind," popular audiences, critics, and scholars have tended to focus more on just that—the "juicy meat" of content.[27] Almost since its inception, television's most outspoken critics and detractors have frequently found the content to be mentally malnourishing at best. They, too, have tended to draw a sharp line contrasting the hot medium of print and the cool medium of TV: the former for serious thought, reflection, and learning, the latter for guilty pleasures, entertainment, and for pushing products. Simply put, books and print culture have commonly represented a vast brain land, while television, in Newton Minow's famous words, a "vast wasteland."[28]

Such a conception, however, takes certain developments in the history of television as inevitable or unavoidable, a belief that Minow, as FCC chairman, was trying to push against in his critical speech. In particular, he strongly believed television was not living up to its potential in serving the public interest: "Program materials should enlarge the horizons of the viewer, provide . . . wholesome entertainment, afford helpful stimulation," and remind them of the "responsibilities which the citizen has towards . . . society."[29] Similarly, Minow was not convinced that broadcasters merely gave the public what it actually wanted, stating that viewers' tastes are not "as low as some of you assume." He cited problems in the inherently limited options available to viewers as well as the overreliance on ratings numbers that did not take into consideration varied levels of viewer engagement. One major issue missing from Minow's emphasis on the public interest, though, was that broadcasters by and large had in effect been defining the public as almost exclusively white. *The Twilight Zone*'s enduring popularity, which Minow even included in his speech as a worthy exemplar of television's potential, demonstrates the validity of many of his points regarding a deeply flawed methodology of privileging ratings figures and appealing to presumed "low" tastes. While *The Twilight Zone* was never in competition for the most highly rated program of its day, it gained a remarkably loyal, engaged, and reflective audience that has extended well into the twenty-first century. It also pointed to the ways television audiences craved content that provoked critical thought regarding important social issues. In other words, some television audiences sought the exact same thing as readers of social commentary—to critically think about and perhaps better navigate the challenges of their rapidly changing world, not merely escape from it.

Indeed, before television became the national craze, a different revolution in consumer culture and marketing was already underway, in the form of the paperback book. Following the success of Allen Lane's Penguin Publishers in the United Kingdom, American publishers, notably Robert de Graff of Pocket Books, began selling mass-market paperbacks for twenty-five cents apiece, at a time when hardcovers cost over two dollars. Previously considered a consumer good primarily for the wealthy, these new and more affordable paperback books opened the floodgates of print culture consumerism after World War II. In a similar manner to many other postwar consumer goods, books transformed from a demand-led market to a supply-led one. Now not only could readers buy classic and contemporary volumes for an affordable fifty cents, but they could also purchase copies featuring an enticing, colorful cover adorned with eye-catching imagery. In addition to these mass-market publications, trade paperbacks burst onto the scene in 1953 as a midrange option between mass-market books and hardcovers. Much like magazines, such as the *Atlantic Monthly* and the *New Yorker*, they appealed to an educated middle class that did not have the wealth usually associated with hardcover connoisseurs but preferred them above the frequently lurid covers and low-grade appeal of many mass-market publications. This two-pronged paperback revolution made reading more accessible, affordable, and more democratic. While presses released reprints of classics and bestsellers, they also released new works of fiction, history, and contemporary social criticism. Paperbacks serve as merely one example among the rise in print culture consumption that included magazines, newspapers, and other publications. Television did not diametrically oppose print culture and the general public's reading habits but developed simultaneously alongside them.[30]

Serling's own career would further illustrate this connection between postwar print culture and television, with his contributions to newspapers, including the *Los Angeles Times,* and several book deals before, during, and after *The Twilight Zone*'s run. Inexpensive paperback books such as *Patterns, Devils and Demons, Witches, Werewolves, and Warlocks,* and *Stories from* The Twilight Zone showed a kind of mutual demand and a more fluid crossover between the worlds of print and television than critics have fully reckoned with. Among such books were titles that could appeal to a younger reading audience with a thirst for fantasy and horror as well as an audience yearning for more social criticism. That throughout his career Serling was involved in both worlds reinforces how the two different media informed each other in content, style, marketing techniques, and consumer appeals right from the start.

The Twilight Zone has certainly not eluded scholarly and popular attention, as several recently published studies demonstrate. Among these, Jon Kraszewski's *The New Entrepreneurs: An Institutional History of Television Anthology Writers* details the institutional struggles of anthology writers, including Rod Serling, Paddy Chayefsky, and Reginald Rose. Viewing these writers through the concept of the "dependent employee," Kraszewski details the professional struggles of postwar writers finding their way in early television.[31] Relatedly, Barry Keith Grant's volume, *The Twilight Zone,* shows how Serling deployed techniques and conventions from other popular genres, such as film noir, science fiction, and horror in order to make his work more accessible and audience-friendly.[32] Grant also examines the series through the concept of single-case authorship, positing that Serling was one of the television's first showrunners. Martin Grams Jr.'s The Twilight Zone: *Unlocking the Door to a Television Classic,* Steven Jay Rubin's The Twilight Zone *Encyclopedia,* and The Twilight Zone *Companion* by Marc Scott Zicree provide readers with extensively researched production information, budget figures, and details for every episode. Mark Dawidziak's *Everything I Need to Know I Learned in* The Twilight Zone: *A Fifth-Dimension Guide to Life* serves as a kind of self-help book featuring life lessons from the show.[33] Biographies of Serling, including Nicholas Parisi's *Rod Serling: His Life, Work, and Imagination*, Anne Serling's *As I Knew Him: My Dad, Rod Serling*, and Gordon F. Sander's *Serling: The Rise and Twilight of TV's Last Angry Man* all provide vitally important details of Serling's life and extensive career.[34]

While these books provide valuable background information regarding the show's production history and Serling's life, my work is less concerned with Serling and his individual career. My intent is to provide a broader intellectual and cultural perspective, situating the series in a rich postwar milieu of social criticism, psychological theories, reform movements, and political struggles. I aim to provide a fuller understanding how *The Twilight Zone* represented a distillation of ideas permeating the public sphere and contemporary works of social criticism. In this way, I position the series not just in terms of Serling's own career trajectory or within the television industry, but in the intellectual thought and social commentary of the early Cold War era.

Among the many works that have analyzed postwar television content, two general trends have emerged, with some scholars emphasizing television's hegemonic, constrictive, and even oppressive social influence and others arguing that television, at least at times, has embodied social openness, progressivism, and reform. Among the former, In his study *Television in Black-and-White America: Race and National Identity*, Alan Nadel illustrates how racial topics, or even the idea of showing a nonwhite representation of American life, became one casualty of television's sponsor-induced limitations. Programming reinforced middle-class whiteness, patriarchy, and conformity, while bypassing Black American communities in order to show there really was "one nation under God," and it was racially homogenous.[35] Similarly, Lawrence R. Samuel has argued how the social "pressure to turn myth into reality intensified" as a direct result of television content and advertising.[36] Serving as one of the many examples of this phenomenon, Stephanie Coontz has explained how popular portrayals of a woman who "can be fully absorbed with her youngsters while simultaneously maintaining passionate sexual excitement with her husband was a 1950s invention that drove thousands of women to therapists, tranquilizers, or alcohol when they actually tried to live up to it."[37]

At the same time, scholarship such as Thomas Doherty's *Cold War, Cool Medium,* maintains that postwar television actually made the United States a more accepting and cosmopolitan nation by increasing the visibility of certain segments of the population. The visibility, for example, of "the junior senator from Wisconsin," Joe McCarthy, hastened his fall from grace, just as Lucille Ball, Desi Arnaz, and Liberace helped to promote acceptance of less traditional expressions of gender and marriage.[38] Scholarship on sixties television, including Todd Gitlin's *The Whole World Is Watching*, and Aniko Bodroghkozy's *Groove Tube* similarly argue that television played a significant, if complicated, role in showcasing elements of sixties countercultural youth movements in news coverage as well as in shows like the *Smothers Brothers Comedy Hour, The Mod Squad,* and *The Monkees.* Lynn Spigel's classic study, *Make Room for TV: Television and the Family Ideal in Postwar America,* demonstrates how television audiences were not merely passive consumers of this new "home theater" either. Her work illuminates the profoundly contradictory ways Americans embraced, resisted, challenged, and adapted to the new medium, which was at once a unifying and a divisive presence within the home.[39] In a similar vein, Susan Douglas's *Where the Girls Are: Growing Up Female with the Mass Media* highlights the "schizophrenic" nature of postwar media that was repressive and objectifying for women on the one hand, and a partial catalyst for feminism and women's empowerment on the other.[40]

Clearly, though, a tension remains in how one ought to characterize TV's role in postwar America, whether it was more repressive or reformatory. In this way, my approach bears some resemblance to the works of Spigel and Douglas, although my work is a cultural history rather than a media studies project. By using *The Twilight Zone* as my main historical lens, I consider these paradoxical tendencies and the inherent contradictions that pervaded American postwar television. The repressive aspects that often originated in marketing concerns, eventually leading to censorship, forced Serling to conceal certain topics and shift from realistic drama to fantasy-based narratives to elude censors. At the same time, however, the show's persistent critical engagement with important social issues and contemporary social commentary demonstrates postwar television's reformatory potentials and ability to critique the dominant status quo.

And while the series questioned and critiqued mainstream white American culture, this focus is not without problems either. As Robert Entman and Andrew Rojecki argue in their classic study, *The Black Image in the White Mind: Media and Race in America,* the conspicuous absence of racially diverse characters appearing on the television screen together has continually served to normalize racial segregation, conflict, stereotyping, and profiling, while also frustrating efforts toward racial harmony and justice.[41] In this way, *The Twilight Zone* serves as an early example of American television's sparse racial diversity—a symptom of a systemic problem that undoubtedly continues to this day. The severe limitations placed on postwar television writers regarding content and nonwhite representations of American life need not be repeated by successive generations in the name of targeting "niche audiences"—a point further emphasized in Taylor Nygaard and Jorie Lagerwey's recent work, *Horrible White People.* Nygaard and Lagerwey argue how contemporary programs including *Girls, Broad City, Catastrophe,* and *Fleabag* collectively help to uphold white supremacy well into the twenty-first century. They posit that this new niche of contemporary television, by centralizing white anxieties, misbehaviors, dysfunctionality, and neuroticism, continues to normalize the overrepresentation of white Americans and underrepresentation of nonwhite Americans.[42] For *The Twilight Zone,* however, the problems of postwar white American society were not meant to be normalized or made more palatable through amusingly quirky or endearing characters, as is the case with some of these more recent programs. Rather, they were nightmarishly unsettling in ways that spoke directly to the marketing of the postwar American Dream.

If *The Twilight Zone*'s socially critical nightmares are to be understood, however, we need to acknowledge the overarching contents of the postwar dream. More specifically, we must consider how marketers such as Ernest Dichter and Louis Cheskin profoundly shaped the all-pervasive world of advertising and consumerism. These motivational researchers relied heavily on Freudian psychology, particularly with regard to the concept of wish fulfillment. As Lawrence Samuel points out, "marketers were very happy to learn about" such concepts, "knowing their ad agencies could figure out ways to complete what was missing from consumers' lives."[43] Equipped with Freud's dream psychology, marketers seemed to find a psychological treasure map, providing the directions to America's buried wishes and loot. But as motivational researchers got to work promoting products with increasing levels of psychological sophistication and promises to fulfill Americans' innermost desires, they left out an important Freudian caveat: "It will be noticed how conveniently everything was arranged in this dream. Since its only purpose was to fulfill a wish, it could be completely egoistical. A love of comfort and convenience is not really compatible with consideration for other people."[44] Undeterred by such concerns, advertisers ensured their marketing creations always catered to the ego and had finality, containing the essential message: "*This* is what you are missing—the key to *your* fulfillment." And in this way, postwar advertisements carried on one of the dominant marketing assumptions of the 1920s, namely that consumers preferred an image of "life as it ought to be" rather than life as it is.[45]

While television sponsors sought to sell consumers' unfulfilled wishes and repressed desires back to them—whether they had to do with purported ideals of whiteness, masculinity, femininity, wealth, power, status, fun, or sex—Serling's writing took a contrasting approach that deliberately left problems unresolved. In this way, his work contrasted with not only the content of most advertising and popular TV programs, but the format as well. By leaving stories more open-ended, he deliberately placed on the audience the burden to think, reflect, question, and act, not simply to passively consume. And while advertisers tended to assure people that they are in control in this world of consumption, Serling reminded Americans that they in fact have little control over many things in the postwar world but can perhaps have more by regaining some of their own consciousness and choosing to stop living in someone else's dream.

Just as Freudian psychology influenced postwar marketing, Rod Serling's approach to scriptwriting arguably related to another renowned dream theorist, Carl Jung. Jung observed that the "more that consciousness is influenced by prejudices, errors, fantasies, and infantile wishes," the more likely we are to "lead . . . a more or less artificial life far removed from healthy instinct, nature, and truth." Jung's goal, like Serling's, was to help close this neurosis-inducing gap between the conscious and unconscious mind. Instead of producing more material that reflected predominant "American Dream" trends in marketing and television content, Serling arguably sought, again in Jungian fashion, "to restore our psychological balance by producing dream material that re-establishes, in a subtle way, the total psychic equilibrium." Jung referred to this as the "complementary (or compensatory) role of dreams in our psychic make-up" and cited, for example, individuals "who have unrealistic ideas or too high an opinion of themselves, or who make grandiose plans out of proportion to their real capacities, have dreams of flying or falling." In this way a frightening or unsettling dream "compensates for the deficiencies of their personalities, and . . . warns them of the dangers in their present course." Finally, Jung concluded, if "the warnings of the dream are disregarded, real accidents may take their place."[46]

Within a culture overflowing with depictions of white supremacy and pronouncements of America's superiority and wealth, Serling attempted, in no small way, to rebalance the psyche of the American TV viewing public at least partially. By inviting viewers to look into the "fifth dimension, beyond that which is known to man," the series ultimately encouraged audiences to reconsider making consumption, global domination, and whiteness the defining features of our lives and dreams. From consuming wartime propaganda to postwar advertisements and consumer goods, Americans needed to find an alternative to this consumption-based existence and pay closer attention to our vulnerable human condition, featuring neglected relationships with ourselves and one another. Modern homes, kitchens, automobiles, fashion, and technology might seem like the keys to unlock our dreams, but they could actually be the very things that keep us from genuine fulfillment.

The multitude of consumer amenities all formed what Roland Marchand once aptly described as the advertisements' highly selective "*Zerrspiegel*," or fun-house mirror, distorting and exaggerating the elements it supposedly reflects.[47] Not only does the advertisers' fun-house mirror distort their products, it also distorts us. *The Twilight Zone* might be similarly described as a selective haunted-house mirror, some nightmares would not make it to the screen, nor would everything be featured in the reflection. But perhaps those who could find their likeness among the haunted mirror's reflections—amid the shadows, cobwebs, and layers of neglected dust— could emerge slightly more conscious. While millions of Americans had plenty of evidence of their dominance of the natural world through modern conveniences and technology, Serling's work critically reminded them that their nation's social character and priorities had yet to be fully determined. In these matters, Americans were likely to be found walking in their sleep, in need of some kind of nightmare to wake them up.

In my work, these various nightmares are organized thematically, with each chapter focusing on a different issue related to postwar life. Typically, two *Twilight Zone* episodes are analyzed in detail, while several other thematically related episodes are discussed briefly. Each chapter brings in contemporary history and print criticism to contextualize what Serling was attempting to achieve.

Chapter 1 is titled "A Haunting Hatred: Living in the Shadows of White Supremacy." The episode "I Am the Night—Color Me Black" serves as an example of the limits of depicting racial issues on television, even in *The Twilight Zone,* while "He's Alive" looks at the many postwar legacies of white supremacy in the United States that ensure the hate-filled ghosts of the past still stalk us (S5, e26; S4, e4).

In chapter 2, "Fighting a War, Combating a Myth: How the Horrors of World War II Shaped *The Twilight Zone*," World War II myth and memory are analyzed in detail. The episode "A Quality of Mercy" tackles racism within the military, especially toward the Japanese, while "The Thirty-Fathom Grave" dramatizes survivor guilt and battle fatigue, or what is now known as post-traumatic stress disorder (S3, e15; S4, e2) . The psychological trauma of real warfare, juxtaposed with simplistic portrayals of combat, serves as a foundation for better understanding Serling and his series.

Chapter 3, "Cold War Space and Technology: A Fertile Frontier or a New Human Wasteland?" focuses on America's space program and pursuit of technological supremacy. The episode "I Shot an Arrow into the Air" serves as a jumping-off point to discuss contemporaneous critiques of manned space flight and the space race. "The Brain Center at Whipple's" illustrates the costs of automation without compensating workers or considering its impact on the labor force (S1, e15; S5, e33).

In chapter 4, "Duck, Cover, and Accuse: Cold War Paranoia Remakes the American Landscape," I analyze two prevailing forms of paranoia during the Cold War—nuclear annihilation and the Second Red Scare. The episode "The Shelter" centers a discussion of nuclear fears and the proposed solution of building bomb shelters (S3, e3). "The Monsters Are Due on Maple Street" shifts attention to the political "fallout" from McCarthyism and the Second Red Scare and the media's relationship with postwar fear-mongers (S1, e22).

Chapter 5, "Cold War Childhood: Containment or Entanglement?" explores childhood and family life during the Cold War. "It's a Good Life" deals with the increasingly complicated nature of parent-child relationships and child-rearing, while "Living Doll" analyzes the burgeoning field of childhood consumerism and the problems of looking to consumption to resolve family issues (S3, e8; S5, e6).

Chapter 6: "White-Collar Weariness: Postwar Work and Leisure Transformed," focuses on the development of suburbia and white-collar work. The episode "A Stop at Willoughby" dramatizes the stresses of commuting, expenses of suburban living, and detriments of trying to live too comfortably and too isolated (S1, e30). "The After Hours" depicts the ways department-store work dehumanizes and objectifies employees (S1, e34).

In Chapter 7, "Consuming Conformity: The Planned Obsolescence of Selfhood in Postwar America's Marketplace," I discuss "Number 12 Looks Just Like You," along with postwar critiques related to consumer culture's oppressive ideals of beauty and femininity, as well as the burgeoning market for psychotropic drugs, such as Valium (S5, e17). The episode "The Lateness of the Hour" serves as the basis for a larger analysis of postwar critiques related to family-focused suburban living and disconnection from society (S2, e8).

Throughout these various nightmares, Serling's work arguably reflected Jung's observation with regard to the Western world: "If we could see our shadow (the dark side of our nature), we should be immune to any moral and mental infection and insinuation. As matters now stand, we lay ourselves open to every infection. Only we have the additional disadvantage that we neither see nor want to understand what we ourselves are doing, under the cover of good manners."[48] And just as the Swiss psychoanalyst endeavored to empower his patients by raising their awareness of certain repressed elements in both the personal and collective unconscious, these arguably were among Serling's main goals. By creating compensatory dreams that attempted to alert dreamers to both real and potential dangers, Serling's *Twilight Zone* worked to produce social nightmares on television before they could ever happen or happen again. Serling's opening narration for "The Shelter" could serve as a kind of mission statement for the entire series: "What you are about to watch is a nightmare. It is not meant to be prophetic, it need not happen, it's the fervent and urgent prayer of all men of good will that it never shall happen. But in this place, in this moment, it does happen. This is *The Twilight Zone.*" It would be up to Americans to define the limits and extent of the spook and determine whether the content of these nightmares stayed in *The Twilight Zone* or continually haunted the nation's sleepwalking inhabitants.

A Haunting Hatred

Living in the Shadows of White Supremacy

Color Me White

"I Am the Night—Color Me Black" aired on March 27, 1964, in *The Twilight Zone*'s final season (S5, e26). Much like his earlier teleplay for the *US Steel Hour*, titled *Noon on Doomsday*, Serling returned to the topic of racist violence, and once again, his desired commentary was for the most part exhumed from the script. Initially, the episode featured Jagger, an African American man who killed a Klansman and was sentenced to be lynched. However, script alterations meant that Jagger was no longer a Black man facing racist terrorism—he was forcibly recast as a white character.[1] While the character's race was changed, the enthusiastic hatred stemming from local law enforcement remained apparent, as the deputy gleefully proclaims, "He's guilty as hell. . . . And man, justice is bein' served deluxe style!" The sheriff, however, does not see things quite so simplistically: "I saw the victim. . . . And when a committee of townspeople came to me and said there'd be no autopsy, I just bent my head and nodded." Adding, "So here we are, gentlemen. All of us treading water in a sewer." The presumed guilt of Jagger and presumed innocence of the Klansman meant no further investigation was necessary. After Jagger is hanged at the gallows, Reverend Anderson, a local Black preacher, challenges the townspeople, "In all of this darkness . . . can anyone make out the truth?" He again questions the crowd, "Do you know why it's dark? Do you know why there's night all around us? Do you know what the blackness is? It's the hate he felt . . . the hate you've felt . . . the hate all of us feel. There was too much . . . there was too much, and we've had to vomit it up and now it's surrounding us and choking us. So much hate. So much miserable hate." As the town is enveloped in blackness, the sky becomes even darker and Serling offers his closing narration: "A sickness known as hate. Not a virus.

"So much miserable hate!" Reverend Anderson confronts Jagger and the towns-people at the execution. Still from "I Am the Night—Color Me Black" (16:44)

Not a microbe. Not a germ. But a sickness nonetheless. Highly contagious. Deadly in its effects. Don't look for it in *The Twilight Zone*—look for it in the mirror. Look for it before the light goes out altogether."

Although Serling successfully concealed a wide range of social commentary in *The Twilight Zone,* this episode served as a reminder of the limits of such an approach. In one of Serling's last scripts for the series, he returned to an issue that he undoubtedly viewed as one of the nation's most pressing problems: the inability to confront racial and social prejudices. Indeed, this very issue arguably led more than anything else to the creation of the fantasy-based program in the first place. Merely three years after the episode aired, Serling explained, "I can't sit on a fence and let carbuncles form. . . . I happen to think the singular evil of our time is prejudice. It is from this evil that all other evils grow and multiply. In almost everything I've written, there is a thread of this: man's seemingly palpable need to dislike someone other than himself."[2] He went on to reflect on the extreme violence meted out to civil rights advocates: "The acts of horror we've been living with the past ten years are nightmarish in themselves. But when we examine the motives to these horrors and background, there's greater cause for worry." He continued, "When a mixed white-black group of Chicago residents paraded on the street asking for better houses for negroes—a charming group of white supremacists threw bricks into their ranks, hitting two nuns, sending them bleeding to the pavement." He concluded, "So long as we hate, so long as we scratch the back of a monster called 'race prejudice, ' so long as we listen to the poison-makers . . . then ladies and gentlemen, we've bought it. We're dead. We've created a garbage dump of a society hardly worth the effort of an appraisal let alone a salvation."[3] "I Am the Night" demonstrated that television sponsors were still unwilling to support content that explicitly depicted the cyclical racial violence and hatred in the United States. This inability to show nonwhite characters as suffering from established social norms illustrated the tense and uncomfortable relationship between American popular television and social injustices that remained throughout the entirety of the series. Despite these continual constraints, the series did find ways to depict white supremacist violence. One of the most memorable instances of this, "He's Alive," featured a Neo-Nazi, played by Dennis Hopper (S4, e4).

Victimizing Hatred

On January 24, 1963, *The Twilight Zone*'s "He's Alive" aired on CBS. The episode begins at night on a city street corner where a young man named Peter Vollmer is delivering a speech to a small crowd: "The economy of our world, now, then, and forever have always found the insidious breed of international bankers. These are the worshippers of purse. Their religion is monetary gain. Their shrine is gold." He continues, "Examine the phenomenon of foreign control. You examine it and you will note with absolute clarity that the lines lead directly to Palestine! They lead directly to Africa! They lead directly to the Vatican!" After he stammers and stumbles a bit, he regains his footing: "There's an insidious, enveloping conspiracy! A conspiracy personified by the yellow man, by the Black man, and by foreigners who come in and infiltrate our economic structure. Oh, there'll come a morning, yes, there will, there will come a morning when these men have taken over your home, taken over your daughters, and they'll be sitting right there on your doorstep." A man from the small crowd irreverently interjects, "If anybody's sitting on your doorstep, buddy, he's a man in a white coat. You better just go with him, quietly." After the two exchange more insults, the man challenges Vollmer, eventually knocking him to the ground. At the sound of police

In front of a pharmacy, Peter Vollmer dispenses some all-too-familiar drugs: white supremacy and conspiracy theory. Still from "He's Alive" (1:24)

sirens, the crowd quickly disperses. When officers arrive, Vollmer tells them, "Communists did this. . . . All of 'em, all of 'em were Communists." Unable to provide the officer with any names, he resignedly says they can handle the situation themselves.

Vollmer's men all reunite around the block as the opening narration comes in:

Portrait of a bush league führer named Peter Vollmer. A sparse little man who feeds off his self-delusions and finds himself perpetually hungry for want of greatness in his diet. And like some goose-stepping predecessors, he searches for something to explain his hunger and rationalize why a world passes him by without saluting. The something he looks for, and finds, is in a sewer. In his own twisted, distorted lexicon he calls it faith, strength, truth. But in just a moment Peter Vollmer will ply his trade on another kind of corner . . . a strange intersection in a shadowland called *The Twilight Zone*."

As the episode continues, Vollmer arrives at an apartment where Ernst, an old family friend, sits playing the cello. After offering Peter some wine, Ernst, in German-accented English, tells Peter he can spend the night if he needs a place to sleep. Peter mentions how that even though they "don't think alike about the same things," he and Ernst remain friends. Ernst responds, "When you were a little kid, Peter, and I used to find you crying at my door late at night. . . . I could pity you then. . . . Now you peddle hate on street corners as if it were popcorn." Peter defends himself: "It's not hate, it's a point of view, it's a philosophy." Ernst assures Peter that he knows the philosophy quite well, having spent nine years in Dachau: "You know who put me there? Peter Vollmer. A lot of Peter Vollmers. Frustrated men . . . sick men . . . angry men. But the result, the effect . . . never mind the cause . . . twelve million bodies in shallow graves. And it all started with young men in uniform talking on street corners." He continues, "I must be one of the worst of your criminals, Peter. Sentimental . . . soft! And very preoccupied with my brother. I should close the door on you. Perhaps this is my sickness. I only see the boy, not the man." Before retiring to bed, Peter tells Ernst that he's like a father to him, while he laments how his drunken father violently abused him and his mother suffered from dementia.

As Peter lays down, his eyes suddenly open, drawn to something outside. He walks over to the window, spotting a mysterious dark figure on the sidewalk. After Peter asks the man who he is, the figure responds in a German accent, "A friend, Mr. Vollmer. . . . You have need of friends, allies." He invites Peter to come outside to talk. After explaining how the two of them believe in the same things, the visitor instructs Peter on the art of working a crowd: "How do you move a mob, Mr. Vollmer? How do you excite them? How do you make them feel as one with you?" He explains,

Speak to them as if you were a member of the mob. Speak to them in their language, on their level. Make their hate your hate. If they are poor, talk to them of poverty. If they are afraid, talk to them of their fears. And if they are angry, Mr. Vollmer . . . give them objects for their anger. But most of all, the thing that is most of the essence, Mr. Vollmer, is that you make this mob an extension of yourself. Say to them things like . . . They call us hatemongers. They say we're prejudiced. They say we're biased. They say we hate minorities . . . minorities. Understand the term, neighbors—minorities. Should I tell you who are the minorities? Should I tell you? We! We are the minorities! That way, Mr. Vollmer. Start it that way.

Vollmer and company on stage in front of Hitler and Goebbels's recognizable faces. Still from "He's Alive" (18:04)

Peter agrees to his new mentor's recommendations.

Instead of a street corner, Peter's next speech takes place in a public hall. His platform features flaming torches as large, dramatic portraits of Adolf Hitler and the former Nazi minister of propaganda, Joseph Goebbels, serve as a backdrop. Taking his mentor's advice, Vollmer thunders to his audience, "We are the minorities! Because patriotism is a minority. Because love of country is the minority. Because to live in a free, white America seems to be of a minority opinion!" He concludes his impassioned speech by promising that they will not stop until their minority is the majority: "This is the promise! And this is the legacy!" as he points to the portraits of Hitler and Goebbels. The meeting room fills with the raucous applause, clearly showing that Vollmer's support is growing.

Following their rally, Peter sees his shadowy mentor appear again, still mysteriously shrouded in complete darkness. After saying that he not only supports Vollmer, but he *is* him, in a sense, he provides further advice: "The organization needs a martyr. . . . You choose one. You take one of no value, and you make him into a symbol. You wrap him in a flag, and you make his death work for you. Find a man who is of no value while he's alive but who can serve you when he's dead." He further instructs his apprentice, "Tell him you have discovered an informer. Tell him the informer has done irreparable damage. Tell him the informer must be . . . put out of the way cleverly . . . so that there is some question as to who is responsible." After some initial apprehension, Peter again agrees to his recommendations, eventually deciding to set up Nick, one of the group's members. Soon thereafter, Peter informs Frank, another member of the group, how Nick has been working as an informant for the police and needs to be eliminated. Peter adds, "Make it look like somebody who hates us did it." Frank understands, telling Pete, "You call it, you've got it." True to his word, Frank fulfills Vollmer's request, as Nick's dead body lies in the street with a handwritten note pinned to his chest: "A good Nazi." The group has their first martyr.

As the episode continues, Pete and his group are gathered backstage preparing for another public meeting. After one of his men laments their fallen comrade, Pete hurls a bevy of insulting remarks about Nick: "He was a fat pig with no guts! He was a greasy bigmouth who copped out at every turn. He was a nickel-and-dime Judas, and he got exactly what he deserved." As Peter takes the stage, however, his tone differs, as he speaks in front of a large portrait of Nick: "A man of honor died last week. A decent, courageous fighter for the cause of freedom gave his life. He gave his life for us! Some skulking assassin murdered him!" He continues, "They stilled his great heart, but they could not stifle his memory. They could not obliterate his courage. They could not wipe away his honor. . . . Nick Bloss died for this. And you and I . . . we must live for this!" The audience enthusiastically applauds Vollmer's passionate speech.

In the following scene, Ernst sits at a bar across the street from where Peter is delivering another speech. As Ernst drinks his beer, he explains to the bartender how he knew Peter when he was a young boy. The bartender says, "Used to be people would laugh at him. But lately, he gets the crowds, and not many people laugh either." Ernst mentions how he has "seen it all before," citing his experience in Nazi Germany. The bartender counters, "That was another time, Mr. Ganz. Another place, another kind of people. That doesn't go here." Ernst, unconfident in such a perspective, replies, "That's what we said, too. They were brown scum. Temporary insanity, part of the passing scene. Too monstrous to be real. So, we ignored them or laughed at them. Because we couldn't believe that there were enough insane people to walk alongside of them." Ernst exhales deeply as he continues, "And then one morning, the country woke up from an uneasy sleep and there was no more laughter. The Peter Vollmers had taken over."

Meanwhile, inside the meeting hall, Vollmer is delivering his speech. He asks the audience, "Do you want the United States of America to remain free?" The crowd passionately answers to the affirmative. Vollmer continues, "Do you want your homes infected with the vermin from foreign shores?" The audience passionately replies, "No!" Then, Vollmer asks, "Do you want a bunch of mongrels to come over here," and the crowd starts murmuring as Ernst walks up on the stage behind Peter. Vollmer realizes his presence as Ernst asks, "You were saying? I can tell them what you were saying. I've heard it before. I've heard it a thousand times before . . . in Munich, in Berlin . . . on a hundred different street corners. It was drivel then, and it is drivel now." Peter urges him to stop, but he persists, "Well, what is this one here? The new model? A 1963 führer right off the assembly line? Well, this one is not so new. He's not so fresh. This one is nothing but a cheap copy. . . . They're all alike. Problem children . . . sick, sad, neurotics who take applause like a needle. . . . Listen to me, Peter, and let them listen. Or else I'll tell them about a quaking, whimpering boy who cried on my couch; who still cries on my couch." Pete's men urge him to do something about Ernst, but Vollmer remains frozen, unsure of what to do or say. Ernst continues, "Shut me up. Stifle me—why don't you? Why can't you? Because this is your courage right here," as he holds up Peter's arm with the party insignia emblazoned on his sleeve. "This . . . and the torchlights, and the crowd. And the *sieg heil*!" Peter finally snaps and hits Ernst across the face. Ernst slowly looks up and remarks, "The rebuttal. The only sort of answer your kind knows how to give. This is your führer. He's yours. I give him to you. A gift from the sewers." Ernst steps down from the stage and slowly walks back outside.

Back in the now-empty meeting hall, Vollmer sits with his head in his hands, dejected by how the latest meeting went. Peter angrily asks his mysterious mentor, who sits in the back, "What are you?! You direct traffic from darkness! You plan the battles, and you're never there when they're fought! Why don't you come out in the light?" After proudly announcing that he, in fact, invented darkness, the mysterious figure emerges, revealing himself to be none other than Adolf Hitler: "You picked me," he announces. "You chose my ideas, you invoked my name, you stole my slogans. So now, you must take whatever else comes with it. In the past, I have given you suggestions. Now I give orders! And from now on, you must be built of steel." Hitler tosses Vollmer a pistol, ordering him to kill Ernst that very night. After initial hesitancy, Vollmer concedes and shoots Ernst, killing him with a single round, successfully eliminating the one voice of love and kindness in his life.

When Vollmer returns to the meeting hall, he sits down to process the recent events. Hitler's voice suddenly comes over the loudspeaker: "What did

"I invented darkness!" In an empty meeting hall, Hitler's shadow instructs Vollmer. Still from "He's Alive" (26:20)

you destroy tonight?" Vollmer responds, "Only a disease. A growth that was on our flesh that had to be removed." Hitler asks his young study how it felt: "It felt like I was immortal," says Peter. Hitler thunders, "We are immortal!" Just then, two police officers arrive at the hall with a warrant for Vollmer's arrest for complicity in the murder of Nicholas Bloss. Vollmer escapes through the back door into the alley. As he frantically climbs up the stairs of neighboring building, the officers fire several rounds into him, knocking him down into the garbage cans below. With his last few breaths, Vollmer tells the officers they have made a "terrible mistake," because he's made out of steel. His bleeding, dying body on top of a pile of garbage tells a different story, however. Following Vollmer's violent end, Hitler's shadow stalks along the walls of the back alley, implying that this is not the end for the hate-filled ideology and rhetoric. Serling's closing narration brings home this final point: "Where will he go next, this phantom from another time, this resurrected ghost of a previous nightmare? Chicago? Los Angeles? Miami, Florida? Vincennes, Indiana? Syracuse, New York? Anyplace, everyplace, where there's hate, where there's prejudice, where there's bigotry. He's alive. He's alive so long as these evils exist.

An appropriate resting place for hatred? The bloodied, hate-filled Vollmer succumbs to his death on top of a pile of garbage. Still from "He's Alive" (49:12)

Remember that when he comes to your town. Remember it when you hear his voice speaking out through others. Remember it when you hear a name called, a minority attacked, any blind, unreasoning assault on a people or any human being. He's alive because through these things we keep him alive."

In probably the most explicit and violent depiction of white supremacy ever featured on *The Twilight Zone*, "He's Alive" dramatizes the persistent lure of racist ideology and conspiracy theory in American life. The episode's main character, Peter Vollmer, closely mirrors the founder of the American Nazi Party, George Lincoln Rockwell, who established the party less than four years before this episode aired. And as biographer Frederick Simonelli explained, "Rockwell was the most widely publicized anti-Semitic and racist political figure in America" throughout the late 1950s and 1960s. While Rockwell's party was new, its ideological basis was not. Just like the character of Peter Vollmer, whose mysterious interactions with a shadow-drenched Hitler fuel his political inspirations, Rockwell once described a mystical experience where he met Adolf Hitler and realized the truth of his teachings, including the Jewish-led communist conspiracy to take over the world.[4] Just like Peter Vollmer, Rockwell brashly carried forth Nazi ideology throughout the United States into the late twentieth century. The episode's title clearly indicates how ideas steeped in bigotry and prejudice can far outlive their most notorious and enthusiastic practitioners, a fact that cannot be relegated exclusively to *The Twilight Zone.*

While Hitler's ideology is clearly the main inspiration for Vollmer and this episode in general, it is important to note that Nazi ideas did not emerge from thin air. While anti-Semitism has existed for centuries, one of its most impactful modern expressions is found in the work *Protocols of the Elders of Zion,* originally published in Russia in 1903. By the 1920s, the text had been translated into German and English and garnered a substantial amount of interest on both sides of the Atlantic. Hitler and Goebbels and, later on, George Lincoln Rockwell consumed this influential volume. As one of the most foundational texts of modern anti-Semitism, the work "exposes" an alleged Jewish international plan for financial and world domination. It declares: "Gold always has been and always will be the irresistible power. Handled by expert hands it will always be the most useful lever for those who possess it. . . . With gold we can buy the most rebellious consciences, can fix the rate of all values, the current price of all products, can subsidize all state loans, and thereafter hold the states at our mercy." The text speaks of the Jews' plan to replace gold with paper money, rejoicing how "our chest will absorb the gold, and we shall regulate the value of the paper which will make us masters of all the positions."[5] Passages such as these were an inspiration for Hitler, as he even explicitly cites *Protocols* in *Mein Kampf.* By the early 1920s, however, several different organizations and scholars had proved the text's plagiarized and illegitimate nature. Among them, Philip Graves established that rather than exposing a Jewish conspiracy, much of the text had been lifted from a nineteenth-century French political attack on the regime of Napoleon III.[6] Undeterred, Hitler merely argued in *Mein Kampf* that cries of "fraud" only prove the text's validity: "*Protocols of the Wise Men of Zion,* so infinitely hated by the Jews . . . are based on a forgery, the *Frankfurter Zeitung* moans and screams every week: the best proof they are authentic." While dismissing that it matters little where the *Protocols* originated or who even wrote it, he claims how with "terrifying certainty they reveal the nature and activity of the Jewish people and expose their inner contexts as well as their ultimate final aims." So important and potentially powerful did Hitler find *Protocols,* he even declared that "once this book has become the common property of a people, the Jewish menace may be considered broken."[7]

Unbeknownst to Hitler at the time, someone across the Atlantic Ocean shared his enthusiasm for this text: Henry Ford. Ford's newspaper, the *Dearborn Independent*, published excerpts of the *Protocols* throughout 1920 in an ongoing featured series called "The International Jew: The World's Foremost Problem." Ford's paper was distributed all over the United States, with a circulation of close to a million copies. According to American Jewish historian Hasia Diner, the significance of Ford's promotion of these conspiracies was substantial: "What Henry Ford says, people stop and listen. There are people who talked about him as a potential presidential candidate in the 1920s. . . . Henry Ford's ability to gain a national audience with his words made him a very dangerous person." In addition to printing passages from *Protocols*, Ford also published articles that blamed a whole host of contemporary issues on the Jewish population. As Diner explains, "Strikes: It was the Jews. Any kind of financial scandal? The Jews. Agricultural depression? The Jews. So 'the Jew,' in a way, became the symbol of a world that was being manipulated and controlled."[8] Additionally, Ford republished these articles in book form with half a million copies in circulation in the United States.[9] Ford's audience grew even bigger when Theodor Fritsch, who published the German editions of *Protocols*, also published the anti-Semitic writings of Henry Ford in Germany.[10] Undoubtedly, these publications had a mutually reinforcing impact on anti-Semites around the world.

Vollmer's speech in the first scene of "He's Alive" in many ways reflects the conspiratorial theories infamously outlined in *Protocols* and *Mein Kampf*—that somewhere there exists a secret international group of "insidious bankers" that controls national economies. Vollmer blames a whole host of nonwhite and foreign coconspirators who seek to infiltrate and destroy the American economy in a way that clearly mirrors Hitler's views: "Peoples who can sneak their way into the rest of mankind like drones, to make other men work for them under all sorts of pretexts . . . under whose parasitism the whole of honest humanity is suffering." By the end of the first scene, Vollmer has surely cast a wide conspiratorial net, from conspiracies about international banking, to accusations about traitorous racial and ethnic minorities, to fears of race-mixing involving "your daughters," and, finally, to telling police officers that those who opposed his speech were all communists. For Vollmer, Rockwell, and Hitler, all these seemingly disparate issues were connected and represented the greatest threat to human civilization and went against nature itself: "The Jewish doctrine of Marxism rejects . . . nature," while it also denies "the significance of nationality and race." Hitler concluded that the result "could only be destruction for the inhabitants of this planet."[11] The stakes of ignoring race, nationality, ethnicity, and Marxism were nothing short of apocalyptic.

By the late 1950s, Rockwell was well versed in many of these conspiracies and texts. Having grown increasingly interested in Nazism by 1952, he now dove even more deeply into studying it. While he was still in the navy, Rockwell was stationed at Keflavik Naval Air Station, in Iceland. During that time, he read through *The Protocols of the Learned Elders of Zion*, Hitler's *Mein Kampf*, and the anti-Semitic writings of Gerald L. K. Smith.[12] By 1960, Rockwell was honorably discharged from the US Navy for his increasingly outspoken and hate-filled views. Soon thereafter, he went on to officially establish the American Nazi Party. The party's platform called for executing "Marxist-Zionist traitors . . . removal of all disloyal Jews from influence in the media, government, education, and the legal system; and the establishment of an International Treason Tribunal to investigate, try, and publicly hang, in front of the U.S. Capitol, all non-Jews who are convicted of having consciously acted as fronts for Jewish treason."[13] And while Rockwell was most notorious for his anti-Semitism, he often defined racial and ethnic minorities, as well as people who espouse a variety of liberal causes, of serving "treasonous" Jewish and Marxist interests. The potential applications could be frighteningly broad.

Even Vollmer's troubled childhood, which may seem clichéd, somewhat reflects Rockwell's own upbringing, as his parents divorced when he was six years old. His father, commonly referred to as "Doc," one of the most successful vaudeville performers of his day, was largely absent from his son's life, while his single mother struggled to make ends meet as she raised three children on her own. Despite these challenges, Rockwell was admitted into Brown University, but he left before graduating, to serve in the US military. He was trained as a pilot in the navy during World War II and was promoted to lieutenant commander in 1945. During his postwar life, however, he would come to sympathize with the Nazi ideology that the US Armed Forces had fought against. While the reasons for his political conversion remain unclear, Rockwell described a kind of supernatural meeting with Hitler in the 1950s.[14]

While the connections to Hitler, Rockwell, and the American Nazi Party seem most evident and obvious in this episode, it also bears repeating that many of the ideas and policies advocated by the Nazi Party's supporters were not theirs exclusively. The cross-pollination between Nazi Germany and the United States has been recently outlined by comparative and foreign law professor, James Q. Whitman in his book, *Hitler's American Model: The United*

States and the Making of Nazi Race Law. Among many provocative and disturbing parallels, Whitman documents how Nazi policymakers cited the extermination and oppression of Native Americans throughout US history as an instructive historical precedent for German expansionism in Europe. Making the point even more succinctly, Nazi politician and lawyer Hans Frank even referred to the Jewish population of Ukraine as "Indians."[15] In addition to the bloody history of US expansion and the ongoing oppression of Native Americans, a variety of US laws related to immigration, citizenship, and anti-miscegenation also piqued Nazi interest. At the time this episode aired, US immigration policy was still largely shaped by a national quota system codified in the 1924 Johnson-Reed Act. This legislation inspired a great deal of interest among Hitler and Nazi officials in the 1920s and 1930s, as it had almost entirely restricted immigration from Asia and Africa and drastically limited immigration from southern and eastern Europe. The act stipulated that the number of visas granted to a specific nationality would be equal to 2 percent of the foreign-born population residing in the United States in 1890. Because many eastern and southern Europeans immigrated after 1890, this sharply decreased the number of visas available to those nationalities. Relatedly, the act also greatly reduced the number of Jewish immigrants, as most Jews had come from eastern Europe.[16] The act also renewed the Chinese Exclusion Act of 1882 and expanded the ban to all Asian nations.[17] While these policies seemed controversial, they had broad bipartisan support. Conservatives who feared the growing influence of socialism, anarchism, and other "anti-American" viewpoints supported it, and many of them also decried the changing ethnic and racial demographics of the United States. At the same time, progressives supported the restrictions based on their desire to improve America's social order by minimizing problems related to poverty, drunkenness, prostitution, et cetera—problems that had become increasingly associated with these more recent immigrant groups.[18]

These new immigration restrictions did not just find favor across the American political spectrum, Hitler praised them in *Mein Kampf.* As Hitler reflected on naturalization and immigration laws throughout the world, he took note of America's interesting example: "There is today one state in which at least weak beginnings toward a better conception are noticeable. Of course, it is not our model German Republic, but the American Union. . . . By refusing immigration on principle to elements in poor health, by simply excluding certain races from naturalization, it professes in slow beginnings a view which is peculiar to the folkish state concept."[19] This "folkish state concept" consisted of citizens, subjects, and foreigners, with full civil rights granted only to citizens. Relegating certain ethnicities to permanent status as subjects and labeling immigrants as "foreigners" meant perpetually depriving these groups a wide array of civil, economic, and social resources and rights. The fact that the majority of African Americans were largely relegated to the status of subjects, unable to vote or hold public office, for example, served as an appealing model to Hitler. Additionally, the fact that the majority of Asian Americans were barred from naturalization until well after World War II meant that the United States proved instructive to Hitler's multitiered plan for codifying citizenship and immigration through racism into German law. By 1935, these ideas became reality in Nazi Germany, as the Reich Citizenship Law defined citizenship as the exclusive right of "pure" Germans, excluding Jews, Romani, and Black Germans.[20]

These twentieth-century immigration and naturalization policies were steeped in the increasingly dominant trends of nativism, eugenics, and scientific racism that held great appeal on both sides of the Atlantic. Race theorists, such as Madison Grant in his *Passing of the Great Race,* argued that the United States needed to uphold racial hierarchies that positioned northern and western Europeans at the top and Asian and African races at the bottom. Grant exhorted, "We Americans must realize that the altruistic ideals which have controlled our social development during the past century and the maudlin sentimentalism that has made America 'an asylum for the oppressed,' are sweeping the nation toward a racial abyss. If the Melting Pot is allowed to boil without control and we continue to follow our national motto and deliberately blind ourselves to 'all distinctions of race, creed or color,' the type of native American of Colonial descent will become as extinct as the Athenian of the age of Pericles, and the Viking of the days of Rollo."[21] Exemplifying just how influential Grant's ideas had become, Hitler wrote to the man, thanking him for his work on race, declaring that the book was "his Bible." Moreover, Grant's text was introduced as evidence at the Nuremberg Trials to defend Nazi Germany's actions as not unique but in line with those of other nations.[22]

Despite the broad-based support for the Immigration Act of 1924 when it passed, an increasing amount of international controversy began to emerge in the 1930s. Amid Nazi Germany's genocidal policymaking, which served as the foundation for the Holocaust, the Jewish population in Germany began to look for ways to emigrate. While about 127,000 Jews arrived in the United States between 1933 and 1940, tens of thousands were unable to do so because of the 1924 immigration restrictions. The controversies regarding how the

United States and other western nations were navigating the Jewish refugee crisis became especially visible in 1939, when the *St. Louis* sailed from Europe with 900 Jewish refugees aboard. The ship first attempted to port in Cuba, as many of its passengers had successfully applied for Cuban visas. When they arrived at Havana, however, they were denied entry. Soon thereafter, they attempted to port in Miami, only to be denied again. Having also applied to land in Canada, the refugees were refused once more. The ship, with no other apparent option, sailed back to Europe, where at least 254 of its passengers died during the war years.[23] Many observers, including Hitler, noted the pretense and duplicity of the United States and other nations. As Hitler explained in an address to the Reichstag on January 30, 1939: "It is a shameful example to observe today how the entire democratic world dissolves in tears of pity, but then, in spite of its obvious duty to help, closes it heart to the poor tortured people."[24] Hitler used widespread international indifference during the Jewish refugee crisis as further justification for his own genocidal policies toward European Jews.

To be sure, while thousands of Jewish refugees faced challenges stemming from these immigration policies, the Jewish population within the United States was not immune to discrimination or violence. The founding of the second Ku Klux Klan, which lasted through World War II, was largely reborn when Leo Frank, a Jewish factory superintendent, was convicted of killing a thirteen-year-old girl named Mary Phagan. When the governor of Georgia changed Frank's death sentence to life in prison, a mob abducted and lynched the man in 1915. A sign of things to come, the second wave of the KKK eventually targeted not only African Americans but many immigrant newcomers and non-Protestant groups as well.[25]

Father Charles Coughlin, one of the most popular radio show hosts of the 1930s, used his platform to spread increasingly anti-Semitic and pro-Nazi views. In addition to his national radio broadcasts, which had millions of listeners, his newspaper, *Social Justice,* included excerpts of *Protocols of the Elders of Zion* and even plagiarized passages from some of Joseph Goebbels's speeches.[26] In an article that struck a typical note for the magazine, contributor Ben Marcin described how accusations of anti-Semitism are largely a product of the inability of Jews to tolerate a different point of view or "critical comment." Rather than the Jewish population actually suffering from hatred, discrimination, abuse, and violent pogroms, the real "reason the Jew was and is persecuted is because he is a victim of his secret government ruled by Jewish leaders."[27] One of Coughlin's most controversial broadcasts aired on

November 20, 1938, two weeks after *Kristallnacht*. Coughlin not only downplayed the violent attacks on Jewish people, businesses, and synagogues but he asserted that Jews in Nazi Germany brought the violence onto themselves because of their centuries-long history of persecuting Christians.[28]

Coughlin's sympathies and even outright support for Nazi Germany became increasingly evident by the late 1930s, as he asserted on multiple occasions that "Nazism must be established to overcome Communism."[29] After the Nazi invasion of Poland, he even urged his listeners to march on Washington to help ensure the United States remained neutral in the fight against Nazi Germany.[30] In 1940, as a result of these escalating controversies, Coughlin was forced off the air. Against mounting pressure from the National Association of Broadcasters, he was unable to renew his broadcasting license. Additionally, the FCC added new regulations that developed into the Fairness Doctrine, requiring programs to include multiple perspectives on controversial topics so as to avoid other Coughlin-like hosts from dominating American airwaves.[31] Coming to his defense, however, the Nazi press predictably declared Coughlin's de-platforming "a typical case of Jewish terrorism of American public opinion."[32] Despite Coughlin's departure from the airwaves, the tremendous popularity of his controversial program, along with the complex questions as to how media companies ought to handle hate speech and disinformation, continue to haunt the United States well into the late twentieth century and beyond.

Not only did Vollmer reflect a lot of the racist views that served as the foundation for US immigration policy and popular media content, he also gave voice to fears regarding miscegenation or "race-mixing." And just as US immigration policies proved instructive to Nazi Germany, American anti-miscegenation laws also had a documented impact on Nazi Germany. In "*Volk*, Race, and State," Herbert Kier he outlined a series of recommendations for race legislation in Nazi Germany that pulled directly from thirty US states that had anti-miscegenation laws: "Thus the thirty states listed here all have prohibitions on miscegenation, which . . . all pursue the aim of safeguarding the American population of European origin against race-mixing with non-European races. . . . Extramarital sex between members of different races is also forbidden in several states, or even subjected to criminal punishment . . . in Alabama and Arkansas."[33] As James Q. Whitman has pointed out, these laws proved particularly influential when Nazi Germany was constructing the Nuremberg Laws, eventually passed in 1935. The Law for the Protection of German Blood and German Honor banned "*Rassenschande*," or race-mixing, making interracial marriage and sexual relations illegal.[34] As for the United States, by the mid-1960s, anti-miscegenation laws still existed in sixteen states. It was not until the Supreme Court's 1967 decision in *Loving v. Virginia*, three years after this episode aired, that anti-miscegenation state laws were ruled unconstitutional and in violation of the Fourteenth Amendment.[35]

While cultural, social, and political exchanges between Nazi Germany and the United States were taking place throughout the 1930s, African Americans attempted to make these connections more visible—to condemn *both* nations and to highlight the hypocrisy and racism within the United States in particular. As Richard Dalfiume has written, "The hypocrisy and paradox involved in fighting a world war for the four freedoms and against aggression by an enemy preaching a master race ideology, while at the same time upholding racial segregation and white supremacy, were too obvious. The war crisis provided . . . a unique opportunity to point out, for all to see, the difference between the American creed and practice."[36] Nowhere was this effort more pronounced than in the Double V Campaign, a movement popularized by the *Pittsburgh Courier*, a Black newspaper. The campaign largely started after James Q. Thompson, a defense worker, was denied the opportunity to work on the floor of a manufacturing plant and relegated to cafeteria work. The Jim Crow segregation that still permeated the military, the defense industry, workplaces, and the nation as a whole inspired Thompson to write the newspaper a letter, which became the basis for the campaign: "I suggest that while we keep defense and victory in the forefront that we don't lose sight of our fight for true democracy at home." He called for all colored Americans to adopt the double V for a "double victory." The first *V* stood for "victory over our enemies from without" and the second "for victory over our enemies from within." He concluded, "Surely those who perpetuate these ugly prejudices here are seeking to destroy our democratic form of government just as surely as the Axis forces."[37]

Thompson's letter and clarion call had a profound impact on the fight for civil rights during the war and beyond. His biting criticism, comparing the menace of American racism and discrimination to the threat presented by Axis forces, struck a powerful chord with African American readers. Civil rights activists, including Ella Baker, A. Philip Randolph, Rosa Parks, and countless other African Americans helped to organize support for the Double V Campaign's principles during the war and well into the 1950s and 1960s. Similarly, the famed writer Langston Hughes called on his countrymen to see the connections between Hitler's Germany and the United States, particularly after race riots erupted across the country. In a poem entitled "Beaumont to Detroit: 1943," he described the similarities among racist segregation laws in the United States, the Ku Klux Klan, and Adolf Hitler. Hughes concludes the poem by simply asking how long he has to fight both Hitler and Jim Crow.[38] By pointing out the shared racism between the United States and Nazi Germany during wartime, African Americans challenged the national status quo and the notion of a unified country fighting the evils of Nazism and racism abroad. The war was never *only* overseas; it had been raging at home for generations.

Despite achieving several notable milestones, including the desegregation of the defense industry during the war and of the armed forces in 1948, the objectives set forth in the Double V Campaign remained unfulfilled in the years after World War II. As Dalfiume explained, "When . . . white acquiescence in a new racial order did not occur, the ground was prepared for the civil rights revolution of the 1950s and 1960s; the seeds were indeed sown in the World War II years."[39] The fight against segregation, anti-miscegenation laws, ethnic and racial discrimination that became the civil rights movement undoubtedly got a substantial boost because of the obvious incongruities between American creeds and practices that were made even more glaring during the war. While African Americans who served during the war wanted to achieve some of the same benefits as white veterans under the Servicemen's Readjustment Act (GI Bill), these hopes were soon frustrated. For instance, Title III of the GI Bill, which granted low-interest mortgages to veterans with no down payment required, had wildly different effects depending on one's race. While white veterans and their families greatly benefited from this government assistance in booming postwar suburbs across the country, Black veterans were mostly denied loans and mortgages. Even though African Americans were technically eligible for these benefits, the program required the cooperation of local banks and lenders. Consequently, the discriminatory lending practices of local banks effectively barred the majority of African American veterans from home ownership. The fact that many planned communities for veterans' families, including Levittown in New York, explicitly prohibited Black families from living there at all added to these severe constraints. Additionally, while the vast majority of Black veterans were typically funneled into unskilled, low-paying jobs, most of their white counterparts gained employment in well-paying, high-skilled positions.[40] Much like the local banks that denied mortgages to most Black veterans, state employment agencies helped to ensure the vast majority of Black veterans had very limited access to jobs that might afford them increased social mobility. When it came to taking advantage of the bill's educational provisions, only 20 percent of the 100,000 Black veterans who applied for educational benefits in 1946 were able to register for college. In the end, only 12 percent of Black veterans registered for college under the GI Bill. Among those who did, 90 percent attended persistently underfunded, under-resourced HBCUs because it was their only option.[41] In these myriad ways, racial inequalities persisted well into the postwar era for those who served during World War II. Simply stated, the Double V Campaign was far from achieving all of its objectives.

If navigating the discriminatory bureaucracies of higher education, job markets, and home finance were not challenging enough, many Black veterans faced constant threats of violence throughout the postwar years. On February 8, 1946, when former Marine Timothy Hood removed the Jim Crow sign from a trolley in Bessemer, Alabama, its white conductor, William R. Weeks, fired off five rounds at Hood. After the badly injured Hood tried to make an escape, he was soon arrested by Police Chief G. B. Fant, who placed him in the back of his squad car, murdering him with a single shot to the head. Fant was never charged.[42] Hood's audacity to carry on the mission of the Double V Campaign demonstrated its potentially fatal consequences.

Similarly, later that same year, World War II veteran Maceo Snipes bravely attempted to exercise his Fifteenth Amendment rights as he cast a ballot in the Democratic primary race for governor in Taylor County, Georgia. The very next day, several members of the KKK, including Edward Williamson, a World War II veteran himself, showed up at Snipes's family farm and shot him. Miraculously, he managed to walk three miles to the nearest hospital, where he was neglected for six hours before the doctors claimed they had no "Black blood" with which to perform a blood transfusion. Snipes died two days later, and no one was charged for his murder. Snipes's tragic death illustrated not only the lethality lurking behind Jim Crow America but how the medical field was far from immune to its twisted ideologies.

Several years before Snipes's death, Charles R. Drew, a prominent African American surgeon and medical researcher, protested how the Red Cross segregated blood by race, citing a complete lack of scientific validity for doing so. The Red Cross, however, stubbornly maintained the practice until 1950. Meanwhile, many states took even longer to change procedures; in Arkansas and Louisiana, for example, the practice of segregating blood persisted until the late 1960s and early 1970s, long after Snipes was told the hospital did not have any "Black blood."[43] World War II medics enthusiastically adopted some of Drew's other notable contributions, including groundbreaking techniques for long-term blood storage, and saved thousands of lives during the war.

The American medical community's failure to racially integrate its blood supply sooner led to countless lives, including Maceo Snipes's, being needlessly lost. Tragically, in promoting the Double V Campaign many other civil rights workers would also lose their lives, including Medgar Evers, another World War II veteran, slain as a result of his efforts to guarantee civil rights to African Americans. The struggle to ensure equal access to blood and health care was merely part of a larger fight that included access to public facilities, voting rights, and civil rights that continued well into the twenty-first century.

Undoubtedly, the civil rights movement was strengthened by the great variety of African American voices pointing out the many striking similarities between the systemic racism of Nazi Germany and the United States throughout the course of World War II. As we have seen, many of the Nazi congruities within US law and policy were not incidental but carefully studied, documented, and legislated by Nazi political officials. In the United States, when this episode aired, the Civil Rights Act of 1964, the Voting Rights Act of 1965, and the *Loving v. Virginia* decision had not yet occurred. The race-based national quota system and racial criteria for naturalization were not yet fully overturned. They remained largely intact until the Hart-Celler Act was passed in 1965, nearly two years after this episode aired. Although the episode did not specifically mention these laws and policies, the ideologies that helped to fuel them and justify them were dramatized in Peter Vollmer's character and platform. And while these civil rights achievements were cause for celebration, complicated legacies remain. Although the race-based quotas were eliminated, immigration, refugee, and asylum caps established by the Hart-Celler Act have resulted in a drastic increase of the number of immigrants considered undocumented or illegal in the United States. The recent repeal of Section IV of the Voting Rights Act of 1965 has resulted in a number of states making it increasingly difficult for many residents to vote, drastically limiting the number of polling places and instituting stricter requirements for casting ballots. Many of these issues are far from resolved.

Just as segregation and racial inequalities persisted well after World War II, race-baiting demagoguery surely did not entirely disappear from American political and social life either. Orval Faubus, who resisted integrating Arkansas schools after the *Brown v. Board of Education* ruling of 1954, served as governor of Arkansas until 1967, while George Wallace announced in his 1963 inaugural address as governor of Alabama: "In the name of the greatest people that have ever trod this earth, I draw the line in the dust and toss the gauntlet before the feet of tyranny, and I say segregation now, segregation tomorrow, segregation forever."[44] While the voices of ardent segregationists could be heard loud and clear in some of the highest political offices in the country, those opposed, including renowned jazz composer and bassist Charles Mingus, were frequently stifled. Mingus's composition "Fables of Faubus" sharply criticized Faubus and Jim Crow segregation. Columbia Records, however, refused to publish the song with its original lyrics. Instead, it released an instrumental version on the 1959 album *Mingus Ah-Um*. Mingus opted to record and release the original song in 1960 on Candid, an independent record label, including the lyrics that sharply condemned Faubus and the hatred of Jim Crow policies.[45] Similarly, following the murder of Medgar Evers in Mississippi and the bombing of the Sixteenth Street Baptist Church in Birmingham, which killed four young Black girls and injured many others, Nina Simone, the brilliant musician and composer, wrote "Mississippi Goddam." Like Mingus, she frequently ran into staunch opposition within the music industry; for example, radio stations destroyed copies of her records and several states banned the song altogether.[46]

While the civil rights movement continued the long struggle of chipping away at the legal foundation of systemic racism, the Black Panthers, Angela Davis, Martin Luther King Jr., and many other activists would soon realize that the economic underpinnings were just as crucial to confront and dismantle, as evidenced in the Black Panthers' Ten Point Program, Davis's work to end mass incarceration, and the MLK-backed Poor People's Campaign. Just as Hitlerian hatred could live on through the campaign slogans and platforms of politicians, it could also achieve some of its ends somewhat indirectly through housing and job markets, state budgets, criminal justice policies, and tax codes. In other words, "He's Alive" and perhaps at his most dangerous when he can live unannounced.

In 1964, Republican presidential candidate Barry Goldwater's slogan proclaimed, "In Your Heart You Know He's Right," alluding to an unspoken, yet understood set of beliefs his supporters shared. Despite Goldwater allegedly being against racial discrimination, he was adamantly opposed to the federal government's involvement in civil rights issues, including the *Brown v. Board* ruling and the Civil Rights Act of 1964. This opposition to the federal government and support for state's rights served as a convenient cloak for those who opposed the civil rights movement. Consequently, segregationists and white supremacists had a somewhat unexpected ally, equipped with a new political tactic. Election night brought the point home further, as Goldwater's only electoral success the 1964 presidential race, other in than his home state of Arizona, was in the Deep South, where support from white people handed him electoral votes. Goldwater's campaign sparked a realignment of the major political parties, while also helping to redefine the Republican Party. Recognizing the importance of these developments, Rod Serling, speaking before the Anti-Defamation League in 1964, expressed how "bias, hate, inequality are specters that have haunted us in other times. What is appallingly different in this nineteen hundred and sixty-fourth year of our Lord, is the strange and apparent respectability which somehow clothes these forces of discrimination and intolerance." He continued, "Where once a German-American Bund, a Silver Shirt, a William Dudley Pelley, a Gerald L. K. Smith, were harmless, insane, and discontinued microbes—the things they believed in, the goals they sought, the causes they espoused, are now integral parts of the John Birch Society, the White Citizens Councils, and—if you will forgive me . . . God help us—a strong element of the Republican Party. . . . We are now witness to an overt and predatory attempt to make this kind of insanity a part of the government of the United States."[47]

Although Goldwater was not successful, the next Republican victor, Richard Nixon, refined and deployed many of Goldwater's tactics in what became known as the Southern strategy. One of Nixon's key advisors, Lee Atwater, explained the Southern strategy: "You start out in 1954 by saying, 'N——, n——, n——.' By 1968 you can't say 'n——'—that hurts you, backfires. So, you say stuff like, uh, forced busing, states' rights, and all that stuff, and you're getting so abstract. Now, you're talking about cutting taxes, and all these things you're talking about are totally economic things and a byproduct of them is, blacks get hurt worse than whites. . . . 'We want to cut this,' is much more abstract than even the busing thing, uh, and a hell of a lot more abstract than 'N——, n——.'"[48] Just as racist scapegoating was frequently deployed as a way to package and conceal other political intentions, economic and fiscal platforms could also be a way to conceal racism and white supremacy.

One of the main aspects of American policy pertaining to race and immigration that the Nazis actually disliked was its convoluted and patchwork nature. The fact that, for example, African Americans had the constitutional right to vote but were disenfranchised at the state and local level through poll taxes, literacy tests, and violence was much more complicated than Nazi policymakers desired. Relatedly, the state laws in the United States pertaining to miscegenation were not all uniform; some states even had no bans on interracial marriage. Nazi officials wanted, instead, clear, unambiguous laws to establish and uphold racial hierarchies. From their perspective, the legacies of Reconstruction and particularly the Fourteenth Amendment, which granted citizens equal protections before the law, necessitated a complex, cloak-and-dagger approach to take certain civil rights away (i.e., poll taxes and literacy tests serving as the cloak and massive disenfranchisement being the dagger). While the Nazis preferred a more straightforward legal approach, the convoluted and cloaked nature of many American laws has enabled many of these systemic inequalities to persist and made dismantling them that much more difficult.

George Lincoln Rockwell represented the explicit, dagger-without-a-cloak approach the Nazis preferred. Rockwell's unsuccessful attempts to garner favor with more mainstream political voices meant that many Americans were reluctant to fully adopt all of Rockwell's ideas as well as his explicit, unfiltered approach. Rockwell's biographer notes how, despite his limited success during his lifetime, his many legacies include "White Power as a unifying concept and an organizing tool; Holocaust denial as a means of rewriting history and muting the moral lessons of anti-Semitism; and the link to the Christian Identity movement that gave the racists and anti-Semites . . . a contrivance to camouflage their purpose with the cloak of religion." He explains how "under the right political, economic, and social circumstances a frightened and angry people could abandon their fragile Republic to the seduction of the man with a quick fix."[49] These sobering legacies remain.

The episode "He's Alive" has proved prophetic in many ways. Not only has race-baiting continued to be a dominant feature of American politics and social life, but the reshaping of the term *minority* has gained considerable traction. Framing a controversial point of view as somehow representing an oppressed minority or marginalized group has been one of the defining features of modern American political and social life. Claiming to belong to a persecuted minority, politicians and pundits alike have attempted to legitimize conspiracy theories and grab attention and power through tropes, cries, and performances of persecution. In doing so, they have also arguably obfuscated the issues of discrimination and oppression, rendering many of the most vulnerable victims increasingly invisible. Just as Governor Wallace decried racial integration in 1963 as "tyranny," constantly redefining political terms has been a way to frustrate, stifle, and confuse efforts toward racial and social equality. Amid a cacophony of outcries, it becomes increasingly essential to distinguish real suffering from the fake, tortured performances of affliction.

The same year World War II ended, in her book *Race and Racism,* anthropologist Ruth Benedict surveyed some of the recent damage racism wrought throughout the world and reflected on the postwar era to come: "If the future of racism is like its past, these theories will depend not on any scientific fact but on . . . what power politics are in the ascendant." She continued, "Racism in its nationalistic phase . . . has been a politician's plaything. . . . It is a dangerous plaything, a sword which can be turned in any direction to condemn the enemy of the moment. The inescapable conclusion . . . is that these racist claims are a front designed to hide self-seeking aggressions and alliances. They are camouflage. For practical guidance . . . we should do well therefore to go behind the racists' slogans and look squarely at the conflict they are trying to foment." In this way, whether the conflict or challenge involves foreign policy, poverty, unequal housing, or education, solving them through racist scapegoating will never bring real, lasting resolution. In the decades that followed World War II, civil rights workers risked and even lost their lives, demonstrating that racist policies were not the solution to the problem but its very crux. Viewers watching this episode who were perhaps inclined to interpret Vollmer's character more generously and sympathetically might say he possibly has a right to be angry and frustrated due to possible unemployment, financial frustration, or for personal reasons (i.e., traumatic experiences during childhood). Whether the conflicts are internal or external, as Ruth Benedict wrote, they "are sometimes justified. . . . But we shall not have decided the matter on the dubious grounds of racism."[50]

The episode makes it explicitly clear that racist hatred is not the answer for Vollmer or anyone, foreshadowing Martin Luther King Jr., that "the price that America must pay for the continued oppression of the Negro and other minority groups is the price of its own destruction."[51] If apostles of hate and white supremacy are to be considered victims, it is only in the reflexive sense—they are victims of their own self-destructive hate. In this way, white supremacy perpetuates damage to all races, including white Americans who may even support Vollmer's cause.

In fact, George Lincoln Rockwell, like Peter Vollmer, met an early demise: one of his compatriots took his life in 1967. Rockwell had decided to "rebrand" in a sense, opting to abandon the swastika and change the party's emphasis from Nazism to "White Power." Several party members were not happy with this, however. Many of those closest to Rockwell believed that a conspiracy lay behind his assassination—the idea was to make Rockwell a martyr—while others would take over the party and uphold its explicit Nazi identity. In much the same way as Vollmer ordered Nick's execution, many within the American Nazi Party believed one of their members, Matt Koehl, had help in killing Rockwell. Following Rockwell's murder, Koehl and the American Nazi Party tried to turn his death and burial into a publicity stunt, unsuccessfully attempting to have him buried at Arlington National Cemetery.[52] Rockwell's life was arguably an example of "the ageless impulse of men and women eaten by the disease of hatred to find a political expression or rationalization for their malady."[53] And according to his biographer, "leashing George Lincoln Rockwell did not leash the beast forever. Each generation must confront that demon anew."[54]

In many ways, white supremacy has been the original promise, hope, and dream that has also left so many Americans unfulfilled. For generations, it has denied millions of Americans citizenship, civil rights, paths of social mobility, education, and self-expression. At the same time, it has left many white Americans disillusioned and disappointed, because the white supremacist promise actually has ensured that poverty, health, community, individuality, and a humane approach to legitimate needs, regardless of race, would be actively neglected. To actively deny the rights and needs of others requires one to also deny their own humanity and basic needs, reflecting what James Baldwin once expressed: "What I'm much more concerned about is what white Americans have done to themselves; what has been done to me is irrelevant simply because there is nothing more you can do to me. But in doing it, you've done something to yourself. In evading my humanity, you have done something to your own humanity."[55] This is shown throughout the episode as Peter Vollmer has one of his best friends killed to artificially create a martyr. When Stanley mentions how he misses Nick, Vollmer disparages Stanley's response to his friend's death: Nick is not even worth missing. While Vollmer took Nick's life, he also took a meaningful relationship away from himself and his cohort. In short, the dehumanizing and degrading racism Vollmer espouses had toxic effects not just outside of the group but within it as well, with one friend murdered and another scorned. Ultimately, when Vollmer chooses to kill Ernst, he has not only taken the life of another human, he has taken one step closer to taking his own life in a sense. By eliminating his closest relationship, he has also killed a part of himself.

In many ways, Vollmer epitomizes the loneliness and self-estrangement that serve as essential ingredients for totalitarianism, according to Hannah Arendt. In her foundational work, *Origins of Totalitarianism*, Arendt argues that totalitarianism is based on the destruction of our relationship to ourselves and others: "Totalitarian government, like all tyrannies, certainly could not exist without . . . isolating men, their political capacities. But totalitarian domination . . . is not content with this isolation and destroys private life as well. It bases itself on loneliness, on the experience of not belonging to the world at all, which is among the most radical and desperate experiences of man." Vollmer refuses belonging to anyone. His time spent alone is not spent in any kind of meaningful inner dialogue—he can hear only the hate-filled demands of Hitler's shadow. By the end of the episode, Vollmer has lost all individuality and has effectively become a mere conduit dispensing hate. Arendt asserts, "Loneliness, the common ground for terror, the essence of totalitarian government," serves as "the preparation of its executioners and victims," and "is closely connected with uprootedness and superfluousness."[56] Vollmer, in this sense, is both the executioner and victim, exemplifying a lack of rootedness, purpose, and importance in the world, while also taking these things away from his friends and family, even if it means murdering them. The disdain Vollmer feels toward others—Jews and immigrants, for instance, is a feeling he clearly holds for himself. According to Arendt, these are totalitarianism's origins.

When he returns to the town hall, Hitler asks, "Sentimentality?" Vollmer simply responds, "None." Hitler then asks, "Steel tonight?" Vollmer confidently responds, "Steel." Having apparently transformed from human to steel, Vollmer has now officially dispensed with the lives of two of his friends while also discarding his own humanity. Vollmer's absence of mind ensures that destructive circle finally closes in on him. While Vollmer insists he is made of steel, in his death he demonstrates, in true totalitarian fashion, that the fantasy and ideology take precedence over reality itself—denying what is true until his last breath. As Arendt had argued years earlier, the "ideal subject of totalitarian rule is not the convinced Nazi or the convinced Communist, but people for whom the distinction between fact and fiction (i.e., the reality of experience) and the distinction between true and false (i.e., the standards of thought) no longer exist."[57] The desperate desire to escape the world and cling to a hate-filled fantasy becomes all-consuming. Vollmer shows this not only in his belief he is made of steel but by clinging to what James Baldwin once called the "lie of whiteness." This false sense of racial superiority threatens life everywhere.[58] Additionally, this negative solidarity, finding a collective identity through hating others, is yet another key component in Arendt's assessment.[59] The alternative, namely confronting the truth of our own vulnerable humanity and the humanity of others opens a world of yet unexplored possibilities. As Baldwin once proposed: "I would like us to do something unprecedented . . . to create ourselves without finding it necessary to create an enemy."[60] The potentialities were, and still are, immeasurable.

"He's Alive" ultimately argues, as Ernst says (and 1948 Republican presidential candidate Thomas Dewey once stated with regard to communism), that one cannot simply shoot an idea with a gun. Just as Nazi Germany was militarily defeated, its ideology could not be entirely vanquished through force of arms. In this sense, the ideology of white supremacy both preceded Hitler and has long followed him. While this episode, somewhat understandably, does not go into detail regarding precedents of and predecessors to Nazi ideology, it does remind Americans that they are not inherently immune or protected from the world's most notorious and destructive ideologies. It also, however, serves as a reminder that for a depiction of white supremacy to be approved of, it must somehow make the ideology seem more foreign in origins, rather than arising from American soil, as Serling attempted in "I Am the Night—Color Me Black." You may not be able to shoot an idea with a gun, but there remain plenty of ways to obfuscate its origins.

The enduring legacies of the Double V Campaign—fighting Hitlers abroad and at home—remind us that military victories overseas do not guarantee victories over ideologies of hate at home. As African American journalist George Schuyler once stated, "Our war is not against Hitler in Europe, but against the Hitlers in America."[61] What was true in the 1940s remained true in the 1960s and beyond. Abraham Foxman noted in his introduction to Hitler's infamous text, "We dismissed him as a madman, and we ignored his wretched book; the result was a tragedy of unprecedented proportions. This is yet another lesson to take from *Mein Kampf*: the lesson of vigilance and responsibility, of not closing our eyes to the evil around us."[62] The United States may have helped defeat Hitler and Nazi Germany militarily, but the passionate and violent backlash to the civil rights movement also helped keep his ideologies alive long after his death. Moreover, the distortion of fact and fiction and the deep disconnection from ourselves and each other continues to provide fertile ground for the potential growth of totalitarianism. How long Hitler's shadowy ghost would potentially be stalking the land would depend partially on Americans' willingness to not close their eyes to the evil around them and, perhaps even more importantly, within them. For Serling, this also meant confronting the neglected ghosts of World War II.

Fighting a War, Combating a Myth

How the Horrors of World War II Shaped
The Twilight Zone

On June 28, 1975, Rod Serling died. He had suffered a heart attack in early May and subsequently experienced two more, with the third proving fatal. Three months prior to his death, Serling gave what would become his final interview. He sat down with Linda Brevelle at La Taverna, one of his favorite restaurants on the Sunset Strip in West Hollywood, and discussed his prolific television writing career. After conversing about some of the challenges of Serling's craft, Brevelle asked him what the emotional low point was in his life. Without hesitation, he replied that it was during the war: "I was convinced I wasn't going to come back." Serling had served in the 511th Parachute Infantry Regiment of the Eleventh Airborne Division in the Pacific theater during World War II. This period in Serling's life not only proved to be his emotional low point, it also served as his primary creative impetus. He told a group of college students in 1970, "I was traumatized into writing by war events, by going through a war in a combat situation and feeling . . . the terrible need for some sort of therapy, get it out of my gut, write it down. This is the way it began for me."[1] In this sense, there is no better place from which to start to understand the creative output of Rod Serling than his military service.

As a teenager, Rod expressed a great deal of eagerness to enroll in the military and fight in the war. Like the 3 million Americans who had enlisted in 1942 alone, Serling was undeniably motivated by the attack on Pearl Harbor and the outpouring of patriotism and war propaganda that followed.[2] Brimming with enthusiasm, he even contemplated enlisting before he graduated from high school, but a history teacher eventually talked him into getting his degree first: "War is a temporal thing. It ends. An education doesn't.

Without your degree, where will you be after the war?"[3] This provocative question led Serling to rethink his situation and stay at Binghamton Central, where he earned his high school diploma on January 15, 1943. The very next morning, he enlisted as a paratrooper. Having gone through basic training in Georgia, Serling became part of the Eleventh Airborne Division. On April 25, 1944, the newly formed unit was ordered to California and soon thereafter to the frontlines in the Pacific Islands. In November, Gen. Douglas MacArthur ordered the Eleventh to secure the Filipino island of Leyte, and when the war ended the following year, Serling's regiment became part of the postwar occupation of Japan. These two years of service would prove to have an incalculable impact on Serling's life and work.

For veterans of any war, it is invariably true that coming back means not only physically stepping foot in one's home country again. Rather, it also means coming back mentally and psychologically. To do this, Elaine Scarry argues in *The Body in Pain,* humans fundamentally need to articulate past suffering: "One of two things is true of pain. . . . Either it remains inarticulate or else the moment it . . . becomes articulate it silences all else."[4] Rod Serling's writing still has the capability to silence audiences into horror, reflection, and suspense— sometimes all at once. This ability was arguably borne out of Serling's lifelong attempts to articulate his own pain, particularly regarding war and ever-present death. Not only did numerous *Twilight Zone* episodes focus on war and mortality, but several of his early teleplays, including *The Strike* (1954) and *The Rack* (1956), dramatically depicted the Korean War. Serling had seen, felt, heard, smelled, and lived warfare, and he nearly died because of it.

In his adult years, he had to cope not only with the experiences of war but with how it was grossly mythologized and romanticized in popular portrayals. World War II veteran and literary scholar Paul Fussell explained how "optimistic publicity and euphemism had rendered their experience so falsely that it would never be readily communicable." Veterans like Serling and Fussell "knew that in its representation to the laity what was happening to them was systematically sanitized and Norman Rockwellized, not to mention Disneyfied." In the United States, "the meaning of the war seemed inaccessible," and "America has not yet understood what the Second World War was like and has thus been unable to . . . arrive at something like public maturity."[5] It is likely that Serling turned to fiction because the medium allowed him to express wartime trauma, emotion, and pain without having to battle public memory and consensus at every turn. For Serling, violence is "nurtured and . . . grows in a soil of prejudice and of hate and of bigotry."[6] While he believed his military service was justified, he also clearly found it important to wrestle with some of the justifications for the violence. These could live on and wreak destruction on generations to come, including the perpetrators of the violence themselves.

Serving as two examples, "A Quality of Mercy" portrays the racist violence that profoundly shaped the Pacific War, while "Thirty-Fathom Grave" illustrates some of the long-term psychological impacts of experiencing real combat (S3, e15; S4, e2). Both aspects of the war, its racially inspired violence and the psychological fallout its survivors experienced, were almost entirely missing from popular portrayals of the war. In this way, not only did combat experiences necessitate a kind of creative catharsis, so too did the war's popular myths. Serling's early encounter with romanticized depictions of World War II arguably prepared him to do battle with the whitewashed portrayals of American life on television throughout the 1950s and 1960s.

And just as World War II inspired much of Serling's work, it profoundly shaped the Cold War. In terms of human cost, World War II represented the worst tragedy in the history of the Soviet Union. As one Soviet reformer pointed out when describing his nation's Cold War policies, "it was widely argued that the people would forgive the leadership anything but a repetition of the tragedy of the beginning of World War II and that this was the primary political priority."[7] Just as the Soviets approached the Cold War as the avoidance of another immense tragedy, and used it to domestically suppress oppositional elements, American policy makers used public perception of World War II myth and memory to ostracize advocates of peaceful alternatives to war, to further justify unprecedented increases in the defense budget, and an ever-increasing number of foreign interventions during the last half of the twentieth century. The war, in other words, was not over.

The Enemy Is a Different Race

"A Quality of Mercy" aired in the third season of *The Twilight Zone*, on December 29, 1961. While this episode deals with the dual realities of racism and brutal violence, it is far from being the only one to explore such topics. "The Purple Testament" dramatizes an officer's ability to foresee which members of his regiment would die before the next mission, illustrating the psychological weight and guilt commanders bore when following orders and leading their men into the next casualty-filled battle (S1, e19). "The Encounter" depicts a young Japanese man and a hardened US Marine who share stories over a beer in an attic filled with war memorabilia (S5, e31). The racial tension and baggage are palpable until the two men come to blows. In the end, the marine is killed with the same samurai sword he took from a surrendered Japanese soldier whom he killed during the war. With these episodes, the unique challenges of combat-related deaths and racial tension during World War II are presented as open wounds that could prove fatal without careful consideration.

"A Quality of Mercy" begins with American infantrymen scoping out a nearby cave with their binoculars. Inside the cave are several Japanese soldiers who stand in the way of the American advance. After repeated mortar blasts miss the cave, the exasperated platoon is pleased to hear that they may be able to simply bypass it: "I've got no big yen to run into anything anymore, not at this stage of the game," Sergeant Causarano says. The men reflect on the pitiful state of the sick and starving Japanese soldiers who also have no idea that the war is essentially over for them. Amid this practically lifeless scene, Serling introduces the episode: "It's August 1945, the last grimy pages of a dirty, torn book of war. The place is the Philippine Islands. The men are what's left of a platoon of American infantry, whose dulled and tired eyes set deep in dulled and tired faces look toward a miracle, that moment when the nightmare appears to be coming to an end. But they've got one more battle to fight, and in a moment, we'll observe that battle. August 1945, Philippine Islands. But in reality, it's high noon in *The Twilight Zone*."

Immediately thereafter, a Jeep carrying a new officer pulls up to the infantry unit and it soon becomes clear that the platoon has gone through several officers, each one killed off by the Japanese. After their new officer, Lieutenant Katell, is briefed on the unit's current situation, he opts to look at the targeted cave for himself. Very quickly, however, his eagerness for action becomes readily apparent as his thirst for killing obviously surpasses any of his recently acquired, battle-weary subordinates. Instead of agreeing to bypass the sick and starved Japanese soldiers, the lieutenant claims that they are going to have to wipe them out. After several of the men mockingly comment that Katell has the wrong platoon, the lieutenant adamantly retorts, "When I tell you boys to jump, you'll jump. If I tell you to stand up on your feet, you'll stand up. If I tell you to head toward that cave with weapons forward and bayonets fixed, that's exactly what you're going to be doing." The soldiers, however, appear deeply unimpressed with the officer's youth and evident lack of battle experience.

Lieutenant Katell asks the sergeant what he thinks. Causarano first tells him to take the gold bars off his helmet and collar so as not to make himself

The unscathed Lieutenant Katell arrives to take command of a war-weary platoon. Still from "A Quality of Mercy" (4:50)

an obvious target to the Japanese. After the sergeant says they should wait to see if another unit's mortar shells can hit the cave, Katell fires back, claiming they could wipe out the Japanese inside of an hour if they throw some grenades into the cave and "pulverize them." Unconvinced, the sergeant advises him, "This is no football game" but "one long, hard gut ache with a lot of torn-up, mangled guys" and explains, "It's going to take a long time for us to forget it. . . . You haven't been shot at yet. And you haven't shot anybody either." Katell states that while the sergeant has been fighting longer, he will soon show his efficiency at killing Japanese. While the other soldiers continue to lie around, exhausted from lack of sleep, one remarks, "This one is bloodthirsty," while another sardonically adds, "You don't think he'll want us to scalp them?" Infuriated by the men's sarcasm and irreverence, Katell asks if they are tired of killing "Japs" or just don't have the stomach for it. The sergeant laments that they have "seen enough dead men to last us for the rest of our lives," but if the lieutenant has some "big yen to do some killing . . . we'll do some killing for you, but don't ask us to stand up and cheer."

As the soldiers reluctantly prepare for the assault and camouflage their faces with mud, Katell, sizing up Causarano, tells him that he either has battle fatigue or is "chicken." The sergeant replies, "Maybe neither, maybe a little bit of both" and offers his honest take on his new commanding officer: "You're a pea-green shavetail just fresh from some campus. You're afraid you won't bag your limit, or worse . . . somebody might spot you as a Johnny-come-lately instead of a killer of men. . . . You want to prove your manhood but it's a little late in the day and there aren't many choices left in how to do it. It all boils down to that lousy cave full of sick, pitiful, half-dead losers and a platoon of dirty, tired men that have their craw full of this war." A frustrated Katell dresses down the sergeant, describing him as "lousy" as well as "the rest of these poor, sad, sensitive, sick boys you want me to bottle-feed!" The newly acquired officer asks his men, "Did somebody forget to tell you, when you fight a war, you fight a war. And you kill until you're ordered to stop killing!" After Causarano asks how many men have to be killed for him to be satisfied, Katell retorts, "Offhand, I'd say all of them. No matter who they are or where they are, if they're the enemy, they get it! First day of the war or last day of the war, they get it!"

When Katell turns back toward his men, his binoculars fall to the ground and he suddenly finds himself transported back to May 4, 1942, as part of a Japanese regiment. His name is no longer Katell, but Lieutenant Yamuri. When one of his fellow soldiers hands him his binoculars, he is shocked to find himself among the Japanese and runs off into the trees. As he races into a clearing, he is quickly fired upon by an American machine gunner and retreats to the unit. Confused, the lieutenant asks, "Those are Americans in the cave?" Sergeant Yamazaki answers, "Yes, sir. We figure there are twenty or thirty of them. Most of them wounded." After the lieutenant proposes that they bypass the wounded men in the cave, his superior officer asks, "Bypass them, lieutenant? Is that tactical, or is that some sudden nugget of compassion that you have unearthed in your fever?" After Yamuri states that they cannot do the Japanese army much harm in their wounded state, he is rebutted once more:

Neither can they sink a battleship, but nevertheless, we have to destroy them. . . . The . . . men in the cave, they are Americans, they are enemy. Healthy, wounded, walking or lying, they are the enemy. . . . The Japanese Army wipes out its opponents. . . . The comparative health and well-being of the enemy, his comfort, or his

> discomfort, the degree of his anguish or his incapacities have no
> more bearing on a military action, a tactical move, or a decision of
> command than the fortunes of an anthill that you step on when we
> move out to attack. . . . This is war and in war, you kill. You kill, lieu-
> tenant. You kill until you are ordered to stop killing.

After Yamuri asks his superior officer how many men have to be killed for
him to be satisfied, the answer eerily reflects the exact philosophy Katell once
uttered to his infantrymen: "Offhand, I'd say all of them. No matter who they
are or where they are, if they are the enemy, they are to be destroyed! First day
of the war or last day of the war, we will destroy them!" When Yamuri again
asks if they might bypass the injured American troops in a cave, the captain
slaps him across the face, and he soon finds himself again an American officer in August 1945.

Before the infantry can attack the cave, the men are suddenly ordered to
pull back after being informed that the United States will soon be dropping
the atomic bomb on Japan. Amid screams of joy and celebration, the lieutenant merely looks dumbfounded and remains silent. Addressing his once
bloodthirsty superior, Sergeant Causarano tells the lieutenant not to worry,
as there will be more wars and more people to kill. Katell, stunned by his
experience, responds somberly, "I hope not," clearly showing his transformed
views of war and death as Serling offers his closing narration: "'The quality
of mercy is not strained, it droppeth as the gentle rain from heaven upon
the place beneath. It blesseth him that gives and him that takes.' Shakespeare,
The Merchant of Venice, but applicable to any moment in time, to any group
of soldiery, to any nation on the face of the Earth—or, in this case, to *The
Twilight Zone.*"

From the opening scenes, the episode's main focal points come into
view—the gruesome, arduous violence and the racist attitudes that predomi-
nately characterized the war in the Pacific. Among the many veterans who
later recollected these aspects of the conflict, Eugene Sledge recalled, "To
deny this hatred or make light of it would be . . . a lie. . . . This collective attitude, Marine and Japanese, resulted in savage, ferocious fighting with no
holds barred. . . . This was a brutish, primitive hatred as characteristic of the
horror of war in the Pacific as the palm trees and the islands."[8] The conflict in
the Pacific theater has since been considered a kind of race war, most notably
by John Dower in his seminal book, *War without Mercy: Race and Power in
the Pacific War.* For American soldiers who experienced the war firsthand,

The transformed lieutenant suddenly finds himself behind Japanese lines. Still from "A Quality of Mercy" (14:44)

like Serling, the brutality typically resulted in a collective weariness, illustrated in the platoon members lamenting how many dead men they have seen. One of the soldiers in Serling's own unit recollected overrunning a Japanese campsite very similar to the one featured in the episode: "Japanese flags were strewn about. . . . Maps, diaries, code books . . . lay on the mossy ground of the village among the dead Japanese. Awe-inspiring above all was the sight of the Japanese wounded, deserted in caves and lean-tos on the side of the canyon. Gagged and bound and left to die, these pitiable creatures would have inspired the revolted pity of the fiercest soldier."[9] This episode's focus particularly on these soldiers—those wounded and "left to die" in a cave and who no longer really represent a major threat—clearly was deliberate to show that killing was neither glorious nor was it always about survival. Like Sergeant Causarano, Serling must have felt a "revolted pity," or, in the words of his script, "a quality of mercy," toward these Japanese soldiers on the verge of death near the end of World War II. Although the war-weary soldiers in this episode have a sense of pity toward their enemy combatants, Katell clearly does not share the same attitude, as his overly simplistic and zealous views become instantly apparent. When one of the men alludes to the inexperienced lieutenant wanting to scalp the Japanese, his sardonic metaphor powerfully reveals these dual wartime realities of racism and savage violence perpetrated by both sides.[10]

In fact, Katell's bloodthirsty sentiments reflect those of Serling's own commander, Gen. Joseph May Swing, who temporarily led the Eleventh Airborne Division. He wrote, in a letter to General March describing the events on Leyte:

> It would do your heart good to see the . . . joyful manner in which they kill the rats. I really believe this is the first time the Japs have run against American troops that never stop coming . . . my troops keep going until dark . . . so they don't know where we are located. As a result, we've killed about twice as many Japs in proportion to our own casualties as had any other division . . . the dawn attack caught 300 Japs sleeping outside . . . and we slaughtered them there with bayonet, knife, and hand grenades.[11]

Swing's boast with regard to the number of kills in his unit rather than any specific tactical or strategic gains reflects the murderous priorities of Katell as well as of many officers during the actual war.

Moreover, Swing's deeply racist language, referring to the Japanese as *rats* and *Japs* also figures prominently in the lieutenant's vocabulary: "We're gonna kill Japs! That's my job!" Far from being a unique case, however, racially charged language was featured all over in the propaganda and news of the day. And although propaganda abounded on every side of the war, the Americans' depiction of the Japanese was particularly dehumanizing and far worse than any characterization of the Nazis. Not only were these representations Japanese even more degrading than those of other American enemies, there existed no concept similar to that of the "good German." While Americans were able for the most part to psychologically separate Nazis from other Germans, no such nuance existed toward the Japanese in wartime propaganda, as the Japanese were indiscriminately characterized as barbarians, apes, and even parasitical insects. One illustration, originally published in *Leatherneck* magazine, depicted the Japanese soldiers as buck-toothed lice and included the caption, "The first serious outbreak of this lice epidemic was officially noted on December 7, 1941, at Honolulu. . . . To the Marine Corps, especially trained in combating this type of pestilence, was assigned the gigantic task of extermination. . . . Flame throwers, mortars, grenades, and bayonets have proven to be an effective remedy. But before a complete cure may be affected the origin of the plague, the breeding grounds around the Tokyo area, must be completely annihilated."[12] In this way, war was much less about fighting for the four freedoms than about wiping out diseased parasites. The character Lieutenant Cable later sardonically expressed this sentiment in the Rodgers and Hammerstein song, "You've Got to Be Carefully Taught" in *South Pacific* (1949). Cable describes how teaching racial prejudice related to skin color, eye shape, and other physical attributes are vital for one's "education."

During the war, these ideas played out with horrific results on the battlefield. As John Dower explains, "Race hate fed atrocities, and atrocities in turn fanned the fires of race hate. The dehumanization of the Other contributed immeasurably to the psychological distancing that facilitates killing. . . . Such dehumanization, for example, surely facilitated the decisions to make civilian populations the targets of concentrated attack, whether by conventional or nuclear weapons."[13] Before civilian populations became the primary targets for two nuclear bombs, the horrors of combat in the Pacific served as a grisly prelude that foreshadowed the small logical step it would take to justify Hiroshima and Nagasaki. Sledge described several such pre-nuclear atrocities in his memoir, *With the Old Breed*: "One day a buddy told me he had a unique souvenir to show me. We sat on a rock as he carefully removed a package from his combat pack. He unwrapped layers of waxed papers that had originally covered rations and proudly held out his prize for me to see. . . . I remonstrated as I stared in horror at the shriveled human hand he had unwrapped." His friend explained how he thought it was a much more interesting souvenir than the common gold teeth other soldiers tended to pilfer, but he still needed to "dry it in the sun a little more so it won't stink."[14]

Sledge also described Japanese atrocities: "The bodies were badly decomposed and nearly blackened by exposure. . . . One man had been decapitated. His head lay on his chest; his hands had been severed from his wrists and also lay on his chest near his chin. In disbelief I stared at the face as I realized the Japanese had cut off the dead Marine's penis and stuffed it into his mouth. The corpse next to him had been treated similarly." After witnessing such horrifying butchery, Sledge honestly stated, "My emotions solidified into rage and a hatred for the Japanese beyond anything I ever had experienced."[15]

Another veteran of the Pacific, Anthony Coulis, begged the question, "Why did we extract such extreme delight in firing a burst of machine-gun fire into already dead Japanese?" As Coulis recalls, he and his fellow marines fired repeatedly at the deceased and watched as their "bodies . . . jerked and quivered," while he and his comrades "would laugh gleefully and hysterically." Only when the Japanese corpses became so badly torn open that they started to emit "a stench that stung our nostrils and turned our stomachs, did we snap back to sanity, turning our backs now on the dead enemy, disgusted with our behavior." Coulis finally and impossibly asks, particularly when it comes to warfare, "When does sanity end and madness begin?"[16] While the question remained a dilemma for most veterans, Dower has shown how incidents like these usually did not inspire philosophical discussions, but instead were opportunistically used on both sides to further justify and intensify the already racially-fueled hatred and extreme violence toward the enemy.

American prejudice and racism existed not just toward the Japanese and Japanese Americans, who were forcibly rounded up during the war in camps, it was also clearly evidenced by the military's treatment of its own Black soldiers. The all-white regiment in this episode merely serves to reflect the realities of segregation in the army. In this way, Jim Crow was at work not only in the southern United States, but in the US military all over the world. In addition to being segregated from white regiments, Black soldiers could not become officers and were frequently assigned only menial jobs such as cooks and mess attendants, leading to the protests encapsulated in the Double V Campaign. The all-Black 555th Airborne Regiment, for example, was never deployed overseas and stationed instead on the West Coast of the United States to put out fires started by Japanese fire balloons. Secretary of War Henry L. Stimson expressed his racial views, which many also undoubtedly shared: "Leadership is not imbedded in the Negro race yet and today to make commissioned officers lead men into battle—colored men—is only to work a disaster to both." In this way, institutionalized racism and segregation in the military created a vicious circle, much like the violent atrocities had on the battlefield. Black soldiers were seen as inherently inferior, and they were never allowed the chance to prove otherwise. However, not all commanders believed segregation necessarily the best practice. General George Marshall knew that segregation and unequal treatment presented a serious problem: "My God! My God! I don't know what to do about this race question in the Army. . . . I tell you frankly, it is the worst thing we have to deal with. . . . We are getting a situation on our hands that may explode right in our faces."[17] Despite an executive order desegregating the military in 1948, unequal treatment of Black soldiers persisted, as they were banned from most veterans' organizations and were funneled into unskilled, low-paying jobs through the GI Bill.[18]

As John Dower aptly explained with regard to World War II, the "propagandistic deception often lies, not in the false claims of enemy atrocities, but in the pious depiction of such behavior as peculiar to the other side."[19] When Katell is forcibly transformed into a Japanese officer and ordered to brutally kill Americans, he suddenly can realize the damaged, vulnerable humanity that lies on the other end of a gun. When his own blind, violent hatred and racially charged rancor is put on display before him, he finally sees its destructiveness. His transformation resembles a scene Sledge describes: "I shuddered and choked. A wild desperate feeling of anger, frustration, and pity gripped me. It was an emotion that always would torture my mind when I saw men trapped and was unable to do anything but watch as they were hit. . . . I turned my face away and wished that I were imagining it all. I had tasted the bitterest essence of war, the sight of helpless comrades being slaughtered, and it filled me with disgust."[20]

As a veteran, however, Serling was no longer capable of viewing any war in simplistic, self-righteous, black-and-white terms. The episode reflects his view that violence "gets nurtured and it grows in a soil of prejudice and of hate and of bigotry."[21] And after coming back home from the front, he eventually bore witness to a new series conflicts being framed in a painfully familiar pattern—the Cold War, the Korean War, the Vietnam War, and a host of other clashes throughout the Middle East, Africa, and Latin America. That the vast majority of Americans were comfortably insulated from having to directly experience any of these engagements meant that they were also in constant danger of perpetually remaining belligerent "shave-tails," noncombatants who, like Katell, lauded combat but could easily maintain a safe psychological distance and self-righteous outlook. Like the lieutenant in this episode, many Americans could be found to have a highly underdeveloped "quality of mercy."

It was arguably Serling's creative intent for Lieutenant Katell to be a stand-in for the American public. Just like Katell, Americans were largely educated during the Cold War with a simple, competitive revulsion for, among other things, any nation or people subscribing to Communism. That many such nations, including China, Korea, and Vietnam were also Asian, made the racial aspects of World War II that much more relevant. By 1971, Serling reiterated his concerns over hate-fueled violence as a foundation for policy: "I don't think we dare succumb to violence. I don't know of any social progress to be born out of the rubble of a bombed building or the ashes of a burned-out street or the body count of men, however impassion and however martyred."[22] Like Katell, millions of Americans internalized this prevailing fighting spirit while also lacking actual experience. Furthermore, just as the atomic bomb "saved" Katell and other American soldiers from more intimately experiencing the horrors of combat, technological innovations in warfare meant that the targeted victims would more exclusively be the ones suffering the trauma of war, leaving their killers physically and psychologically relatively unscathed. And while Serling was not wholly pacifistic himself, his experiences had clearly led him to conclude that violent combat was not the ultimate solution and it was certainly not something to approach with the naïve, boyish eagerness exemplified by Katell. Instead, war, if it was to be viewed realistically and maturely, should be considered an altogether unexciting, desperate affair. And before war is ever hastily declared, it should be primarily informed by the traumatized, yet living minds of those who have been reared by the merciless hand of real warfare. A character reflects in an episode from Serling's series *The Loner:* "I sometimes think a man can die from killing as well as from being killed."[23] The next episode explores the slow, painful death that can take place in such a combatant.

The Horror of Surviving

While Katell mostly escaped war's traumatizing effects, millions of other veterans were not as lucky. For those who had experienced the horrors of warfare, peacetime would not necessarily be altogether peaceful. *The Twilight Zone's* "Thirty-Fathom Grave" explores the psychological impacts of battle fatigue, now called *post-traumatic stress disorder,* or *PTSD,* could potentially have on an individual (S4, e2). In a similar manner, the episode "Judgment Night" featured a Nazi U-boat officer who in 1942 ordered an attack on the SS *Queen Glasgow,* a British passenger liner (S1, e10). Having killed hundreds of civilians, Captain Lanser is condemned to perpetually relive the attack, but rather than in his German submarine, he is aboard the very ship he destroyed. In a similar vein, the episode "King Nine Will Not Return" tells the story of Captain James Embry, aboard the B-25 Mitchell bomber *King Nine* when it crashed in North Africa in 1943 (S2, e1). Envisioning himself back at the crash site, Embry searches for the other crew members, to no avail. Eventually, the former captain is shown in a hospital back in the states, suffering from survival guilt after he reads a newspaper headline that reveals the discovery of the crashed bomber. Furthermore, "Deaths-Head Revisited" dramatizes the psychological torment of former SS captain Gunther Lutze, who upon visiting Dachau, is painfully tortured by the eerie ghosts of his Holocaust victims (S3, e9). Lutze eventually is interred at a mental institution, where the doctor asks why Dachau is still standing, while Serling's closing narration offers an answer: "All the Dachaus must remain standing. The Dachaus, the Belsens, the Buchenwalds, the Auschwitzes—all of them. They must remain standing because they are a monument to a moment in time when some men decided to turn the Earth into a graveyard. Into it they shoveled all of their reason, their logic, their knowledge, but worst of all, their conscience. And the moment we forget this, the moment we cease to be haunted by its remembrance, then we become the gravediggers." In all of these episodes of *The Twilight Zone*, the tremendous mental weight of surviving war is depicted as a necessary, and even helpful, psychological torment. By giving honest expression to the horrors of war, the survivors pass valuable, if painful, insight to future generations. And like Serling's closing narration articulates, the haunting remembrances perform an important service—that of helping to minimize the number of future gravediggers.

"Thirty-Fathom Grave" begins on an American naval destroyer in the South Pacific Ocean in 1963. In the opening scene, a ship crewmember reports finding some recent storm damage on one of the motor whale boats. Captain Beecham, the officer in charge, angrily responds that the boat was not properly secured for torrential weather and that even a "thirteen-year-old sea scout" would have known what to do. Chief Bell, the boatswain's mate, whose duties include securing the boats in the time of a storm, immediately reports to the captain's office. When he arrives, the captain sardonically orders, "At ease, chief. That shouldn't be too difficult for you, should it? . . . You're the champion of the fleet when it comes to being at ease, Bell." After Beecham chastises Bell for his negligence, the reprimanded Bell explains in a hushed voice that he did his best but had not been feeling up to par. Altering his tone, the captain says that he is not interested in pistol-whipping his crew and cares when one of his crewmembers has a problem. Bell says that he has performed his duties exceptionally well, but noticed his focus slipping the past few days. After the captain tells him to stop by if he needs to discuss anything further, Bell steps out of his office looking pale and dizzy.

In the sonar room, several crewmembers begin to detect a tapping sound in the waters below. Thinking it may be a submarine, they immediately notify Captain Beecham, who checks the scope for himself. With two mysteries now established—Bell's apparent compromised health and some peculiar metal tapping in the waters below—Serling introduces the episode, "Incident one hundred miles off the coast of Guadalcanal. Time: the present. The United States naval destroyer on what has been a most uneventful cruise. In a moment, they're going to send a man down thirty fathoms and check on a noise maker—someone or something tapping on metal. You may or may not read the results in a naval report, because Captain Beecham and his crew have just set a course that will lead this ship and everyone on it into *The Twilight Zone*."

Beecham soon orders his men to shut off all the engines so they can better hear the mysterious tapping noise from below. As the men stand around listening closely, Chief Bell, still appearing woozy, faints and collapses on the top deck. When he awakes, he finds himself in bed in the sick bay. Eager to get up, Bell is urged by the medic to get some rest instead. He explains how he has a "funny feeling" but cannot really describe it, and the medic gives him a shot to help him relax. Meanwhile, on the main deck, Captain Beecham plans to send a crewmember down to investigate the noise. Worried that his superior officers will think he lost his mind, the captain tells one of his men that he will need several witnesses to back up his report. When one of his crewmembers tries to reassure him that it is probably just a submarine, the captain replies, "Sure it could be a sub, that's probably what it is. But what about this sub? Has it got two arms and a fist? Somebody's making that noise down there. . . . Maybe it's just our imagination."

The diver slowly descends to the ocean floor, where he locates an old submarine. Hearing the tapping once more, he knocks a couple times on the submarine, hoping for a response, but there is only silence. After he inspects the submarine, he notices that its whole deck has severe shell and machine gun damage. Suddenly, he hears the tapping again and determines that it is coming from the middle of the ship. He returns to the surface, where the disturbed and confused captain explains, "That sub was hit by shell-fire. Whatever action took place must have happened within a period of hours or else there wouldn't have been anyone still alive. But there's been no action, or we'd have seen it or heard it. Now put all that together, and it spells nothing."

Back in the sick bay, Chief Bell awakens and tells the medic that he feels like he can't stay in one place: "This crazy feeling that I'm, that somebody, is ordering me some place, is pulling me some place. And if I didn't stay put, if I didn't fight it, I'd go up on that deck and never come back. Sound pretty nuts?" The medic tries to relax Bell again, reassuring him that he just needs

"Doc, what's happening to me?!" Chief Bell visits the doctor, who tries to calm his nerves. Still from "The Thirty-Fathom Grave" (35:46)

some more rest. Meanwhile, the diver converses with Captain Beecham, declaring, "There is somebody inside her, Sir. I'll lay odds on that." The sonar room again detects noise from the ocean floor, but this time it appears that the sub is moving. The captain orders the diver to explore the situation once more, hoping that the submarine's shifting position will reveal the number on its hull. When he arrives at the sub, he spots the numbers *714*. Excitedly, the captain searches a reference book for ship 714, reading its description aloud: "714 commissioned December 1941, sunk in action, first Battle of the Solomons, August 7, 1942." In disbelief, he slowly repeats the date, "August 7, 1942," realizing the sub was sunk more than twenty years ago.

Now back in his office, the captain is visited by the medic who wants to discuss Chief Bell's health: "Well, it's an illusion, or a psychosis or whatever that's a little out of my line. . . . I do know that he needs help. Psychiatric help . . . he has a look about him. . . . It's not a look you see very often. Usually it's an hour after a battle when the eyes face upward but you know they're really looking inside. That's what he looks like. Like a man who's been just picked up off a raft of dead men." The captain agrees to keep Bell in sick bay and

"They were dripping wet and they were not alive!" Chief Bell sees his deceased World War II crew aboard the ship. Still from "The Thirty-Fathom Grave" (35:12)

hospitalize him when they port again. As the captain sits down to have coffee with some of his men, he mentions how their problems are further compounded by the fact that Chief Bell has "something eating at him." One remarks that he may be "dredging up a couple of memories" from World War II: "He was picked up here after sinking. . . . He was on a ship that was hit, the only survivor, or something like that, they pulled him out of the water."

Left alone, Bell gets up from his bed to look at himself in the mirror. To his surprise, his face is not the only one he sees, as several young men, soaking wet, wave for him to follow them. Horrified, Bell quickly retreats and throws a metal dish at the mirror, shattering the glass. After hearing the commotion, the medic rushes back into the sick bay, and Bell tells him, "I was looking in the mirror and I saw faces. . . . They were staring at me, they were pointing at me. Now, I know this sounds crazy, but they were there. It's as if they were ordering me into the mirror, pulling me in." After the doctor tries to reassure Bell that they will conquer whatever is ailing him, Bell quickly gets up when he senses something out in the passageway. The doctor assures him that nothing is out there but an empty hallway. Feeling the compulsion increase all the more, Bell goes out to the passageway only to see several men once again motioning to him: "Oh my dear God in heaven. Did you see them, doc? Men. Men looking at me they were wet they were wet they were dripping wet and they were not alive!" The doctor tries to convince Bell that he talked himself into what he wanted to see but is then shocked to find a wet pile of seaweed on the passageway floor.

When McClure dives down again to the sunken submarine, he finds dog tags with Chief Bell's name on them. When the captain takes the tags to Bell, he decides to ask when he lost them. Bell explains when he was a signalman, he mishandled the signal light, giving away their ship's location. When the Japanese opened fire on the ship, Bell was flung off the side. He continues, "All the time I was in the water there I could hear the voices of our guys. They were *screaming!* I know what it was now. . . . See them guys down there in that sub, they know I'm up here. That's what this thing has been, see I should be down there with them. I should be down in that sub. I should be dead. And all this noise see, this pounding this clanging, that's them guys down there they're calling muster on me."

After listening to his disturbed crewmember's account, the captain does his best to rid Bell of his wartime demons:

> One man does not sink a sub, and one lousy circumstance does not decide a battle and one case of sudden fear does not add up to a coward. You've been taking a dirty rap for twenty years. You've slept with it, you've hung it around your neck, you've let it dig deep down inside and tear you to pieces. Now let me tell you something, Bell. It's not deserved, it's not right. . . . A frightened sailor didn't destroy that ship or kill off that crew. Bell! You've got to understand. A war did! A set of circumstances did! Bell, you've got to believe me.

Bell, still consumed with his own hallucinations and guilt, rushes out of the office to the deck, diving into the depths of the Pacific Ocean.

When the crew frantically attempts to rescue Bell, one of the men informs the captain that they have been searching for ten hours, to no avail. McClure comes up to report on the submarine to the captain one last time, explaining that its periscope shears had been cut in half and eight men remained in the ship while one of them was holding a hammer. Adding a final note to the mystery-tinged suicide, Captain Beecham reflects, "Funny thing, how long it takes some men to die or to find any peace at all.

Sometimes I think that's the worst thing there is about war—not just what it does to the bodies but what it does to the *minds.*" He steps out onto the deck and looks out at the great expanse of the ocean and addresses his former crew member: "Rest in peace, Chief Bell. I think it's your due now." Serling then closes his episode: "Small naval engagement, the month of April 1963. Not to be found in any historical annals. Look for this one filed under *h* for *haunting* in *The Twilight Zone.*"

In this episode, Serling dramatizes the psychological effects of combat, particularly as they relate to battle fatigue, or PTSD. Prior to World War II, the US military believed that battle fatigue or *shell shock,* as it was termed in World War I, was largely the result of a soldier's preexisting psychological issues. As a result, the armed forces assumed that psychological breakdowns, as well as the undesired presence of gay men, could be mostly evaded through a psychiatric screening process.[24] This process, headed by psychoanalyst Harry Stack Sullivan, first implemented in 1940, resulted in the exclusion of about 2 million men of the 15 million who were interviewed.[25]

Despite the dominant assumption that the military could limit the psychiatric damage wrought by war by excluding those allegedly predisposed to, or with a history of, psychological problems and anxiety, the war soon proved otherwise. Instead of confirming these assumptions, World War II further complicated them and eventually resulted in the desperate need for psychiatric disorders to be reconsidered. This need, borne out of the psychiatric fallout of the war and the increased involvement of psychiatrists on the front lines led to the formation of the first *Diagnostic and Statistical Manual of Mental Disorders* in 1952. As the war dragged on, psychological attrition rates increased dramatically and steadily, casting doubt on the dominant belief that combat-related psychological disorders resulted from preexisting conditions. Faced with an ever-increasing number of soldiers being repatriated back to the United States for psychiatric issues, the military increasingly sought out assistance from psychiatrists. While a mere thirty-five psychiatrists were involved in the military at the start of the war, by the end, this number had increased to one thousand, representing a third of all American psychiatrists.[26]

Among the psychiatric professionals who became involved in the war, Roy R. Grinker and John P. Spiegel proved among the most influential. Having worked with soldiers on the front lines of North Africa, they eventually published their firsthand wartime experiences, treatments, and conclusions in two separate books: *War Neuroses* and *Men under Stress.* Their work exemplifies the general shift away from viewing veterans with mental disorders as cowards or malingerers toward, instead, seeing mental illness as a direct result of combat-related experiences. Rather than further pathologizing anxiety-ridden veterans, the psychiatrists pronounced that it "would seem to be a more rational question to ask why the soldier does *not* succumb to anxiety, rather than why he does."[27]

Grinker and Spiegel explained how after World War I, recorded data showed that 65 percent of patients with war neuroses had a "personal or family history of nervousness," compared to only 45 percent of nonneurotics. However, they questioned the fairness and accuracy of these findings, explaining how those "who develop war neuroses have their attention directed to nervousness and 'remember' more of similar events in their past than more normal soldiers unconcerned with the problem at the moment. The latter have a tendency to deny all previous anxieties or phobias. Their pasts are too healthy to be true." Additionally, Grinker and Spiegel noted that although "it might speculatively be held that those with no previous anxiety will do better in battle than their less stable brothers, observation has led us to suspect that is not always the case." They cited individuals who gave no history of previous anxiety but "crack rather early under shellfire, just as there are many persons with a history of previous anxiety who endure many battles before being overwhelmed." They concluded that "in certain instances of lifelong anxiety states, the ego's capacity to endure anxiety is relatively great" because anxiety "is nothing new to these people; they have always had it, and know how to deal with it."[28] In this way, Grinker and Spiegel urged their fellow psychiatrists to reconsider trauma and the development of mental illnesses in their patients.

During World War II, psychiatrists explained how the "holocaust of battle exposes the primitive forces within every man's personality." And even though war was brutal, unforgiving, and horrifying, it presented for that very reason, unique opportunities for understanding human psychology in profound ways. They explained how war, perhaps more than any other occasion or set of circumstances, "permits detailed studies to be made of . . . ego reactions in various stages of dissolution and repair." They argued also that their observations were not merely limited in value to wartime alone but "furnish experimental data for the understanding of anxieties from the stresses of civilian life."[29] Their research would have implications far beyond combat.

While psychiatrists worked to change prevalent misconceptions both within the field and outside of it, the task was not an altogether easy one. One of the most respected generals in the army, George S. Patton, exemplified some of these challenges. Unlike Captain Beecham in this episode, Patton believed that soldiers who showed signs of anxiety or mental trauma were merely faking it in order to shirk their duties. The general even once fantastically claimed that there was no such thing as shell-shock and claimed it was "an invention of the Jews."[30] In his directive to the Seventh Army, dated August 4, 1943, a day after he slapped a soldier he mistook for one of his men suffering from battle fatigue, Patton wrote, "It has come to my attention that a . . . number of soldiers are going to the hospital on the pretext that they are nervously incapable of combat. Such men are cowards and bring discredit on the army and disgrace to their comrades, whom they heartlessly leave to endure the dangers of battle while they, themselves, use the hospital as a means of escape. . . . Those who are not willing to fight will be tried by court-martial for cowardice in the face of the enemy."[31] Convincing certain military personnel, who could also be apparently showing signs of mental disturbance themselves, would not be an easy task.

Not only was increasing psychiatric awareness a challenge within the ranks of the military, it was also a serious concern for the civilian population, which had remained insulated from many of the disturbing realities of the war. The traumatized veterans of World War II had to contend with the already predominant notion of "the good war." While Americans at home went to see films such as *The Flying Tigers* and *The Fighting Seabees* as the war was going on, productions such as these John Wayne films arguably served to only widen the psychological gap between civilians and enlisted servicemen. One veteran described how the romanticized depictions of death, such as a military hero slowly and dramatically dying in his friend's arms, for example, is so utterly far from the reality of warfare: "All of this play acting is just so much rot, an insult to those who died in real battles. Death cannot be imitated by such a display of mock heroics dreamed up by fifty-thousand-dollar-a-year script writers. . . . Death is a reality, the thought of which terrifies, yet fascinates me. I shall always remember those who died on my ship . . . those poor dead faces, the sightless eyes, the clenched hands. . . . No speeches. No cigarettes. No drama."[32] Not only were the realities of romanticized and simplified in these movies, but the vast majority of war films conspicuously lacked any allusion whatsoever to the psychiatric problems combat might have on an individual. One of the few exceptions to this, however, was William Wyler's *The Best Years of Our Lives* (1946), which depicted a wide array of struggles experienced by soldiers readjusting to civilian life. By and large, though, popular depictions of returning soldiers returning to were grossly romanticized and simplified.

Psychological trauma was arguably the most relevant and significant effect of war, as it would not only impact veterans' futures but their families' as well. This relative gap in understanding meant that adjusting to peacetime would be even more jarring and challenging to all parties involved. If veterans attempted to follow Patton's intolerant lead regarding their own mental health or families internalized John Wayne's many invulnerable characterizations of a combatant, the long-term effects of psychological trauma could potentially worsen. As Spiegel and Grinker explained, "the difference between the ideal and the fact is sometimes so great, a severe intrapsychic tension is established which, with an increase in the degree of external stress, often leads to psychological illness." They pleaded, "Too high a priority cannot be given to this problem" of "appreciably large numbers of men with regressed attitudes and damaged confidence" entering civilian life, as "it may be too late to correct or control the immediate emotional reactions which will be aroused by their impact upon civilians who have had no experience or knowledge of the war." They remarked how in the "absence of an intimate knowledge of the feelings and problems of the combat veteran, it is easy to see how oversolicitous or overharsh attitudes in the nonmilitary public could lead to a vast confusion." And although those who fought in World War II have since been lauded for their stoicism and silence regarding their experiences, they offered a warning about such thinking: "It has been sometimes stated that the veteran does not want people to pay attention to him, that he wants to be let alone and ignored." They claimed that these assumptions do not "coincide with our experience," which has shown that "the veteran does not want to be ignored; he wants to be understood and helped. It is only because of his inability to understand himself, and of his lack of faith in the capacity of others to understand or help him, that he prefers to be alone with his difficulties or in the company of other combat veterans."[33] The public's general lack of awareness, combined with the relative silence of veterans, resulted in postwar psychiatric challenges that could seem cryptic to common civilians. "Thirty-Fathom Grave" attempts to at least partially address this knowledge gap.

Throughout this episode, Bell's symptoms closely resemble those recorded by psychiatrists during the war. After observing a variety of battle fatigue cases near the frontlines, Grinker and Spiegel explained that severe "anxiety states produce an intensely striking, unforgettable picture." Patients in such a state appear "terror-stricken, mute and tremulous." Their facial expressions are frequently "vacuous or fearful and apprehensive," while their speech is "usually impossible except for a few stuttering attempts to frame an occasional word." In spite of their severely compromised state, those suffering from battle fatigue "persist in attempting to communicate with attendants" and commonly experience "sudden fits of crying or laughing . . . without reason." To most observers, their behavior is "extremely bizarre and attitudinizing," consisting of "apparently senseless gestures alternating with periods of excessive activity, characterized by running about the ward and leaping over beds." And like Chief Bell hearing the underwater clanging and noises in the hallway, the psychiatrists noted how any "sharp or sudden noise produces a marked startle reaction . . . the patient jumps, trembles violently, and turns toward the source of the noise with an expression of fear on his face."[34]

Although the concept of survivor guilt was not codified until the sixties, it is clear that many World War II veterans, like the fictional Chief Bell, experienced it nonetheless. In his memoir about the war in the Pacific, Eugene Sledge recounted a psychological disturbance not unlike Bell's: "I imagined Marine dead had risen up and were moving silently about the area. I suppose these were nightmares, and I must have been more asleep than awake, or just dumbfounded by fatigue. Possibly they were hallucinations, but they were strange and horrible. The pattern was always the same. The dead got up slowly out of their waterlogged craters or off the mud and, with stooped shoulders and dragging feet, wandered around aimlessly, their lips moving as though trying to tell me something. I struggled to hear what they were saying. They seemed agonized by pain and despair. I felt they were asking me for help. The most horrible thing was that I felt unable to aid them."[35] When Grinker and Spiegel discussed treating a patient with similar symptoms, they explained how the "socially acceptable outlet for suicidal drives consists in volunteering to return to combat duty, where a less sordid death is sought."[36] Not only could battle fatigue and survivor guilt weigh on a combatant's mind, they could drive the soldier to a semi-military-assisted, socially acceptable form of suicide, like Chief Bell's.

While veterans who came home were sometimes doted on by their families and entertained by friends and neighbors with parties, food, and drinks, they could also appear "somewhat reticent and sad instead of gloriously happy" because the "more he receives, the guiltier he feels toward those he left behind . . . the effect is a gloomy reaction." Consequently, a veteran not uncommonly "dismisses his personal exploits from the conversation and is reticent about talking of himself, not because of any inherent modesty, but because 'Joe,' who died on the very same mission, haunts his memory with reminders that he has not done as much." As a result, a veteran's guilty feelings can "reach such an intensity that the returnee thinks of asking to return to combat as soon as his overseas leave is finished." Instead of combat turning men into pillars of strength, they more than likely "have had their birthright of independence exchanged for . . . inferiority feelings or socially unadapted behavior . . . shattered confidence and continued helplessness which . . . have enforced a regression to and perpetuation of dependent and immature attitudes."[37]

As a survivor of the war, Serling undoubtedly wrestled with such psychological dilemmas and challenges. His own regiment, the 511th Parachute Infantry, suffered a staggeringly high casualty rate of 50 percent—roughly one thousand men died in his regiment of approximately two thousand.[38] And although death during wartime is anticipated, the way it came was frequently unexpected. During the 511th's two-week siege in Leyte as cargo planes were dropping food crates for the American soldiers, a horrifying example of this reality took place. While Serling and the rest of his regiment took cover under a palm tree, one of the food crates plummeted from the sky. As it fell through the tree leaves, the enormous crate decapitated one of the 511th's men, Corporal Melvin Levy, killing him instantly. After this nightmarish incident, which made death seem both highly uncertain and patently absurd, Serling led the burial services for the deceased man, who, like Serling, was a Jewish New Yorker.[39] During the war, the overwhelming, omnipresent possibilities of death, disaster, and tragedy could even come in the form of a food crate descending from the sky.

While Serling witnessed countless deaths, such as Corporal Levy's, he also inevitably had several close calls that could have easily resulted in his own demise. In one instance, during the Battle of Manila, Serling spotted a Japanese soldier staring back at him with his rifle ready and aimed to fire. But before the Japanese soldier pulled the trigger, another American soldier intervened and shot Serling's potential killer, saving him from an early death.[40] While Corporal Levy was freakishly killed by a supply crate, Serling was unexpectedly saved by no merit of his own. Why did Levy die and Serling survive? Death, survival, and heroism in combat seemed all too arbitrary in the real-life fields of battle.

In their published work, Grinker and Spiegel explained how battle fatigue and its ensuing psychological problems were not exclusively the result of intense and prolonged periods of combat. One patient who "kept thinking of his dead friend," whose "face constantly appeared before him," provided some evidence of this. After they had given him a small dose of Pentothal, a barbiturate, he "expressed a strong desire to return to China" because he "felt guilty about the other soldier's death . . . and felt guilty about leaving the squadron with the job unfinished," while he also expressed how "the Chinese people were the only ones who appreciated his efforts" and "Americans had no concept of war and didn't care."[41] Thus, survivor guilt and public indifference could combine to create profound psychological dilemmas.

In a related sense, wartime psychiatrists witnessed how a lack of morale and support could also have devastating effects on a combatant's psyche. Enlisted African Americans, for example, who were segregated and mostly based within the United States during the war, frequently showed even greater battle fatigue–related symptoms. Just as the previous patient lamented the lack of care and concern for all of his efforts, the rates were even greater among African Americans who had been rewarded for their efforts with continual prejudice, violence, and discrimination at home.[42] Similarly, women who also participated in the war effort by taking positions in manufacturing and were subsequently laid off also remained relatively under recognized and forgotten. Just as many combatants suffered more intensely because of public indifference and lack of understanding regarding the actual experiences of war, stress-related mental disorders involving racial and sexual minorities were arguably even less publicly recognized, as their efforts were not nearly as acknowledged during and after the war.

Chief Bell's psychological trauma in "Thirty-Fathom Grave" not only illustrates the effects of survivor guilt and the complicated aspects of public understanding and support, it also illuminates the important dynamics of group cohesion during World War II. Psychiatrists' experiences with combatants further revealed just how vital was a unit's camaraderie, cohesion, and sense of community. More powerful than abstract ideals of liberty, democracy, or even hatred for the enemy, group morale and solidarity kept the vast majority of soldiers fighting and forging ahead.[43] Although fighting primarily for each other could effectively sustain units that had lower casualty rates, for those that lost most, or even all of their members, the long-term impacts could be devastating. And while military psychiatrist Albert Glass later asserted that "the most significant contribution of World War II military psychiatry was recognition of the sustaining influence of the small combat group," relying primarily on the group could make a sole survivor particularly susceptible to developing a mental disorder, dramatized in this episode of *The Twilight Zone*.[44]

Psychiatrists noted that if a soldier's superego unrelentingly identified "with the spirit of friends on the battlefield—both dead and alive—it will remain angry and demanding." And while those with moderate levels of anxiety were usually able to break free from such psychological torture after proper medical attention in a secured environment, in "the more severe cases . . . this identification is surprisingly strong" and the "patient stubbornly regards himself as the missing, weak link in his company or platoon."[45] Although Captain Beecham tries to free Bell from his unrelenting psychological association with the dead members of his former unit, Bell's severe state of anxiety clearly demands professional attention beyond the abilities of anyone on the ship.

Overall, the efforts and involvement of psychiatrists during World War II helped to solidify many important insights regarding the psychology of warfare. Among the most significant were the primacy of group dynamics and the reality that everyone, not merely those with a history of anxiety, was susceptible to battle fatigue and other related mental disorders. These crucial observations would help improve understanding and the quality of care in the future. Additionally, the importance of immediate psychiatric attention was also recognized by psychiatrists who noted that the time it took to transport mentally disordered combatants could considerably worsen their anxiety states. Despite these important discoveries, the long-term impacts of battle fatigue were relatively undervalued and not wholly understood. While psychiatric professionals noticed significant improvement and recovery in their patients, the likelihood of symptoms to reemerge and the need for continual care was still relatively underestimated at the war's end.[46]

While the majority of veterans did not want special care or attention, those suffering from serious mental disorders, such as acute battle fatigue, were helped with the postwar expansion of the Department of Veterans Affairs and the passage of the National Mental Health Act, which established the National Institute of Mental Health in 1946. Serling, who had experienced the gruesome, horrifying realities of war and death as well as the psychological burden of surviving it, found various ways to recover from such horrors, particularly through his writing. Psychiatrists similarly noted how a patient who "kept all the experiences to himself and deliberately tried to forget," continually suffered a "load on his stomach" but was finally able to progress by choosing "to suffer the pain of remembering first."[47] Unfortunately, for many veterans, being cured represented a lifelong struggle. Completely forgetting their experiences was impossible.

In his memoir, Sledge explained: "Under that cap were the most ghastly skeletal remains I had ever seen—and I had already seen too many. Every time I looked over the edge of that foxhole down into that crater, that half-gone face leered up at me with a sardonic grin. . .maybe he was mocking the folly of the war itself: 'I am the harvest of man's stupidity. I am the fruit of the holocaust. . . . People back home will wonder why you can't forget.'"[48] Continually confronting and even occasionally reexperiencing the nightmares of war proved vital for Sledge, Serling, and other veterans who at least partially restored their mental health and reengaged with civilian life. Immersing oneself in a repressed nightmare could be the key to experiencing freedom, release, and growth. In this manner, nightmares represented not merely a debilitating event or a frightful problem; embedded within them were the necessary and vital elements for personal growth and social progress alike.

By seeking to expose the nightmarish realities of a mythologized war and the excessively idealized pictures of American postwar society, technology, family life, consumerism, and suburbia, Serling intended not merely to inspire disparagement, derision, and disgust. Rather, as his wartime experiences revealed, the unpleasant and horrifying nightmares that lurk behind the veils of mass-produced, deceitful dream imagery could potentially reopen the possibilities for future growth, progress, and change for the individual and the nation alike. Throughout Serling's life as a civilian writer, he continued to reflect what World War II veteran Daniel A. McDonald articulated in his published piece, "Out of Uniform: A Strange New World":

It is not your fault that you came back and they didn't, but you feel guilty for being the one to survive. This feeling will live with you for years to come. . . . Then we begin to realize that all sacrifices are not made in the field of battle. . . . The guns are silent, but there are still wars to fight, wars against disease, poverty, illiteracy, and injustice. These enemies are still taking their toll of lives and happiness. We are being discharged from one army and folding our uniforms to reenlist in a new army . . . and fight the battle for success. Although the experience of war has taken something out of each of us, it puts something into us, too.[49]

Just like real combat, success was not guaranteed in of postwar life, but the causes were certainly worth a uniform change for Serling and millions of other veterans. Between the race-fueled war in the Pacific, Japanese

American internment, segregation in the military, the unequal, discriminatory impacts of the GI Bill, and the living trauma that veterans and civilians alike struggled with, World War II had profound impacts on life in the United States. In the ensuing years, Americans worked collectively and individually to restore a sense of normalcy, predictability, and comfort, having just endured the challenges of the Great Depression as well as the war. How normalcy, predictability, and comfort would be defined and who benefited from those definitions would be up for serious debate, however. As we will see, the dominant conceptions of the American Dream, which promised Americans happiness and harmony, all but guaranteed that profound racial and social dissonances remained obscured beneath a cloak of whiteness.

Cold War Space and Technology

A Fertile Frontier or a New Human Wasteland?

In 1961, in his work *Science since Babylon*, Yale historian Derek de Solla Price captured many of the prevailing beliefs regarding science and technology during the first decades of the Cold War. Price argued, above all, for the inherent beneficial progress that comes with continual investment in science, increasing the number of scientists, and escalating the amount of federal funding allocated for research and development: "We have the position, then, that in normal growth, science begets more science and technology begets more technology."[1] According to Price, for the state department and the vast majority of Americans, who were furnishing their homes and garages with the latest technological gadgets, more science and more technology were unquestionably good. However, Price's work also reflected David Noble's observation that because of "both of our ignorance and incessant inculcation by our established institutions," we have come to believe in a false Darwinian logic as it relates to technological development. Noble later explained, "We believe that the process of technological development is very much like the biological evolution of the species through 'natural selection' and because this view is ideological, deeply ingrained as a habit of thought, we rarely if ever actually think about it."[2]

In this manner, also characteristic of the time, *Science Since Babylon* conspicuously lacked serious consideration of the value judgments, moral implications, and ideological complexities that always are an intrinsic part of scientific development. Cold War science and technology represented a kind of disembodied intelligence. For Price and so many other Americans at the time, science was considered largely free from the baggage of politics and complex social dynamics. As Audra J. Wolfe has recently shown, though, this belief was contradicted at the time by the massive amount of defense-driven federal investments in science laboratories and university research. In unprecedented ways, the "idea of 'open science' sat uneasily next to the reality of a research infrastructure that was largely backed by . . . military interests." Military power and scientific advancement became more closely linked than ever before as the "battle for hearts and minds turned all kinds of science— military and civilian, basic and applied, big and little—into proxy areas in which to demonstrate the superiority of the American way of life."[3]

When the Soviets successfully launched Sputnik 1 into orbit in 1957, American politics and popular culture reflected an increasing sense of fear that the Soviets were outpacing Americans in space and science technology. In one of many examples, *Life* magazine published an article in its March 24, 1958, issue detailing how Soviet teenagers were much more studious, self-disciplined, and educated than their American counterparts, who instead spent most of their time worrying about dating and driving cars.[4] As a result of these growing concerns, funding for American science programs as well as grants and fellowships sharply increased the following years. The space race, as the predominant sign of scientific advancement and Soviet superiority to the Americans, remained at the forefront of concerns. The newly formed National Aeronautics and Space Administration (NASA) and the mission to put men on the moon would soon take center stage in American Cold War policy. But as Serling's "I Shot an Arrow into the Air" and several other episodes illustrate, manned space flight was a deeply flawed enterprise from the outset, for the very reason that it sought to prove political and military superiority rather than attain significant scientific discoveries that might benefit all mankind (S1, e15).

While NASA's Mercury Program was taking off, the Department of Defense was also funding huge portions of research and development at General Electric, Westinghouse, RCA, and other major corporations—which meant that industries could pursue technological innovation with ever-increasing, deliberate speed. With the aid of the defense department's budget, a variety of industries looked to develop and invest in technology that could maximize earnings and limit production costs. While American corporations reaped great benefits from these federally allocated funds, they did not always result in improving the lives of working Americans. Consequently, many critics pointed out that scientific and technological growth did not necessarily equal social or cultural progress. One particularly vitriolic critique came from Philip Wylie, who explained in his 1942 work *Generation of Vipers*, "A people already conditioned psychologically to identify material construction with spiritual progress became, automatically, suckers for the illusion that movement connoted advancement."[5] In "Brain Center at Whipple's" Serling dramatized how new technology does not automatically bring progress or a better standard of living (S5, e33). Instead, in this episode, new technology raised challenges and questions that cannot be answered by merely celebrating its arrival. Thus, Serling reminded Americans that technology was not a mere product of evolutionary biology but had profound implications regarding socioeconomic class structure, racial issues, and foreign policy.

Humans in Space: The Promise or the Problem?

When "I Shot an Arrow into the Air" aired on January 15, 1960, it was *The Twilight Zone*'s fifteenth episode, but it represented the fifth time space exploration served as the show's subject matter, illustrating the urgency and fascination with the space race. That the space race was driven more by a thirst for political and military power than by scientific concerns was also later dramatized in "The Little People," which frames the desire for manned space flight in particularly biting fashion (S3, e28). After the ship crash-landed on a distant planet, one of its crew members, William Fletcher, works on repairs, while Peter Craig scouts the area and happens upon a tiny civilization. Craig quickly inspires fear in them by easily crushing several of their buildings, making him feel godlike in his power. When he returns to the ship, Fletcher announces that he has successfully fixed the damages and they can return to Earth. Craig, however, wants to stay on the planet to rule over the "little people." After some arguing, Fletcher returns to Earth by himself, leaving Craig behind. After Fletcher leaves, an alien spacecraft soon lands on the planet, revealing a lifeform much larger than Craig, making him the fearful, subservient subject now. The episode's final twist reveals the space race's faulty objectives and how instead of asserting man's strength, it makes his profound ego-fueled weaknesses all the more apparent.

In a similar manner, "People Are Alike All Over" features a crash-landing on a distant planet (S1, e25). The only surviving crewmember explores the surroundings and eventually comes across an alien civilization. He soon finds himself locked up in a zoolike cage for public display, revealing the darker meaning of the statement "people are alike all over" and the colonial ambitions of humans in space. In these episodes, Serling sought to reveal the real intentions and dangers behind space exploration, specifically manned space flight, and how they were not necessarily the missions of science, peace, and knowledge they were purported to be.

Airing less than three years after the successful launch of Sputnik 1 and not even two years following the creation of NASA, "I Shot an Arrow into the Air" was filmed in otherworldly Death Valley, California. The episode begins at a rocket launch site with a view into the control room, full of technicians, flight controllers, and high-tech machinery. Serling's introduction describes the rocket about to take flight: "Her name is Arrow One. She represents four and a half years of planning, preparation, and training, and a thousand years of science and mathematics and the projected dreams and hopes of not only a nation but a world. She is the first manned aircraft into space. And this is the countdown, the last five seconds before man shot an arrow into the air." Following a seemingly successful launch into space, the camera cuts back to the control room, with one flight controller writing "unreported" on a radar map, while another nervously flips through his charts on a clipboard: "I still don't understand how we could've lost them with all the monitors we have going." To make matters worse, mission control soon realizes it has lost not only sight of the rocket but contact with the crewmembers as well. As one of the flight controllers looks up at the stars in the night sky, he muses, "I shot an arrow into the air, it landed I know not where. Nursery rhyme for the age of space. . . . Gentlemen, wherever you are, God help you." Brass instruments play in a crescendo, foreshadowing more dramatic tension to come before the screen fades to black.

As "I Shot an Arrow into the Air" continues, the astronauts find themselves on a hot, dry, rocky, and desolate terrain when the colonel in charge of the mission sits down to write the mission's first log in his book: "First entry, log, Arrow One, Colonel R. G. Donlin commanding. We have crash landed on what appears to be an uncharted asteroid, cause of malfunction and ultimate crash unknown. There was an explosion. The electrical system went out. That's all any of us remember . . . any of us being flight officers Corey and Pierson and navigator Hudak, who has been seriously hurt, and myself. The rest of the crew—dead. There is very little left of the aircraft. The radio is gone. The bulk of the supplies have been destroyed in the crash. And as of this moment, there is little certainty that we have been tracked and our whereabouts known." Just then, flight officer Corey snatches the logbook from Colonel Donlin, telling him, "This is no time to write your memoirs." The colonel, reprimanding Corey's insubordination, angrily tells him that they are still a crew and still need to follow protocol and command. As Donlin tends to the injured Hudak, giving him some water to drink, Corey protests again, claiming that Hudak is going to die anyway and the men should conserve the mere five gallons of

Corey looks on, disapprovingly, as Colonel Donlin gives a dying crewmember a drink of water. Still from "I Shot an Arrow into the Air" (5:44)

water they have left. As they unpack their tools to dig graves for their dead crewmembers, Pierson calls attention to how the sun looks very similar to how it does from Earth, concluding that they must have landed on an asteroid in the same orbit as Earth's. After Hudak breathes his last breath and adds to the mission's death count, Pierson catches Corey trying to steal the water at Hudak's side, leading to a fight: "For the record, Corey, there's just three of us now, and the big problem is going to be to stay alive, I mean, the three of us—but if I catch you filching just once more, just once, I'll kill you!" Corey quickly retorts that the same applies for him.

After Corey and Pierson each explore a several-mile radius area of the terrain, night falls on the mysterious celestial rock. When Corey returns without Pierson, the colonel angrily tells him that he ordered the men to stick together. After seeing Corey hurriedly gulping water from his canteen, Donlin asks how he came back with even more water than he set out with. Corey explains how he took Pierson's, because he found him face-down on the ground, dead. Donlin, remaining skeptical of Corey, orders Corey to show him the whereabouts of Pierson's body. The men head out, the colonel, gun in hand, carefully following behind Corey.

Along the way, the men stop for a brief water break. While Corey pretends to tie his boot laces, he reaches for a rock, clearly thinking of killing his commanding officer. Before he can do so, the colonel orders him to keep moving, and they make their way down to the valley, where Pierson is supposedly lying dead. When they reach the spot, the man is nowhere to be seen: "Well this is where he was. I swear this is where he was. . . . He must have crawled away," Corey says. The colonel, in disbelief, exclaims, "You said he was dead . . . you were so sure he was dead, Corey . . . did you do anything for him at all? Did you check him? Did you do anything for him, Corey, or did you just steal his water and make a beeline back?!" Corey only continues to insist that he genuinely thought Pierson was dead when he saw him lying there in the valley.

Donlin pushes on ahead, repeatedly calling out for Pierson. When the colonel finally finds Pierson, he is lying on his back with blood on his forehead, apparently from Corey smashing him with a rock. Clearly on the verge of death and struggling to speak, Pierson draws three intersecting lines in the sand with his finger, two horizontal and one vertical. Unsure of what the symbol means, Donlin makes his way up the mountain to try and see what Pierson might have been trying to tell them. But before he makes it to the top, Corey picks up the gun that the colonel left behind and explains how two men can live for five days with the resources they have, but one could live for ten. He fires a round at Donlin, killing him instantly. Unfortunately for Corey, the canteen lying next to Donlin's corpse is completely empty, as the bullet penetrated it before Donlin. Corey now speaks to the colonel's body: "You brought the book to the wrong place, you brought protocol, the chain of command, and the numbers, and none of them fit here. . . . This is a jungle where only the tough animals survive, and they don't do it according to the rules. You know your trouble, Colonel? You were looking for morality in the wrong place."

As Corey makes his way up the mountain, he takes one last look at the two men's bodies. Serling's voiceover begins:

Now you make tracks, Mr. Corey. You move out and up like some kind of ghostly billy club was tapping at your ankles and telling you that it was later than you think. You scrabble up rock hills and feel hot sand underneath your feet and every now and then take a look

"You know your trouble, Colonel? You were looking for morality in the wrong place!" Desperate for more water, Corey shoots and kills Colonel Donlin. Still from "I Shot an Arrow into the Air" (19:02)

over your shoulder at a giant sun suspended in a dead and motionless sky like an unblinking eye that probes at the back of your head in a prolonged accusation. . . . Mr. Corey, last remaining member of a doomed crew, keep moving. Make tracks, Mr. Corey. Push up and push out because if you stop—if you stop, maybe sanity will get you by the throat, maybe realization will pry open your mind and the horror you left down in the sand will seep in. Yeah, Mr. Corey, yeah, you better keep moving. That's the order of the moment. Keep moving.

While Corey staggers along, the camera becomes increasingly shaky, reflecting Corey's physical exhaustion and unstable mental state. He looks over the edge of the mountain, begins laughing hysterically, and finally recognizes what Pierson was trying to draw—telephone poles. The camera pans, revealing telephone wires, a tour bus driving by below, and a sign for Reno, Nevada: the men never made it to outer space but merely crashed right back on Earth. Serling announces, "Practical joke perpetrated by Mother Nature and a combination of improbable events. Practical joke wearing the trappings of nightmare, of terror, of desperation. Small human drama played out in a desert ninety-seven miles from Reno, Nevada, USA, continent of North America, the Earth, and of course—*The Twilight Zone*."

This episode, on the heels of the previous week's "Third from the Sun," which dealt with the idea of other life forms escaping to Earth, returned to the topic of space exploration (S1, e14). While these space-themed episodes collectively did not necessarily seek to condemn the aspirations and curiosity to explore space, they did encourage viewers to reconsider how space exploration was being framed socially and culturally in the United States—in other words, to rethink how manned space flight and the moon were being mass-marketed.[6] Among the tropes employed to market space exploration was one already familiar to many Americans: the frontier myth. As De Witt Douglas Kilgore has recently explained in his work *Astrofuturism: Science, Race, and Visions of Utopia in Space*, "the idea of a space frontier serves contemporary America as the West served the nation in its past: it is the terrain onto which a manifest destiny is projected. . . . But it is also the space of utopian desire. Astrofuturist speculation on space-based exploration, exploitation, and colonization is capacious enough to contain imperialist, capitalist ambition and utopian, socialist hopes."[7] And similar to the frontier of old, space represented a racial rebirth for white Americans in particular, as any representation of nonwhite human beings in popular portrayals of space was practically nonexistent.

Television's first space-themed show, *Captain Video and His Video Rangers*, clearly shared many plot points with popular westerns. The show's introduction even sounded like it could have been written for a western: "Fighting for law and order, Captain Video operates from a secret mountain retreat. . . . Captain Video asks no quarter, and gives none to the forces of evil." Instead of a sheriff bringing justice and order to a frontier outpost, Captain Video brought morality and peace to a troubled, violent galaxy. Airing every weeknight at seven o'clock from 1949 to 1955, the program included several-minute scenes from old westerns.[8] The apparently seamless aspects between westerns and space, coupled with the marketing possibilities of selling space blasters and other space-themed toys, helped to proliferate the theme of space exploration both on television and in the toy store. *Space Patrol* (1950–1955) *Tom Corbett, Space Cadet* (1950–1955), and the radio program *Dimension X* (1950–1951) soon followed *Captain Video*, and these represented but a few among several new space-themed shows of the fifties.

Early television writers, toy manufacturers, and marketers were not the only ones who saw this connection between westerns and space. Serious science fiction fans did too, much to their chagrin. Seeing the rampant degradation of the science fiction genre being sold as merely westerns with space rays, the first issue of *Galaxy Science Fiction*, released in 1950, satirized this phenomenon. The magazine's back cover featured two excerpts, one allegedly from a western and another from a science fiction story. The western excerpt read, "He spurred hard for a low overhang of rim-rock . . . and at that point a tall, lean wrangler stepped out from behind a high boulder, six-shooter in a sun-tanned hand. 'Rear back and dismount, Bat Durston,' the tall stranger lipped thinly. 'You don't know it, but this is your last saddle-jaunt through these parts.'" Directly next to it was the sci-fi passage: "He cut out his super-hyper-drive for the landing . . . and at that point, a tall, lean spaceman stepped out of the tail assembly, proton gun-blaster in a space-tanned hand. 'Get back from those controls, Bat Durston,' the tall stranger lipped thinly. 'You don't know it, but this is your last space trip.'"[9] While framing outer space as a kind of new western frontier helped to sell televisions, toys, and the space race itself, it also helped solidify a niche market for "real" science fiction, one unpolluted by western tropes.

Aside from popular "space opera" programs, arguably the most significant representation of space on American television in the fifties was Walt Disney's "Man in Space," the episode of *Disneyland* that originally aired on March 9, 1955. The program was both wildly popular and actually based on real science. It was also largely influenced by a series of space exploration issues published by *Collier's* magazine in the early fifties, as several of the magazine's contributors eventually worked on both projects. The periodical series began with a bang and declared "Man Will Conquer Space Soon" on its front cover and featured vivid illustrations as well as serious articles by rocket scientists, all making the case for space exploration. Two of the contributing authors in *Collier's* were aerospace engineer Wernher von Braun and science writer Willy Ley, both of whom were featured in "Man in Space" and quickly became household names during the space race. Disney also hired animator Ward Kimball to create a program that promoted both manned space exploration and his new theme park in California.[10]

The hour-long program briefly detailed a history of rocket technology and how rockets could feasibly propel man into outer space, but it did so with overtly racial typecasting. Citing one of the first uses of rockets—at the Battle of Kai-fung-fu in thirteenth-century China—the animation depicted Asians with huge oversized teeth and tiny eyes, ceaselessly, madly firing rockets at one another back and forth. The episode later describes European contributions to rocket technology in utterly peaceful terms, including V-2 rockets, which Nazi Germany used numerous times to bomb civilian targets. Disney's special, however, makes no mention of this controversial history. While the science may have been accurate, the historical and social complexity regarding rocket technology was not. In seeking to promote space exploration, the social message of Disney's production was clear: the Western world only uses rockets for peaceful purposes and the East will only use rockets to perpetuate war and violence. The clear racial and geographical delineation of what became part of the Disneyland theme park's Tomorrowland fit seamlessly with the cowboys and Indians of Disney's Frontierland. Race and ethnicity served as a consistent and familiar dividing line between good and evil in Disney's universe.

"Man in Space" was a success not just with home audiences; President Eisenhower also became an enthusiastic fan. The day after he viewed the program in the White House, Eisenhower called Disney's studio to request a copy, and he eventually showed it to Pentagon officials.[11] Just three years later, NASA was created with its chief objective being the very same as the Disney special: to see man in space. And while Disney studios went on to produce other space-themed episodes in the fifties—"Man and the Moon" and "Mars and Beyond"—"Man in Space" continued to be shown to audiences in an abbreviated format alongside film screenings of *Davy Crockett and the River Pirates*. The connection Disney made was again emphasized, just as it had been on other television programs—Tomorrowland, that is, space, is the Frontierland of the twentieth century. And just like the frontier of old, it is up to American pioneers like Davy Crockett to ensure peace and order. As Alan Nadel has succinctly explained, Disney provided a place for America to integrate "its history and destiny, its technology and its geography, its family and industry . . . where all the significant elements of that unprecedented integration were white."[12] Whether it was America's past or future, the Alamo or outer space, Disney made sure any signs of either racial integration or oppression would be wholly absent.

By the time John F. Kennedy delivered his acceptance speech at the Democratic National Convention in 1960, space exploration already seemed almost inextricably linked to the American frontier. Standing at the podium in Memorial Coliseum in Los Angeles, Kennedy, like so many others before him, summoned frontier mythology to rouse the nation: "I stand here tonight facing west on what was once the last frontier. From the lands that stretch three thousand miles behind us, the pioneers gave up their safety, their comfort, and sometimes their lives to build our new West. They were not the captives of their own doubts, nor the prisoners of their own price tags. They were determined to make the new world strong and free, an example to the world—to overcome its hazards and its hardships, to conquer the enemies that threatened from within and without." In citing the United States' success in bringing freedom to the western frontier, Kennedy described what now could be termed the *New Frontier*. He declared: "Beyond that frontier are uncharted areas of science and space, unsolved problems of peace and war, unconquered problems of ignorance and prejudice, unanswered questions of poverty and surplus."[13] Kennedy defined this new frontier as not just space exploration, but a confrontation of social and economic injustices as well.

Combining all these challenges under the title *New Frontier* did not necessarily mean these separate issues would be given equal priority. As the nation would soon realize, these supposedly joint issues of space exploration, poverty, and social prejudice were far from symbiotic in their management.[14] To be sure, Kennedy was not solely responsible for deprioritizing social welfare issues. Political lobbies and social and fiscal conservatives in Congress certainly played a major role in stifling the New Frontier's social programs. However, a speech Kennedy delivered merely four months into his presidency provided more than a clue as to where his new administration's priorities primarily lie. Speaking to a joint session of Congress, Kennedy now described the nation's lunar aspiration in very different terms. A manned space flight no longer represented an exclusively peaceful venture, but was part of "the battle that is now going on around the world" and described how "no single space project in this period will be more impressive to mankind." To his credit, Kennedy explained how putting Americans on the moon demanded "a major national commitment of scientific and technical manpower, matériel and facilities, and the possibility of their diversion from other important activities where they are already thinly spread."[15] But while social issues were once seen to have a symbiotic relationship with manned space flight, Kennedy now suggested having to sacrifice them.

Conspicuously absent from Kennedy's speech, however, were the scientific perspectives and judgements of his recently formed Committee for Space. The Wiesner Report, composed by Jerome Wiesner of MIT and several other scientists on the committee, explicitly criticized Project Mercury, which had begun under Eisenhower and ran until 1963. The ongoing project merely "strengthened the popular belief that man in space is the most important aim of our . . . space effort." The committee explained in no uncertain terms how "a crash program aimed at placing a man into orbit at the earliest possible time cannot be justified solely on scientific or technical grounds."[16] The committee criticized not only the science behind the project but also the unnecessary risk of death in the endeavor. By way of speeches as well as policy, the new administration was hastily placing the irresistible potentials of prestige and public relations before science and safety.[17] In the midst of the Cold War, the space race formed an element of Kennedy's prioritization of foreign policy issues. As several international events—including the failed Bay of Pigs coup attempt and Yuri Gagarin's successful voyage to outer space—shaped his administration's first months, the president most likely viewed the potential lunar landing through a kind of foreign policy lens: landing on the moon was the best means to recuperate the international prestige of the United States and its foreign policy.

A year and a half later, Kennedy delivered his much more well-known moon speech at Rice University in Texas but noticeably left out the realistic economic appraisal he had offered Congress. Speaking to a regional audience, Kennedy brushed aside the national economic picture in favor of a local one, emphasizing how the space program would create a number of new jobs in Houston. In a similar manner, his words also belied the complexity of issues involved in the lunar project, as he stated that the nation would undertake this objective for the same reason Rice University plays the University of Texas in football—simply "because it is hard." And instead of the moon being prey to "a hostile flag of conquest," the United States, just like the pioneers of old, would come bearing "a banner of freedom and peace . . . with instruments of knowledge and understanding."[18] Kennedy returned to the classic motif of a free and peaceful frontier to sell his policies to the public.

In the coming years, space exploration was put front and center, even to the detriment of the social issues Kennedy had once mentioned; the New Frontier would come to embody, almost exclusively, space exploration. And as historian James Patterson explained, the Kennedy administration "devoted only sporadic attention to domestic affairs and . . . his administration, hamstrung by Congress, accomplished little of significance in the realm of social legislation. In this respect . . . there were no new frontiers here."[19]

In "I Shot an Arrow into the Air," *The Twilight Zone* dramatized many of these issues related to America's lunar ambitions, tackling the space-as-frontier mythology as well as the notion that American pioneers are the guarantors of peace and freedom. From the outset, the episode makes it clear that these space pioneers are not necessarily the living embodiments of peace, knowledge, and understanding—resembling neither Captain Video nor a Disneyfied Davy Crockett. Having faced several casualties and looking at potentially even more because of their desperate lack of resources, the crashed crew illustrates some of the complications involved with manned space flight. First, Serling explores the fact that when it comes to human survival, lofty ideals of peace and freedom only go so far, especially when resources are desperately insufficient, reflecting in many ways what Amitai Etzioni later outlined in his scathing indictment of the space race, *The Moon-Doggle*. Etzioni's 1964 book argues among many other things, that just as much, if not more "could be achieved on the moon by robots, who do not eat or drink; who require no return ticket; and who can be sent up regardless of the safety margin."[20] By obsessively pursuing manned space flight through a "cash-and-crash" approach rather than by satellites or robots, the United States was spending approximately 98 percent more than it really needed to, while also unnecessarily risking human lives and taking resources from other equally important projects.

At the same time, this episode also comments on the underacknowledged barrenness and poverty on Earth, particularly with regard to the United States, where resources are supposedly abundant. While the American frontier described by television shows, Walt Disney, and the president seemed like an enviable place to live, bursting with opportunities, peace, and freedom, it quickly becomes apparent in this episode that the new frontier, much like the old, is actually prone to violence and desperately bereft of certain essential resources. Thus while the mythological frontier seemed inextricably tied to space exploration, Serling illustrates how the actual American frontier, as well as the nation as a whole, truly is connected to the space race with regard to resource management and distribution. Nobel Prize winner in physics Polykarp Kusch raised this very issue when he testified before the Senate Committee on Aeronautical and Space Sciences in 1963. Kusch deplored what he saw as the short-sighted funneling of resources away from earthly needs to put men on the moon, and he even specifically mentioned water resources: "I think a real challenge to our technology and science is to develop sources of water and techniques . . . which would halt the drop in the water table, and perhaps restore it to previous levels. I think we are under a moral obligation not to bequeath to our successors an arid continent."[21] And while Kusch advocated for more attention be paid to other scientific fields, such as oceanography, his critiques were equally as relevant to the largely forgotten economic and social issues throughout the United States and the world: the now abandoned fragments of the New Frontier.

In dramatizing a space mission gone wrong, Serling invites the home audience to question the notion that humans, Americans or otherwise, are aptly suited to spread peace throughout the galaxy. Once again, the course of events in this episode reflects an observation Etzioni later articulated: "As man moves deeper into space, he is not just advancing as an explorer or entrepreneur, he is also projecting his international problems into a new environment."[22] That the space race was unquestionably part of the Cold War, despite efforts to market the mission as being above politics, meant space would be subject to human baggage, particularly the management and fight for resources. As the main characters in "I Shot an Arrow into the Air" are seen turning against each other with both suspicion and firearms, the episode illustrates the absence of humanitarianism in manned space flight and, instead, the predominance of militarism and a budget largely backed by the Department of Defense. Moreover, in an environment that makes survival increasingly difficult, the needs of man become even more costly. Throughout the episode, Corey's need to keep moving while he absorbs all the resources around him reflects the hurried, strenuous pace of the United States' own mission to propel man onto the moon. In this way, the negligence, manipulation, and selfishness regarding both resources and humanity on earth, will not be cured by exploring space but will only be intensified.

As this episode illustrates, putting men in space did not mean leaving behind humanity's baggage. Instead, like the men in this episode, manned space flight could seek the outer reaches of space, but as long as fighting for resources, military strength, and political power remained primary concerns on Earth, explorers could always expect to crash right back into them no matter where they landed. Despite all the political speeches, Disney specials, and children's shows, Serling sought to dramatize how the space race really was not necessarily about utilizing resources wisely or being scientifically sound or promoting peace. In fact, NASA's current website openly admits that the landing on the moon was "first and foremost political."[23] Yet, one must again question political effectiveness here and ask who exactly is defining what is, in Kennedy's words, "impressive," particularly as it relates to the Cold War and American foreign policy. While Kennedy proclaimed that space exploration has a profound "impact . . . on the minds of men everywhere, who are attempting to make a determination of which road they should take," there are many reasons to doubt such a claim.[24] As Etzioni, among many others at the time, pointed out: "heading the list of values of the developing nations are . . . economic, social, and political progress." Moreover, because much of the third world was nonwhite, such thinkers are also very concerned with our race relations: "Nothing we can do in outer space will substitute for the impression we give by our failure to accept the colored people of our country. If we are really concerned with the 'impression' we make on other nations . . . we must succeed in introducing reforms in this country, both on economic and social fronts."[25] In this way, the forgotten aspects of the New Frontier, which included such issues, looked very similar to the rocky, barren terrain incidentally explored by American astronauts. Using space as an extreme version of white flight, the United States of the sixties neglected these social issues, which would require even more struggle and desperate demonstrations before Washington would take another look at the unforgiving desert in its own backyard.

At best, the use of the frontier image with regard to the space race was misguided and premature; at worst, it was a gross mischaracterization. In a practical sense, the "settling" of the historical frontier was, to a large extent, about gaining natural resources and making them accessible to Americans back east. As David Potter pointed out with regard to the nineteenth-century frontier,

> if we are to appreciate the links with the past, we must recognize . . . that one of the key principles was . . . the constant endeavor of government to make the economic abundance of the nation accessible to the public. . . . In the early nineteenth century the major form in which abundance presented itself was the fertility of unsettled land. For a people of whom 90 percent followed agricultural pursuits, access to abundance meant opportunity to settle the new lands . . . it became clear that access to soil did not mean access to wealth unless it was accompanied by access to market . . . the market was the source of wealth to which access was needed.

Potter concluded that the "frontier ceased to operate as a major force in American history not when it disappeared—when the superintendent of the census abandoned the attempt to map a frontier boundary—but when the primary means of access to abundance passed to other focuses in American life."[26] In this way, the supposed New Frontier never truly even opened in the first place; it had not yet proven to have the economic potential western lands once carried. American suburbs and cities could arguably be more accurately described as the new frontier, as they offered more practical, economic potentials for most Americans than western lands or the moon. The moon was never presented in a practical way as the New Frontier: it did not seem to hold, at least not yet, much economic opportunity for the public at large. The remarks of Wallace Reid, a World War II veteran, regarding the cost of war, also applied to space flight: "When you and I divide the cost of childbirth into the cost of firing one gun for eight hours, we find that the country could pay for bringing three hundred babies into the world with the money it spent in that one day."[27] And merely a year after the successful moon landing, a young Gil Scott-Heron released his first studio album and struck a similarly critical tone in his song "Whitey on the Moon," which lamented the lack of affordable health care, housing, and basic utilities for Americans on Earth, while we publicly funded putting white men on the moon.[28] Rather than a frontier bursting with the potential to increase the amount of accessible resources, both Scott-Heron and Serling depicted manned space flight perhaps more accurately as a potential Death Valley for national resources.

For Whom the Computer Automates

If "I Shot an Arrow into the Air" explored the frontier of space exploration, "Brain Center at Whipple's" looks at the frontier of technology, specifically the advent of computers. Among many other episodes that dramatized modern technology, "From Agnes—With Love" tells the story of a computer programmer who becomes the object of the computer's romantic infatuation and its prisoner (S5, e20). In *Twilight Zone* fashion, the programmer becomes the programmed, as the computer manipulates the mind of the episode's protagonist. In the end, Serling concludes, "Machines are made by men for man's benefit and progress, but when man ceases to control the products of his ingenuity and imagination he not only risks losing the benefit, but he takes a long and unpredictable step into . . . *The Twilight Zone.*" Another episode, "A Thing about Machines," features a food critic named Bartlett Finchley, who lives alone and is constantly having trouble with his appliances and other machines (S2, e4). He continually calls repairmen to fix his unruly machinery, but the problems worsen as his appliances order and chase him out of his own house. Eventually, Finchley's car chases him until he falls into his pool and drowns. In all these episodes, the possibilities for technology to actually control humans more than humans do machines is dramatized with horrifying results.

On the night of May 15, 1964, *The Twilight Zone's* "Brain Center at Whipple's" captured this theme as well. The episode opens with Wallace V. Whipple, the owner of a manufacturing corporation, and William Hanley, the plant's chief engineer, viewing the 1967 year-end report on a projector screen. Intended for the families and stockholders of the Whipple Corporation, the short film stars Whipple, who describes his corporation as one that "only takes steps forward." The film highlights the company's assembly lines and various plants throughout the country, citing how just one plant, impressively, employs 34,827 men. After noting these laudable employment numbers, Whipple introduces his stockholders to a new piece of machinery, the X-109B14, a "modified, transistorized, totally automatic assembly machine." He boasts how this new piece of technology will eliminate sixty-one thousand costly jobs, seventy-three outdated machines, eighty-one thousand man hours per eleven workdays, and $4 million in yearly expenditures for employee insurance, hospitalization, welfare, and profit participation. Within six months, factories will be completely mechanized and automated, operating from a "brain center."

When the short film ends, Whipple admiringly states how his production "speaks for itself." Hanley, noticeably underwhelmed, asks if he really expects to automate the plants within six months. Whipple explains that the date could be even sooner and adds that a lot of the factory's fixtures, such as time clocks, will be going in the trash heap. After Hanley protests that these changes will lead to mass unemployment, Whipple, unbothered, responds, "That, unfortunately, is progress, Hanley. You know, you're a solid man when it comes to assembly line planning, but when it comes to the aforementioned progress . . . you're a foot-dragger." Whipple, addressing his new machine as "sweetheart," excitedly says how much time they will be spending together. Serling introduces the episode: "These are the players, with or without a scorecard: in one corner, a machine; in the other, one Wallace V. Whipple, man. And the game? It happens to be the historical battle between flesh and steel, between the brain of man and the product of man's brain. We don't make book on this one, and predict no winner, but we can tell you that for this particular contest there is standing room only—in *The Twilight Zone.*"

As the episode develops, Whipple tells Hanley he is "holding on tight to this nineteenth century," while Hanley explains that it is not the nineteenth century he is hanging onto, but principles of loyalty and labor. Whipple coldly retorts that if Hanley feels such remorse over the changes, he should

"Well, little sweetheart, you and I are going to spend a great deal of time together!" Mr. Whipple lovingly attends to his machine as Mr. Hanley looks on in disgust. Still from "The Brain Center at Whipple's" (4:27)

have a sign made for his desk stating, "Mr. Walter Hanley, plant manager in charge of regrets." Hanley argues, though, that replacing men with machines means exchanging "efficiency for pride . . . craftsmanship, what a man feels when he makes something." Whipple scoffs, stands up from his desk chair, and gets right in Hanley's face: "What the devil can I do with pride?! Can I bottle it, wrap it, produce it? I'm not selling pride, I'm selling product." After Hanley mentions that Whipple's father ran the plant for forty years in an efficient manner but also with good will toward his employees, Whipple again scoffs, stating that while his father doubled the size of the plant, his competitors, who perhaps were less concerned with the "goodwill and welfare" of his employees, quadrupled theirs. Whipple points out how other factories were able to outpace his father's because they were more willing to mechanize their factories and also did not have "plant managers who went off into a crying jag every time a pink slip was attached to a time clock."

After two technicians have installed the new computers, Hanley and the factory's foreman, Dickerson, can do little but look and reflect on the steel and blinking lights that signal the end of a lot of careers. Dickerson, breaking the silence, asks Hanley, "Ever notice how it looks like it had a face? An ugly face. A miserable ugly face. Whipple, he thinks it's a machine. It's not a machine, it's an enemy. It's an opponent. I swear we've got to hate a thing like this!" Undoubtedly feeling helpless about the plant's future as well as his own, Dickerson ends up at a local bar, drinking himself into a stupor. With slurred speech and outstretched hands, he asks the bartender if he knows what they are. "Pair of hands," the bartender simply replies. "You know what else they are? . . . They're obsolete, they're off the market. They're like wooden wagons trying to roll down a freeway. Flesh and bone and muscle and nerve, but that don't cut mustard anymore," Dickerson responds as he slams his fists down on the bar. After explaining how he is going to turn the machine into mere "nuts and bolts," Dickerson enters the plant, set on destroying Whipple's new profit-boosting device.

Before Dickerson can get to the computer, however, Whipple confronts him, having been informed of his breaking and entering. After Dickerson pleads that he has worked there for thirty years and has rights at the factory, Whipple tells him bluntly, "You're drunk, disorderly, and trespassing on private property, and therefore subject to arrest!" When Dickerson asks who will be there to mourn his boss at his own funeral, Whipple ignores the question and gleefully describes all the advantages his machine has over men such as Dickerson. The new machines do not age or need paid vacations, reflecting what one of Kurt Vonnegut's characters slyly expressed in the novel *Player Piano*: "He would make a good lamp post if he'd weather better and didn't have to eat."[29] Infuriated with the plant owner, Dickerson shouts in his gravelly voice how "men have to eat and work . . . you can't pack 'em in Cosmoline like surplus tanks or put 'em out to pasture like old bulls! I'm a man! And that makes me better than this hunk of metal! You hear me?! Better!" Dickerson picks up a lead pipe and begins pounding at the newly installed computer, causing it to burst into flames. While the indecisive security guard looks to Whipple for instruction, Whipple snatches the guard's pistol and fires a round at Dickerson. The grimacing factory veteran collapses, addressing the battered machine as he falls: "You see, it took more than you to beat me. It took man," emphasizing that it is not so much technology that dehumanizes and devalues man but other human beings and how they handle technological change.

The following day, Hanley reassures Whipple that the technicians are downstairs repairing the X-109B14 that Dickerson damaged. Unable to

"It took more than you to beat me. . . . It took man." Mr. Dickerson falls to his death after Whipple shoots him for trespassing, proving that machines do not threaten workers as much as the policies and choices of business owners. Still from "The Brain Center at Whipple's" (13:04)

control his excitement, Whipple shows off another new piece of technology: a "tape-controlled seven axis," or a "sentry." Whipple explains how this new machine is designed to oversee plant operations and collect data on man hours, cost hours, product rejects, et cetera. While Whipple giddily states that it is "the most sophisticated machine" he's ever encountered, Hanley only asks how many men will lose their jobs because of it. Whipple disingenuously responds, "Oh well this should please you, Hanley. Only one, just one . . . it replaces you." After Hanley unemotionally explains that he had only come to Whipple's office to give him his notice, Whipple coolly responds that he expected as much, knowing Hanley as a "reasonable man," and guarantees him a generous severance payout and pension. Hanley thanks him and offers to give him something as well, delivering a strong back-handed slap to Whipple's face: "That's for you, Mr. Whipple, from me. It's for your lack of sensitivity, your lack of compassion. Your heartless manipulation of men and metals. You can take my severance pay, my pension, and your goodbye speeches and feed them into your machine. Because when I walk away from you, I walk away clean. And that, Mr. Whipple, is one hell of a trick!" As Hanley leaves the office, he finds that even walking away clean means surrendering to Whipple's technology one last time, as he cannot even open the office door without scanning his ID card in the new security device.

The scene is followed by a montage interspersing clips of manual laborers eating in the cafeteria with Whipple in his office tweaking his machinery. As Whipple flips one of the switches on his machines, an empty cafeteria and a vacant parking lot is revealed, quickly followed by a close-up of him twirling his gold pocket watch. The meaning of the juxtaposition is clear— the obsession with profit margins and technological efficiency is costing people their livelihoods just as it is taking the life out of the plant, quite literally. As one of the technicians, a young African American man, comes by to check in, he states that the incessant equipment checks Whipple has him doing are superfluous. In response, Whipple threatens that he is merely employed "for the moment," and he demonstrates one of his other machines that can take dictation perfectly. This machine, Whipple promises, will make secretaries obsolete as well as "powder rooms . . . coffee breaks . . . work stoppages due to various and sundry inconveniences, such as maternity and that sort of thing." In disbelief, the technician counters, "Inconveniences like maternity? You'll have to forgive me . . . but if we keep up with this sort of thing, we're going to have wonderful products but mighty few people to buy them." Impervious to the technician's words, Whipple responds that he is not concerned with such matters but merely focused on providing efficiency. The technician states that although the plant can boast a certain level of efficiency, it lacks people, laughter, and everything that makes people feel connected to others. Instead, the plant stands as a lonely, desolate place devoid of life and human vitality. As the technician announces his resignation, before he makes his final exit, he advises Whipple to run an equipment check on himself.

Alone again in his office, Whipple lovingly tends to the machines he has clearly become infatuated with, but something goes wrong. When he flips a switch and pushes a button, he hears voices of his former employees coming through the machine: "Did it ever occur to you, you might be trading efficiency for pride?" "When you're dead and buried, who do you get to mourn for you?" "I think it'd be a good idea if you ran an equipment check on yourself!" All the machines start to malfunction, buzzing and flashing, while the office door opens and slams shut repeatedly, barring Whipple from escaping the cacophonous electrical chaos.

In the following scene, Whipple walks into the bar where Dickerson drank himself into a stupor before attacking the plant's machinery. As Whipple sits down, Hanley is seated on the opposite end of the bar. As he asks Hanley how his retirement is going, it becomes clear that Whipple, with an unshaven face and loosened necktie, is not quite himself. Whipple soon reveals that he now has been laid off from the plant: "It's not right, Hanley. It's not right. Cold, dispassionate, impersonal . . . they chuck a man out right in his prime, chuck him out like he was some kind of a part . . . said that being alone with the machines had warped me. That was the expression they used, 'warped!' It's not fair, Hanley, it's not fair! A man has value! A man has worth! They just snap their fingers, and they bring in a replacement. . . . It isn't fair the way they diminish us." As the camera pans to the window toward the Whipple Manufacturing plant across the street, it reveals a robot occupying Whipple's old office, twirling a gold watch just like the former executive used to do. Serling offers his closing remarks: "There are many bromides applicable here—too much of a good thing, tiger by the tail, as you sow so shall ye reap. The point is that too often man becomes clever instead of wise, he becomes inventive but not thoughtful—and sometimes, as in the case of Mr. Whipple, he can create himself right out of existence. Tonight's tale of oddness and obsolescence from *The Twilight Zone*."

In "Brain Center at Whipple's" Serling dramatically depicts the potential social impacts of computer technology, another postwar American frontier. And just as the frontier is an image of American opportunity and ingenuity in terms of territorial expansion and space exploration, new technologies also represented another endless expanse bursting with new possibilities. While several different segments of the population, including manufacturers, marketers, and the defense industry, celebrated nearly any kind of technological innovation that could be sold as a consumer good or used for national defense, a substantial amount of uneasy criticism could be heard from various fiction writers and industrial workers. Automation served as the subject matter for Kurt Vonnegut's first novel, *Player Piano* (1952), and many of Philip K. Dick's early works while also creating enough of a national stir to prompt two separate congressional hearings on the topic of automation in the 1950s alone. Like *The Twilight Zone*'s Wallace V. Whipple, many business executives, including D. J. Davis, the vice president of Ford, welcomed in the new age with a calm confidence. Appearing before Congress, Davis declared, "Automation is just another normal step in our continuous technological progress. Certainly, such progress will create changes. But progress in itself is change—a change always for the better."[30] Automation's impact on workers and the general public, however, proved to much more complex than a mere step forward.

Like so many other issues affecting the United States during the early Cold War, automation technology could be traced largely back to World War II. As *Electronics*, the industry's trade magazine, explained, the field of electronics during wartime had undergone "a period of extraordinary creativity and growth. Under the stimulus of a multi-billion-dollar flow of funds, it changed from a timid consumer-oriented radio industry into a heroic producer of rugged, reliable military equipment."[31] The emergence of the digital computer, initially designed to measure and calculate ballistics and to analyze atomic bombs, was arguably the most significant of these wartime developments. In 1944, Franklin Roosevelt, already looking forward to peacetime, asked Vannevar Bush, director for the Office of Scientific and Research Development, about the potentials of scientific innovation for civilian life. Recognizing that the war would be won or lost largely because of technological innovations and projects, including the Manhattan Project, of which Bush was a part, the president optimistically stated: "New frontiers of the mind are before us, and if they are pioneered with the same vision, boldness, and drive with which we have waged this war we can create a fuller and more fruitful employment and a fuller and more fruitful life."[32]

Bush's response did not arrive before Roosevelt passed away; President Truman received it in July 1945. Bush's report, *Science: The Endless Frontier,* struck a similarly optimistic tone and explained how the "pioneer spirit is still vigorous within this nation. Science offers a largely unexplored hinterland for the pioneer who has the tools for his task. The rewards of such exploration both for the Nation and the individual are great. Scientific progress is one essential key to our security as a nation, to our better health, to more jobs, to a higher standard of living, and to our cultural progress." While Bush went into much greater detail as to how scientific research should be conducted and funded in the future, the emphasis his response and Roosevelt's initial inquiry both placed on jobs was instructive—among the most important aims of science and technology was providing work for the general American public. In fact, Bush even qualified his statements, adding that science "by itself, provides no panacea for individual, social, and economic ills. It can be effective in the national welfare only as a member of a team, whether the conditions be peace or war."[33] Thus, the director reminded the president that science and technology should never be pursued as ends in themselves but remain in cooperation with the team of humanity, while helping to address social needs.

Bush's qualification points out how both political and private business rhetoric celebrating "technological progress" could obfuscate issues as much as illuminate them. And while almost any state regulation could be seen as a suspiciously socialistic overreach in the context of the Cold War, continual government funding of major private industries was for the most part above suspicion. In 1964, the same year this episode aired, two-thirds of research and development costs in the electronic equipment industry—including that of GE, Westinghouse, RCA, AT&T, Philco, and IBM—was financed by the federal government.[34] But by aligning technology with the mythological frontier, rhetoricians concealed the federal government's central role in the development of both. This concealment also enabled Cold War pundits to paint technological advancement as inherently patriotic and good for the nation, while sustaining the false belief that free market capitalism was the sole driver of such change. Thus, the pervasive celebration of technological innovation also reflected assertions that market forces are inherently good for society. Although both technological development and market trends were profoundly shaped by state policy throughout the Cold War and after, isolating them from private- and public-sector decision-making furnished them with a seemingly natural, if magical, allure.

In their letters, President Roosevelt and Vannevar Bush proudly mentioned science's impressive historical record of creating new industries and lines of work, including automobile manufacturing. However, there was no note of the fact that industries did not necessarily share these goals of universal employment—something Roosevelt's unpopular predecessor, Herbert Hoover, learned the hard way. CEOs could more predictably be expected to primarily seek to increase their own profits, while limiting expenditures rather than to create jobs. Corporations likely saw workers as more of a liability than an asset. And while federally funded wartime manufacturing created many new job opportunities for Americans in the forties, after the war the increasingly automated manufacturing plants posed a whole new set of dilemmas. The close relationship between private industry and federal funding, however, persisted without much serious challenge, as did the continual promotion of new technology as a benefit to the entire nation.

In this context, "Brain Center at Whipple's" casts serious doubt on the popular belief that the technological frontier of postwar America was a good in itself. Rather, this frontier would only be as "good" as its ability to improve the standard of living for average Americans. In a similar manner to its treatment of space, *The Twilight Zone* framed the postwar technological frontier with ominous ambivalence—it could help or seriously hinder the distribution and creation of new wealth and opportunities, depending on how it was being managed. In this way, technology was not offered up as some kind of Promised Land or as the inherent representation of progress, as Whipple described it. Instead, Serling encouraged his viewers to consider technology in terms of its ability, both potential and real, to create employment opportunities and median wealth and to raise the standard of living for the general public, not just CEOs.

The episode's climactic confrontation between Dickerson and Whipple dramatically depicts many of new technology's potential threats. As corporations decentralized their operations and automated their plants, Dickerson exemplifies the gradual disempowerment of workers, small businesses, and labor unions. Among many corporations transitioning during this period, Ford Motor Company opened its first automated plants in the fifties, beginning with the Brook Park Plant outside of Cleveland, Ohio, in 1952. Recognizing the dramatic shift in labor relations this represented, the United Auto Workers held a convention in March 1953 to discuss the impacts of automation on their work. The union's resolution declared that if automation was "improperly used, for narrow and selfish purposes," it could "create a social and economic nightmare in which men walk idle and hungry—made obsolete as producers because the mechanical monsters around them cannot replace them as consumers," calling attention to the need for businesses like Ford to sustain national purchasing power. Meanwhile, in Detroit, Ford's River Rouge plant went from employing over 100,000 workers in the 1930s to merely 30,000 by 1960. As automotive labor historian Stephen Meyer has pointed out, workers at the River Rouge plant historically "were among the industry's most well-organized, racially and ethnically diverse, and militant. When Rouge workers walked out on strike, the company's entire manufacturing operations crashed to a halt."[35] To avoid more confrontations and controversies, and also to invest in more fully automated factories, Ford shuffled his operations throughout the country and in the second half of the twentieth century, to foreign countries. By 1990, the River Rouge plant's workforce had shrunk to just a little over 6,000.[36] And while automation did create new positions, among them machine operators, those employees were often paid less than assembly workers, even though these new positions were part of drastically increasing productivity rates. As Meyer pointed out, in the 1950s an operator was paid $1.75 per hour and a setter about $1.85 in Cleveland's new Brook Plant, but these rates were lower than some of the machining and assembling jobs in Detroit's River Rouge plant.[37] Thus, increased productivity and new machinery did not benefit all employees proportionately.

To be sure, automation's impact was felt not only in the automotive industry but many others as well. Speaking before Congress, James Carey, secretary-treasurer of the International Union of Electrical Workers, called attention to how new technologies were affecting electrical manufacturing. Carey explained that in the part of the industry that produces electrical generators, transmitters, distributors, and industrial apparatuses, the number of production workers declined 11 percent and nonproduction workers by 2 percent. Moreover, in the industry's electrical appliance division, production worker employment dropped 13 percent. Carey also called attention to the fact that while man-hour output at Westinghouse had increased by 50 percent since 1949, wages had increased less than half that amount, when accounting for inflation. He asked, "Will business take the lion's share of the benefits of technological progress, as it did in the 1920's, or will society receive a share? Wage and salary increases are an important part of the answer. But if society, as a whole, is to receive the benefits of sharp increases in man-hour output, industry will have to share the benefits of technological progress with consumers through reduced prices."[38]

As for the growing obsolescence of certain positions, Carey advocated that it was companies' responsibility to retrain workers for different jobs in automated factories and/or offices. He insisted, "The cost of retraining such workers, and of maintaining their incomes while they are being retrained, should be considered a regular part of the investment cost of changing over to automation."[39] Companies like Westinghouse, however, opted to relocate many of their operations to, among other places, the southern United States because of cheap labor and right-to-work laws banning union organization. Following these congressional hearings and further labor unrest, one resolution materialized in Washington—the Manpower Development and Training Act of 1962. This legislation called on companies to retrain workers for other positions instead of simply laying them off. Federal funds, however, as historian James Patterson has noted, "mainly subsidized officials and private interests who provided the training" and "had at best a marginal impact on unemployment."[40]

The dialogue between Whipple and his workers highlights the potential plight of not just working men in the age of automation but women as well, explicitly referring to "maternity leave." One of the most vocal advocates for working women at the time was Myra Wolfgang, the "Battling Belle of Detroit," who took issue with both Betty Friedan's brand of feminism and corporate industry alike. Wolfgang proclaimed that the Friedan-endorsed ERA did not go far enough, particularly for full-time working women who had to work to just survive.[41] Wolfgang helped to form the Federation for the Advancement of Women, while also supporting the Network for Economic Rights. Both institutions' chief objectives included voluntary overtime, childcare, maternity protection, welfare reform, and improved labor standards. Wolfgang explained: "We, who want equal opportunity and responsibility and equal status for women, know that it is frequently necessary to obtain real equality through a difference in treatment rather than an identity in treatment."[42] Working women also had to be particularly concerned about the supposed advantages automation brought, especially as they related to access to health care, childcare, and family leave.

As Whipple finally becomes a casualty of his own philosophy and loses his job, the episode dramatizes that not just manufacturing positions but white-collar positions are being automatized. Here, Whipple serves as the personification of Howard Coughlin's declaration before Congress: "There will be serious problems caused by the introduction of automation in offices. Many individuals who have spent their lives acquiring certain skills and have come to believe implicitly in their own indispensability are in for a rude shock. They will see machines do in seconds work that takes them days and weeks to accomplish. They will see machines replace the jobs they and their coworkers have come to feel are their permanent niches in the office world. A lot of people will lose their jobs."[43] Whipple, having also been deemed "warped" by working alongside machines, reflects what UAW critic Hyman Lumer observed: that "the task of keeping an eye on a multitude of instrument panel lights and watching for the faulty performance of tools and machines . . . can be . . . as nerve-wracking and exhausting as the hardest physical work." Backing his claims with a Yale University study, Lumer explained that the "new machines have eliminated drudgery, but the strain of watching and controlling them makes the workers 'jumpy.'"[44] Automation presented problems not just for those laid off in industrial production but also for those hired to take these newly created computer-oriented roles. The psychological strain and stress, coupled with the lack of human interaction, meant that the burden of adapting to this new technological frontier would be on humans, not on machines.

While postwar corporations such as Ford and Westinghouse excitedly welcomed the possibilities of this new age of automation, it is clear that working people did not always have reason or even the ability share in this excitement. And in the context of the Cold War, those concerned for the rights of working-class Americans were particularly vulnerable to being treated as suspect and even promoting Marxist causes. And to be sure, while the age of automation had not yet occurred when Marx wrote the words, he did comment on how the "instrument of labour, when it takes the form of a machine, immediately becomes a competitor of the workman himself. The self-expansion of capital by means of machinery is thenceforward directly proportional to the number of the workpeople, whose means of livelihood have been destroyed by that machinery."[45] But as seen in this episode of *The Twilight Zone*, as well as in the public statements of US unions and labor organizers, it was not so much automation that was the problem. The vast majority of labor advocates recognized that technology was here to stay. But what needed to be more deeply considered were the corporate and political responses to these changes. Union leaders, including Dick Greenwood of the International Association of Machinists and Aerospace Workers, urged employers to share with labor the productivity gains resulting from automation: "At this point, the objective is not to block the new technology, but to control its rate and manner of introduction, in order that it is adapted to labor's needs and serves people, rather than our being servile to it or its victims. It can go either way, and it's headed the wrong way right now."[46] This "wrong way" was how the burden of a rapidly changing economy and labor force was placed more on the public to stop the bleeding of unemployment and wage reductions. As Philip Wylie lamented, "Business was able to kick around and decimate the people and their needs with virtually no punishment, whatever the result."[47]

While many commentators asserted that technology would create more jobs, just like mechanization did in the early 1900s, this was soon shown to be a gross miscalculation. Mechanization in the twenties certainly allowed workers to be more directly involved in producing finished goods, helping to spread wealth in different ways. But now, the necessity of access to extremely expensive computer technology in order to be a competitive producer severely limited the numbers of American producers and people who could be actively involved with production, including small businesses and laborers. As the authors of the Port Huron statement had pointed out, "automation brings unemployment instead of mere leisure for all and greater achievement of needs for all people in the world—a crisis instead of economic utopia. Instead of being introduced into a social system in a planned and equitable way, automation is initiated according to its profitability. . . . Technology, which could be a blessing to society, becomes more and more a sinister threat to humanistic and rational enterprise."[48]

The Cold War interests of asserting national superiority through manned space flight and computer technology are depicted as inherently flawed in these episodes of *The Twilight Zone*. While manned space flight seemed to offer political prestige on the Cold War's grandest stage, these objectives woefully neglected public and scientific concerns. Instead of federal funds supporting a new frontier of possibilities for the public, these new technologies in effect robbed humanity, as they were narrowly funneled into supporting the needs of putting a few white men in space, rather than millions of humans on Earth. Moreover, by channeling funds to this end, the United States seriously limited its potential for scientific discoveries in outer space and in other equally critical fields, such as oceanography. And while new computer technology carried promises for US economic strength, *The Twilight Zone* exposed how economic productivity matters little if it mainly results in laying off workers and shrinking the number of American consumers. At the March on Washington in 1963, civil rights activist and labor organizer A. Philip Randolph asked what good automation would do if it "destroys the jobs of millions of workers Black and white" without ensuring employment. He implored, "It falls to us to demand new forms of social planning, to create full employment, and to put automation at the service of human needs, not at the service of profits—for we are the worst victims of unemployment," pointing out how rising unemployment numbers were worse for African Americans in particular.

With "I Shot an Arrow into the Air," Serling illustrated how human personalities and egos were unnecessarily front and center in space exploration. Human presence actually complicated space missions and made them costlier and more dangerous. By forcing humans into the spotlight of outer space, the United States effectively kept scientific understanding of the rest of the universe in relative darkness. And while space exploration unnecessarily forced humans into the picture, automation was forcing them out in a way that dangerously neglected public needs. In "Brain Center at Whipple's," viewers witnessed how the disembodied intelligence and production potential offered by automation technology displaced the human element from the production–consumption cycle. Automation technology seemed to carry enormous potential for humans everywhere, including creating cheaper access to finished goods and permitting more leisure time. However, the introduction of new computer technology frequently took power from workers by separating them from production processes and severely limiting their ability to benefit from new, increasingly efficient technologies. In the words of Philip Wylie, "Starting with the thesis that competition is the essence of democracy . . . the businessman undertook two main lines of bastardization of that truth. First . . . was the elimination of competition wherever possible and by all means imaginable. Second, was the establishment of the notion that business competed only with *itself* and never with any other requirement of mankind." If businesses could define their conduct and responsibilities as only competing with other businesses, they could force the welfare of workers and the general human population out of the equation. Making an exclusive group of white American pioneers the focal point of space exploration and by ensuring computer technology benefitted white business owners more than the racially diverse working population all but guaranteed many workers would be transferred from a dream into a nightmare in and out of *The Twilight Zone.*

Duck, Cover, and Accuse

Cold War Paranoia Remakes the American Landscape

Although there were plenty of reasons for Americans to celebrate the end of World War II, the postwar era ushered in a host of new challenges for the nation and world alike. Edward R. Murrow, capturing this somewhat ambivalent landscape, declared, "Seldom if ever has a war ended leaving the victors with such a sense of uncertainty and fear, with such a realization that the future is obscure and that survival is not assured."[1] This questionable survival and obscure future were largely a result of the very forces that brought the war to a close—American nuclear technology and Soviet military power. While the Soviets proved to be by far the most critical force in defeating Nazi Germany, the United States' nuclear power, which ended the Pacific War by decimating the civilian populations and infrastructure of Hiroshima and Nagasaki, foreshadowed some of the moral dilemmas to come. While Soviet strength and American nuclear technology ruthlessly brought the war to a close, they also introduced unprecedented quandaries and possibilities for future devastation and destruction. In 1949, following the Soviets' successful test, the United States no longer possessed a monopoly on nuclear technology. As both superpowers developed hydrogen bombs throughout the 1950s, the victorious alliance between the two nations during World War II seemed a distant memory.

Within the United States, national nuclear safety programs attempted to provide a sense of security for Americans, just as hardline anti-Communist policies and politics worked to guarantee the survival and purity of America's brand of consumer capitalism. While fallout shelters emerged as a popular and marketable solution for Americans fearful of nuclear annihilation, McCarthyism and the legacies of the Second Red Scare shaped the American political landscape throughout the 1950s and 1960s. Although McCarthy's red-hunting tactics and nuclear fallout shelters were intended to provide

Americans a sense of security, Serling dramatically illustrated that these solutions could endanger our neighborhoods, society, and nation. He demonstrated how the claustrophobic, constrictive conditions of fallout shelters were also reflected in the repressive and restrictive politics endorsed by McCarthyism's supporters. Rather than ensuring security, "The Shelter" and "The Monsters Are Due on Maple Street" argue how the resolutions offered by fallout shelters and McCarthyism all but guarantee that the United States will become an intellectually narrower, politically and socially claustrophobic nation, rather than a strong, robust one (S3, e3; S1, e22). Serling encouraged postwar Americans to more actively consider their individual roles in either dismantling or sustaining a free and democratic society.

Our Subterranean Salvation

In the third season of *The Twilight Zone,* "The Shelter" aired on September 29, 1961. Prior to this, *The Twilight Zone* also dramatized nuclear fears in "Third from the Sun," depicting a family's attempt to escape to Earth from another planet in order to avoid nuclear catastrophe on their home planet (S1, e14). The episode concludes with an ominous, open ending, as it becomes clear that the family is merely headed to another planet that is also in danger of nuclear destruction. Another one of the series' most iconic episodes, "Time Enough at Last," portrays the lonesome experience of a bookworm who has survived a nuclear explosion (S1, e8). When the attack occurs, Henry Bemis, a banker, miraculously survives, having been in one of the bank's vaults during the attack. Realizing he is now finally left unbothered to read, Bemis excitedly plans his schedule, but when he steps on his eyeglasses, his hopes are dashed. In these episodes, the attempts to avoid nuclear war through escape, security, or seclusion are depicted as largely futile, as Serling consistently illustrates that the best way to avoid nuclear disaster arguably is to work toward mankind's peaceful coexistence and to help ensure nuclear weapons will not be used at all.

In a similar vein, "The Shelter" dramatizes the inadequacies of fallout shelters. The episode begins in a suburban home where a surprise birthday party is taking place for Dr. Bill Stockton. After finishing dinner, Jerry, one of the party guests, stands up to give a toast, declaring the guests' unanimous love and affection for their "man with the little black bag." While thanking him for his medical service, another guest sarcastically adds how they also owe a debt of gratitude for all the noise and chaos resulting from the doctor having a fallout shelter recently constructed in his basement. The guests all laugh and drink to Jerry's heartfelt speech, but immediately thereafter, the doctor's son, Paul, comes rushing into the dining room explaining that the television just went out after an announcer instructed everyone to turn on their CONELRAD stations. Bill Stockton, with a distressed look on his face and after-dinner coffee in hand, goes to turn on the radio, hearing a chilling announcement:

> Four minutes ago, the President of the United States made the following announcement, I quote: "At 11:04 Eastern Standard Time, both our distant early warning line and ballistics early warning line reported radar evidence of unidentified flying objects flying due southeast. As of this moment, we have been unable to determine the nature of these objects, but for the time being, in the interests of national safety, we are declaring a state of yellow alert. The civil defense authorities request that if you have a shelter already prepared, go there at once. If not, use your time to move supplies of food, water, and medicine to a central place. Keep all windows and doors closed. We repeat, if you're in your home, go to your prepared shelters or to your basement."

The guests, without saying a word, scatter and run back to their homes while jets fly overhead. Serling introduces the episode: "What you're about to witness is a nightmare. It is not meant to be prophetic, it need not happen, it's the fervent and urgent prayer of all men of good will that it never shall happen. But in this place, in this moment, it does happen. This is *The Twilight Zone.*"

When the episode returns, Stockton; his wife, Grace; and their son work feverishly to bring water, food, and other essentials down to their fallout shelter. When their son runs upstairs to get a toolbox, the husband and wife privately discuss the dire situation. Bill tells Grace that even if the object turns out to be a bomb, there is no guarantee that it would land near them. She responds, "But if it does, Bill, New York is only forty miles away. And New York's going to get it. We know that. So, we'll get it too. All of it. The poison, the radiation, the whole mess. We'll get it." Her husband tries to assuage her fears by saying that they will be safe in the shelter and have plenty of food and water to last them for several weeks. Clearly not comforted, Grace retorts, "Then what? We crawl out of here like gophers to tiptoe through all that

"Why is it so necessary to survive?" The Stocktons discuss the dilemmas of surviving a nuclear attack in their fallout shelter. Still from "The Shelter" (8:08)

rubble up above? The rubble and the ruin and the bodies of our friends? Bill, why is it so necessary to survive? What's the good of it? Wouldn't it just be better, and easier, just quicker if we just . . ." Grace begins to sob as her husband explains that their twelve-year-old son is the real reason they need to survive. Grace wipes the tears from her eyes as Paul comes down the stairs.

Suddenly, there is a knock on the Stocktons' door. Jerry, the friend who had given the toast at the party, frantically explains that he does not have a basement and pleads with Bill to let his family stay in their shelter: "Bill, you've got to help me! You've got to keep my family alive!" Bill, however, does not budge an inch and adamantly retorts, "When that door gets closed and locked, it stays closed and locked. . . . I'm sorry, Jerry, as God as my witness, I am sorry, but I built that for my family!" Jerry, grabbing desperately onto Bill's shirt asks, "What about mine? What'll we do? Just rock on the front porch while we burn to a crisp?" Bill replies, "That's no concern of mine. Right now, it's my family I have to worry about. . . . I kept telling you, Jerry, all of you, get ready, build a shelter. Forget the card parties and the barbecues for maybe a few hours a week . . . and make the admission that the worst was possible. But you didn't want to listen. None of you wanted to listen. . . . So now you've got to face something far worse!" Bill runs into his shelter, slams the door and shouts, "It's out of my hands! It's got to be God! It's got to be God!" One by one, all of the families that were at the party earlier come to the doctor's house, demanding to be let into his shelter. When neighbor Marty is not allowed entrance, he rebukes Bill, telling him he may survive but he will also have blood on his hands: "You're a doctor! You're supposed to help people!" But Bill stubbornly refuses.

As the neighbors are now in a collective state of increasing panic, they all discuss what action to take. While one says they should all pool their things and stay together in a basement, another declares that they should break down the door to the fallout shelter. The group's distress intensifies while Marty states that maybe they should draw lots so at least one family could stay in the shelter. After Marty pleads that he has a three-month-old baby, his neighbor Frank screams back at him, "You shut your mouth, Weiss! That's the way it is when the foreigners come over here! Pushy, grabby semi-Americans!" Marty, seething, with clenched teeth, shouts back, "Why, you garbage-brained idiot!" and the two men nearly come to blows, but Jerry intervenes.

The group eventually decides to break down the shelter door, using a steel pipe as a battering ram. One of the neighbors cries out to Bill, "You've got a bunch of your neighbors outside who want to stay alive! Now you can open that door and talk to us and figure out with us how many can come in there or you can just keep on doing what you're doing, and we'll bust our way in there!" After Bill again refuses, Frank proposes gathering some heavy pipe from a nearby house, but another neighbor quickly rebuts: "Who cares about saving him? No, if we do that, if we let all those people know that we have a shelter on our street, we'd have a whole mob to contend with. A whole bunch of strangers!" Another neighborhood woman reinforces the group's increasingly tribal mindset: "What right have they got to come over here? This isn't their street! This isn't their shelter!"

Jerry, however, sensing the irony in this discussion now says, "Oh, this is our shelter, huh? And on the next street, that's another country. . . . You idiots, you fools, you're insane—all of you!" After saying that everyone is acting like a mob and "a mob doesn't have any brains," Marty expresses his agreement, only to be met with more xenophobic rage from Frank, who delivers a right cross to Marty's face. With Marty knocked down, the rest of the group rushes off to fetch some piping. Staccato, dissonant music accompanies their anger-fueled mission. The white suburban mob furiously and repeatedly crashes the shelter door, and just when they break through, an announcement comes through on the CONELRAD station: "The previously unidentified objects have now been definitely ascertained as being satellites. Repeat, there are no enemy missiles approaching. . . . We are in no danger. The state of emergency has been officially called off." The neighbors breathe a collective sigh of relief but are noticeably ashamed of themselves.

As the neighbors realize there was in fact no nuclear threat, some begin to attempt to make amends. Frank approaches Marty, explaining, "I just went off my rocker. . . . I didn't mean any of those things I said to you. We were all of us so scared, so confused." Jerry proposes that they raise money to cover the damages they all exacted on Bill's house, and Marty recommends they throw a party the next day to get back to "normal." Bill, though, clearly distressed after the madness mutters, "Normal? I don't know what normal is. I thought I did once. I don't anymore." After one of his neighbors reiterates that they would pay for the damages, the doctor responds, "Damages? I wonder if any one of us has any idea what those damages really are. . . . Maybe one of them is finding out . . . the kind of people we are just underneath the skin . . . a lot of naked, wild animals who put such a price on staying alive that they'll claw their neighbors to death just for the privilege. We were spared a bomb tonight, but I wonder if we weren't destroyed even without it."[2] Serling offers a closing narration to the fear-filled madness, "No moral, no message, no prophetic tract. Just a simple statement of fact—for civilization to survive, the human race has to remain civilized. Tonight's very small exercise in logic from *The Twilight Zone*."

This episode clearly deals with Cold War fears and paranoia regarding nuclear war, fears that were steadily on the rise throughout 1961. The reemerging Berlin Crisis again threatened to oust the Western powers from Berlin and give the Soviets sole control over the city. And while both sides dug in their heels, in late July Kennedy delivered a speech denouncing Khrushchev's plans, asserting American legality to be in West Berlin, and reiterating US commitment to the city's inhabitants. In the same speech, he also soberly discussed the prospect of nuclear war. After expressing his responsibility to let citizens know "what they should do and where they should go if bombs begin to fall," Kennedy announced: "Tomorrow, I am requesting of the Congress new funds for the following immediate objectives: to identify and mark space in existing structures—public and private—that could be used for fallout shelters in case of attack; to stock those shelters

Damaged beyond repair? After the neighbors break into the shelter and offer to pay for the damages, Dr. Stockton reflects, "I wonder if any one of us has any idea what those damages really are." Still from "The Shelter" (20:12)

with food, water, first-aid kits and other minimum essentials for survival; to increase their capacity; to improve our air-raid warning and fallout detection systems, including a new household warning system which is now under development; and to take other measures that will be effective at an early date to save millions of lives if needed." He continued, striking a more optimistic tone, that in "the event of an attack, the lives of those families which are not hit in a nuclear blast and fire can still be saved—if they can be warned to take shelter and if that shelter is available. We owe that kind of insurance to our families—and to our country . . . the time to start is now. . . . With your help, and the help of other free men, this crisis can be surmounted. Freedom can prevail—and peace can endure."[3]

In tackling the very real potential of nuclear war, Kennedy offered US citizens one clear resolution: fallout shelters. This clear connection between nuclear security and shelter access created a stir throughout local and national media. Several aspects of this heated public debate would be at the crux of Serling's episode, reminding home audiences that while they cannot necessarily dictate American foreign policy, they can control how they handle the ever-increasing threat of nuclear war in their homes and neighborhoods. Serling illuminates how placing security above all else, and defining it simply as having access to a shelter, could potentially have disastrous results when put into practice.

In fact, Grace's character articulates what Serling once expressed regarding shelters: "We've been talking, my wife and me about the possibility of building a shelter and we were struck with the moral and ethical problem what would happen if there were an alert sounding. . . . It's my feeling now that if we survive what do we survive for? What kind of a world do we go into? You know if it's rubble and poison water and inedible food and my kids have to live like wild beasts, I'm not particularly sure I want to survive in that kind of a world."[4] And while protagonist Bill Stockton dismisses this viewpoint, many public figures and intellectuals expressed similar concerns. President Eisenhower, for example, claimed that if he was in a shelter when nuclear war broke out he would merely walk out, not wanting "to face that kind of a world and the loss of my family."[5] Political leaders were not the only ones commenting on the grim prospects either, as Gerard Piel, publisher of *Scientific American,* claimed, that "the firestorms of a thermonuclear war would work an irreversible disruption of the social and moral fabric of Western Civilization."[6] Geneticist Bentley Glass reflected that "life would be very primitive for the survivors for a long time to come," and asked, if "America survived at all . . . would the more fortunate lands take pity on the country that first produced and used the atom bomb, and later engaged in the accelerating arms race?"[7] Biochemist Albert Szent-Gyorgyi predicted that American democracy would not prevail if such a nuclear catastrophe occurred and instead, "we will have here only a crude, barbaric dictatorship of half cripples."[8] For many intellectuals, scientists, and politicians, mere survival was not altogether desirable.

Bill Stockton, however, gives voice to the more optimistic pro-shelter enthusiasts, including the Kennedy administration and the Office of Civil Defense, which was tasked with developing a national fallout shelter program. Striking a tone very similar to Bill's, Steuart L. Pittman, the assistant secretary of defense, called on Americans to have "the courage to face a disaster far enough ahead to have a chance in the crisis" and "to do all they can to take care of the people or children they look out for."[9] In September 1961, *Life* magazine featured a dramatic cover layout, replete with a man in a civilian fallout suit and, in big, bold letters, the words "HOW YOU CAN SURVIVE

FALLOUT." The article therein fantastically declared that no fewer than ninety-seven of a hundred Americans could be saved in a nuclear attack if they took cover in fallout shelters, an estimate that the magazine's editors renounced in a later article.[10] The same issue also included a letter from President Kennedy stating how the "government is moving to improve the protection afforded you in your communities through civil defense. We have begun . . . a survey of all public buildings with fallout shelter potential, and the marking of those with adequate shelter for fifty persons or more."[11] In this way, just as Kennedy's Berlin speech had done, *Life* magazine promoted shelters in both the public and private sectors.

To be sure, these views were not limited to the Office of Civil Defense, the Kennedy administration, contractors, or popular middle-brow magazines; they were also articulated by public intellectuals. Roger S. Cannell, of the Stanford Research Institute, claimed that shelters would enable Americans to "rebuild our civilization" and would serve "to justify the faith placed in us by our own families and by the peoples of the free world."[12] In all these iterations of pro-shelter discourse, the individual human will and that of the nuclear family to survive are connected to the survival not only of the United States, but as Herman Kahn argued, of "Western ideals and institutions."[13] Shelters would not merely provide sanctuary to families, but they would guarantee the survival of American ideology. In this manner, the Stocktons' son represents the future of not only their family but also American democracy in a world ravaged by nuclear war. As the Stocktons find out, however, their preparations for their family's security did not necessarily guarantee survival; they even jeopardized it.

The feverishly panicked scenes in "The Shelter" dramatize what Eisenhower's civil defense director Leo Hoegh revealed when he testified before Congress in 1960: many owners did not want their shelters to be made "public knowledge and, therefore, have everyone in the neighborhood rush in and take over."[14] This kind of awareness foreshadowed some of the moral dilemmas raised by shelter critics. Two particularly powerful metaphors emerged among the many derisive ones. The first compared shelters to the Maginot Line, reflecting the inefficacy and false sense of security shelters provided but also subtly implying that the barrier could not guarantee safety from one's neighbors, either.[15] The second was that of a cave. And while many critics argued cavelike shelters were, on a practical level, akin to burial vaults or coffins, others raised more psychological concerns. P. Herbert Leiderman and Jack H. Mendelson, for example, alleged that taking cover in a shelter seemed like a way to turn back the evolutionary clock: "It is one matter for man to have evolved from living deep in a Paleolithic cave to the city apartment or the garden home in the suburb, but an entirely different matter to consider whether he can successfully return to the cave."[16] Meanwhile, Erich Fromm and Michael Maccoby sardonically wondered whether "this troglodytic life" was "the fulfillment of the American Dream."[17] Striking a similar tone, Rabbi Maurice N. Eisendrath, president of the Union of American Hebrew Congregations, asked whether Americans might resort to exhibiting "the morality of moles or other underground creatures, slithering in storm cellars."[18] And the governor of New Jersey at the time, Robert B. Meyner, argued that "when primitive man left his cave and began to live in the light, he was meant to travel onward and upward; not to circle back."[19] The Stocktons' neighbors, however, would eventually do just that, circle back to overrun the Stocktons' Maginot Line and gain entrance into the Cold War cave known as the fallout shelter. And in doing so, they would also exhibit the barbaric behavior popularly associated with our cave-dwelling ancestors.

The intense exchanges between neighbors in "The Shelter" illustrate another prevalent social feature of the time: xenophobic rage. Even though Marty Weiss presumably had his US citizenship, that he is the first whom Bill denies shelter and the first whom Frank insults and attacks exemplifies the haste to associate immigrants with questionable loyalty and a sense of entitlement. This rage, which resulted in several pieces of legislation, was partially due to the fact that during the postwar period popular rhetoric and the state department alike linked immigrants and any subtle suggestion of "foreignness" to Communism. Although immigrants such as Klaus Fuchs and Julius and Ethel Rosenberg were found guilty of leaking intelligence to the Soviets, other immigrants who were instrumental in developing the space and hydrogen bomb programs, such as Wernher von Braun, were given less critical consideration. Before the Cold War even began, the second Red Scare was beginning to take shape in the 1930s and 1940s as right-wing politicians attacked New Deal liberals with charges of Communism. In 1938 the House Committee on Un-American Activities began its operations, interrogating anyone suspected of having socialist leanings and in 1940, the Smith Act was passed, requiring all US residents who were not citizens to register with the federal government and be fingerprinted. It also allowed the government to deport any individuals ever affiliated with the Communist Party.[20]

The Immigration Act of 1952 solidified many of these measures, forbidding immigrants who were ever affiliated with the Communist Party from entering the country, while also reestablishing a preference system for nationalities, making Eastern Europeans among the least favored. In protest, President Truman vetoed the act and declared, "Today, we are 'protecting' ourselves as we were in 1924, against being flooded by immigrants from Eastern Europe. This is fantastic. . . . We do not need to be protected against immigrants from these countries—on the contrary, we want to stretch out a helping hand, to save those who have managed to flee into Western Europe, to succor those who are brave enough to escape from barbarism, to welcome and restore them against the day when their countries will, as we hope, be free again."[21] Truman's veto, however, proved unsuccessful, as both the Senate and the House voted to overrule it.

Nuclear fears not only exacerbated citizens' animosities toward unwanted neighbors and immigrants, they also created extraordinary complications for whole cities and urban communities. In many cities, such as Las Vegas, Nevada, with its proximity to Los Angeles, authorities were concerned about what to do during and after a nuclear attack with "a swarm of locusts" from southern California, who might "pick the valley clean of food, medical supplies, and other goods."[22] Even though Las Vegas was dependent on Los Angeles for much of its food supply, J. Carlton Adair, the head of Las Vegas's civil defense agency, supported the creation of a five-thousand-person militia to protect the city from potential Los Angelino invaders. While a variety of plans to build fallout shelters for urban residents were proposed, including even moving cities entirely underground, the fallout shelter program was less focused on city dwellers, leading John Kenneth Galbraith to sardonically state that the program was a "design for saving Republicans and sacrificing Democrats."[23] Part of the reason for this anti-urban bias was, according to pro-shelter advocate Bernard Brodie, "the ever-recurrent suspicion that they would probably be of no use . . . the case for the shelter against radioactive fallout in the county is much easier to make."[24] If a major city, such as New York, Los Angeles, or Chicago, was hit, the fallout would be the least of the city's concerns. In the end, instead of massive fallout shelters being constructed for the urban populations of America's cities, public buildings already in existence, such as schools, churches, and government and business offices, were designated to serve as the temporary shelters and were stocked with supplies. Of the 160 million sites designated as such, most were within urban areas that had little chance of surviving a direct hit.[25]

Far from being an airtight solution, however, the designation of public buildings for shelter use raised concerns not only regarding their effectiveness but also their potential availability to minority populations. Giving voice to such fears was Langston Hughes, whose story "Radioactive Red Caps" dramatized how segregationist practices could potentially affect access to shelters. Simple, the main character, states, "If I was in Mississippi, I would be Jim Crowed out of bomb shelters. . . . By the time I got the N. A. A. C. P. to take my case . . . the war would be over, else I would be atomized. . . . Down there they will have some kind of voting test, else loyalty test, in which they will find some way of flunking Negroes out. You can't tell me them Dixiecrats are going to give Negroes free rein of bomb shelters."[26] While Kennedy turned focus away from private shelters, the prospect of public shelters, particularly for marginalized groups, also presented a host of problems stemming from social inequalities.

The episode's climactic scene, with the neighbors ramming their neighbor's door down, touched on another controversial dilemma of the shelter debate: how shelter owners should respond to their neighbors' desperate actions. An August 1961 *Time* magazine article titled "Gun Thy Neighbor?" exposed some of the troubling implications of shelter survival. It began with the words of a Chicago suburbanite: "When I get my shelter finished, I'm going to mount a machine gun at the hatch to keep the neighbors out if the bomb falls. I'm deadly serious about this. If the stupid American public will not do what they have to to save themselves, I'm not going to run the risk of not being able to use the shelter I've taken the trouble to provide to save my own family." The article also included the views of Reverend Hugh Saussy of Holy Innocents Episcopal Church in Atlanta: "If someone wanted to use the shelter, then you yourself should get out and let him use it. That's not what would happen, but that's the strict Christian application."[27] Other religious leaders, however, disagreed with Saussy, claiming he was wrongly implying "that we must love our neighbor, not as ourselves, but more than ourselves." This view, articulated by Father L. C. McHugh, was featured in the Jesuit publication *America* in its September 1961 issue. McHugh also implored that one should "think twice before you rashly give your family shelter space to friends and neighbors or to the passing stranger." Further, he stated, if some neighbors did attempt to break in, they could be "repelled with whatever means will effectively deter their assault." He concluded by somewhat casting aside his spiritual authority, stating that ultimately the choice to have a firearm in order to break up "traffic jams" at one's shelter door is the individual's.[28] But the implications were clear—those who had shelters could practically find themselves playing God and determine who gets to survive. In this way, the seemingly noble responsibility of protecting one's family had some potentially very ignoble social implications.

In an interview, Bob Crane asked Rod Serling about the reaction among home viewers. Serling responded, "We had 1300 letters and cards inside of two days. I think we hit some kind of a nerve. . . . I used the show, I wrote it because I felt, number one, it had great immediacy." The characters' raw emotions, while dramatic, touched on what all too many Americans were feeling. But as historian Kenneth Rose has explained, "What is clear is that at the height of Cold War tensions Americans *talked* a great deal about fallout shelters, but relatively few Americans actually *built* fallout shelters."[29] And while the National Fallout Shelter Survey persisted through the 1960s, identifying 160 million spaces that could be used for public shelters, private shelter numbers were estimated to be a relatively meager two hundred thousand by 1965. While Rose cites many reasons for this, including the development of intercontinental ballistic missiles, the Limited Nuclear Test Ban Treaty of 1963, and the increasing focus on Vietnam, he also claims that shelter critics won the "metaphor war." These metaphors, comparing shelters to caves with the potential to transform Americans into barbarians, clearly had an impact as well. This particular episode of *The Twilight Zone*, taking place close to the peak of nuclear fears, dramatized several aspects of this national shelter debate.

While the Office of Civil Defense, the Kennedy administration, and numerous private contractors all worked to promote shelter construction, *The Twilight Zone* encouraged viewers to consider that dominant national agendas do not necessarily line up with their own or those of their families. Like Herbert Marcuse, who observed that "life as an end is qualitatively different than life as a means," Serling urged his viewers to question the point of their lives beyond mere survival.[30] And while Kennedy cited Epicurus's declaration that "a man who causes fear cannot be free from fear," his resolution to construct shelters was misleadingly simple, as the national debate over shelter morality soon showed. In contrast, Serling's "The Shelter" dramatized the views George Kennan had once articulated: "Are we to flee like haunted creatures from one defensive device to another, each more costly and humiliating than the one before . . . concerned only to prolong the length of our lives while sacrificing all the values for which it might be worthwhile to live at all?"[31] Serling showed that more important than human life were the values, morals, and ideals for which humanity strives. Without them, life would be hardly worth saving.

"Suspect Thy Neighbor"

While "The Shelter" exposed the moral fallout that could result from an over-reliance on shelters, "The Monsters Are Due on Maple Street" attempted to expose the destructive effects of McCarthyism on American society (S1, e22). Far from the only episode to deal with political scapegoating, "Four O'Clock" featured a political fanatic, named Oliver Cringle, who obsessively sought to collect people's personal information and expose anyone, including health care professionals, with seemingly questionable backgrounds (S3, e29). His plan to shrink everyone whom he deems evil in the world ironically results in himself shrinking to miniature size. "He's Alive" (discussed in chapter 1) features Peter Vollmer, a neo-Nazi politician on the rise, dramatically showing how certain political tactics, such as the scapegoating of racial, ethnic, and religious minorities, ensures the continued "survival" of Adolf Hitler. After Vollmer's racist rage is largely met with public derision, he gains increasing popularity after Hitler's ghost instructs him to have one of his deputies purposefully assassinated by one of his group's other members. Having victimized his cause and himself, Vollmer, with his neo-Nazi politics, gains traction until he murders his close friend, Ernst, and is shot and killed by a police officer. In both of these cautionary tales, the accusatory bullies are hoisted by their own petards, as their tactics and politics are revealed to be profoundly misguided, corrupt, and even life-threatening.

In a similar manner, "The Monsters Are Due on Maple Street" dramatizes the social repercussions that result from an unsuspecting community falling prey to a feverish obsession with finding a scapegoat. Originally airing on March 4, 1960, the episode begins with a picturesque suburban neighborhood slowly coming into focus, accompanied by Rod Serling's opening narration: "Maple Street, USA, late summer. A tree-lined little world of front porch gliders, barbeques, the laughter of children and the bell of an ice-cream vendor. At the sound of the roar and the flash of light, it will be precisely 6:43 p.m. . . . This is Maple Street on a late Saturday afternoon. Maple Street—in the last calm and reflective moments before the monsters came." As two men wash a car, a sudden burst of light appears overhead. They initially presume it to be a meteor, but the residents soon discover something peculiar—all things powered by electricity, phone lines, portable radios, and car engines are completely nonfunctional. Pete Van Horn, one of the residents, who had been doing some woodwork in his front yard, checks a nearby street to see if its residents, too, are without power. As he leaves, the camera focuses in on something he is carrying in the loop of his overalls—a hammer, likely an allusion to the Soviet flag's hammer and sickle. This deliberate object placement and camera focus serves as the first major clue that Serling is exploring McCarthyism and postwar anti-Communist paranoia.

The neighborhood residents quickly huddle together to plan their course of action. One of the neighbors, Steve Brand, decides to take a drive downtown, but as he turns the key in his car's ignition, he finds that he cannot start it. Not to be deterred, Steve and his neighbor Charlie decide to walk downtown to see if they can figure out what is causing the outage. As they leave, Tommy, a neighborhood boy, mysteriously protests, "They don't want us to leave . . . that's why they shut everything off." The boy eventually claims that the cause is a spaceship that flew by. The adults initially scoff at the young boy's idea, one resident remarking, "He's been reading too many comic books or seeing too many movies or something." Charlie and Steve, who seem convinced of this diagnosis, start toward downtown again, but Tommy persists, "You might not even be able to get to town. It was that way in the story. Nobody could leave . . . except the people they'd sent down ahead of them. They looked just like humans. . . . They sent four people—a mother and a father and two kids who looked just like humans but they *weren't*." A hush falls over the residents as the camera slowly pans over their worried faces. In an attempt to break the mood and the silence, Steve jokingly remarks that they will need to "run a check of the neighborhood and find out which ones of us are really human." Soon thereafter, another Maple Street resident, Les Goodman, attempts to start his car, repeatedly, without success, but when he walks over to join the rest of the neighborhood, his car inexplicably starts. The neighbors immediately direct their suspicions toward Les: "How come his car just up and started like that?" asks one. "He never did come out to look at that thing that flew overhead. He wasn't even interested," adds another. "He always was an oddball, him and his whole family," says a third.

The group ultimately decides to question Les, as the camera focuses down on their legs, they move in unison, rushing to meet him. Steve suddenly protests, though, and implores: "Wait a minute! Now let's not be a *mob!*" As Les stands in his front yard, he explains that, just like the rest of the group, he has no idea how his car started on its own. Sensing Les's confusion, Steve brings him up to speed, explaining that the general consensus is there may be a family on Maple Street whose members are not quite what they appear to be, but rather, "monsters from outer space." As Les asserts his humanness, his car mysteriously starts up again, while a neighbor expands

"He always was an oddball, him and his whole family. Real oddball." The mob of Maple Street springs into action, on the way to interrogate Les. Still from "The Monsters are Due on Maple Street" (8:47)

the line of questioning: "How do you explain . . . well, a couple of times I've come out on my porch and I've seen Les Goodman here in the wee hours of the morning standing in his yard just looking up at the sky . . . as though he were waiting for something . . . as though he were looking for something." Les, disgusted by these mounting charges, says that the only thing he is guilty of is insomnia and moves toward the group of neighbors, causing them to recoil and retreat: "You scared, frightened rabbits, you. You're sick people . . . and you don't even know what you're starting here. . . . You're starting something here that . . . you should be frightened of. . . . You're letting something begin here that's a nightmare!"

As night falls on Maple Street, most of the residents remain outside in their front yards. While Charlie drinks a beer, he shouts across the street at Steve, warning him that he is not "above suspicion" and should be careful whom he is seen with. Here, Charlie directly mirrors McCarthy in his aggressive accusations based on being "guilty by association." Immediately thereafter, one of the other residents mentions how Steve's wife has been "doing some talking" about his late-night habits. Steve, clearly growing tired of the mounting absurd allegations, retorts, "Let's get it all out. Let's pick out every idiosyncrasy of every man, woman, and child on this whole street. And then we might well set up some kind of a kangaroo court. Now, how about a firing squad at dawn . . . ?" As Don explains that he has heard about Steve working on a radio set in his basement, Charlie steps forward with his hands in his pockets and appears more self-assured as accusations against Steve accumulate. Charlie smugly asks Steve whom he talks to on his radio set, and Steve replies with biting sarcasm, "I talk to monsters from outer space, I talk to three-headed green men who fly here in what look like meteors!" After Myra, Steve's wife, explains that he has simply been working on a ham radio set and that they could see it for themselves, Steve objects, claiming they do not have to show the neighbors anything unless they obtain a search warrant.

Steve's frustration continues to build as he rebukes the group's accusatory attitude: "Don't tell me who's safe and who's a menace. . . . You're all standing out here all set to crucify somebody! You're all set to find a scapegoat. You're all desperate to point some kind of a finger at a neighbor. . . . The only thing that's gonna happen is that we're gonna eat each other up alive!" His neighbors fall silent, seemingly reprimanded, for the time being. The silence is soon interrupted by footsteps. Someone is walking down Maple Street, but no one can see who it is because of the darkness. Tommy suddenly cries out, "It's the monster!" and Don rushes off, coming back with a shotgun. Steve protests bringing a gun into the situation, but Charlie welcomes it. The camera reveals to the viewing audience that the figure approaching is Pete Van Horn, the man with a hammer in his jeans who went to check on a nearby street. As he walks down the street, the camera again focuses on the hammer in his pants loop. Blinded by his own fear, Charlie fires the gun, killing Pete instantly, as his body collapses onto the unforgiving pavement of the street where he lived.

When the Maple Street crowd descends on the corpse, to their shock, they discover the mysterious figure is their neighbor, Pete Van Horn. Charlie repentantly pleads to the others that he did not realize who the man was: "How was I supposed to know he wasn't a monster or something? I was only trying to protect my home." Just then, the lights turn on in Charlie's house, and the suspicious crowd shifts to Charlie, who calls the situation a "gag." Steve angrily grabs Charlie's shirt collar and tells him that a man lying dead in the street is far from a gag. Charlie runs from the crowd, and they all give chase, picking up rocks and throwing them as they run after their neighbor-turned-murderer.

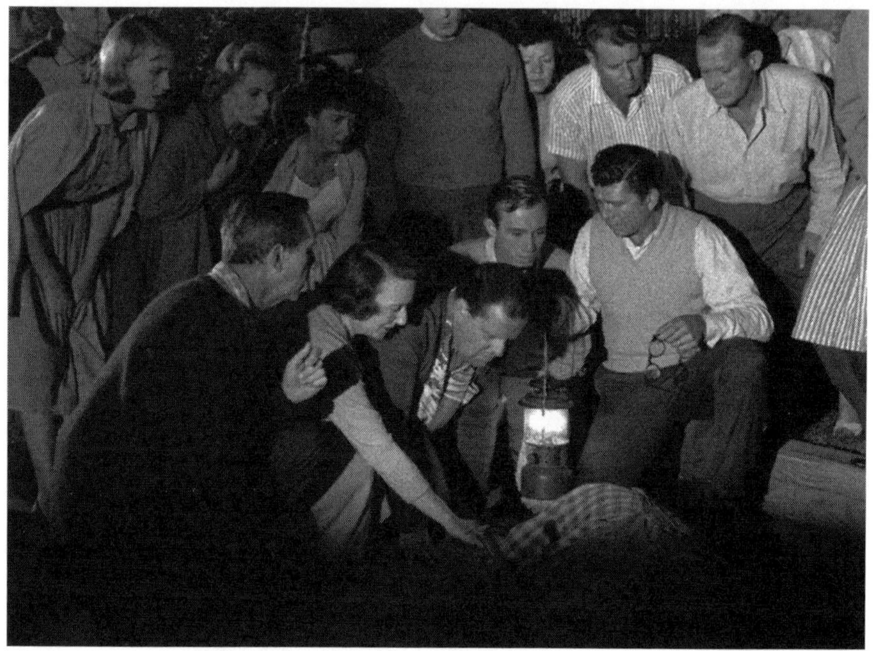

"How was I supposed to know he wasn't a monster or something?" Charlie and his fellow Maple Street residents inspect his kill: their neighbor, Pete Van Horn. Still from "The Monsters are Due on Maple Street" (19:05)

Charlie, with a bloodied forehead and in sheer desperation and fear, suddenly says he knows who the monster is and accuses Tommy. The crowd soon descends into madness, with each resident accusing someone else. With glass shattering, guns firing, and bricks flying, Maple Street could hardly be more different than the serene, peaceful place it once was.

The camera slowly zooms out onto the neighborhood, eventually revealing two space aliens next to their ship witnessing the chaos from above: "Understand the procedure now? Just stop a few of their machines and radios and telephones and lawnmowers, throw them into darkness for a few hours, and then sit back and watch the pattern. . . . They pick the most dangerous enemy they can find, and it's themselves. All we need do is sit back and . . . let them destroy themselves." As their ship ascends to the reaches of outer space with Maple Street in the throes of violent chaos below, Serling offers his closing narration: "The tools of conquest do not necessarily come with bombs and explosions and fallout. There are weapons that are simply thoughts, attitudes, prejudices to be found only in the minds of men. For the record, prejudices can kill, and suspicion can destroy. And a thoughtless, frightened search for a scapegoat has a fallout all of its own for the children and the children yet unborn. And the pity of it is, that these things cannot be confined . . . to *The Twilight Zone.*"

In "The Monsters Are Due on Maple Street," the alleged monsters from outer space serve as an obvious metaphor for the threat of Communist infiltration in much the same way Arthur Miller's 1953 play, *The Crucible,* uses Puritan New England to explore the witch-hunting tactics of McCarthyism. The idea of monsters disguising themselves as a normal suburban family was reflected in the popular belief that Communists would likely do the same to subvert the United States. This idea was also popularly captured in the 1956 film *The Invasion of the Body Snatchers.* The extreme use of these ideas, although derisively referred to as "the paranoid style" by Richard Hofstadter, permeated contemporary popular culture and politics alike. Furthermore, the anti-Communist propaganda of the postwar era bore striking resemblance to the World War II propaganda Serling was intimately acquainted with: "Communism, in reality, is not a political party. It is a way of life—an evil and malignant way of life. It reveals a condition akin to disease that spreads like an epidemic; and like an epidemic, a quarantine is necessary to keep it from infecting the nation."[32] Just as he had seen the Japanese dehumanized, representing diseased lice, Communism was not a political idea worthy of debate, rational rebuttal, or coexisting with, it was an epidemic that needed eradication.

Following the passage of one of the most significant pieces of anti-Communist legislation, the McCarran Internal Security Act of 1950, the federal government required official registration from the Communist Party, its members, and its front groups. Additionally, the act created the Subversive Activities Control Board, which was responsible for investigating persons suspected of having Communist ties. The act also warned that one common "device for infiltration by Communists is . . . procuring naturalization for disloyal aliens who use their citizenship as a badge for admission into the fabric of our society." In addition, the act explained how "Communist organizations . . . are organized on a secret, conspiratorial basis and operate to a substantial extent through organizations, commonly known as 'Communist fronts,' which in most instances are created and maintained, or used, in such manner as to conceal the facts as to their true character and purposes and their membership." In this way, the "monsters from outer space" in this episode reflect these two core fears and suspicions: alien immigrants and the mysterious, covert nature of Communist front organizations.

Despite the McCarran Act's eventual passage, President Truman had expressed strong opposition before he vetoed the bill. The Internal Security Act, he believed, would not actually weaken Communist efforts. Rather, it "would . . . help the Communists in their efforts to create dissension and confusion within our borders." And while the idea of requiring Communist organizations to publicly register themselves sounds "simple and attractive," he claimed it was "about as practical as requiring thieves to register with the sheriff." Additionally, he noted that the act could have the somewhat indirect, long-term result of severely constricting open and honest political expression within the nation's borders. He explained the new "provision could easily be used to classify as a Communist-front organization any organization which is advocating a single policy or objective which is also being urged by the Communist Party. . . . Thus, an organization which advocates low-cost housing for sincere humanitarian reasons might be classified as a Communist-front organization." He added that it "is not enough to say that this probably would not be done. The mere fact that it could be done shows clearly how the bill would open a Pandora's box of opportunities for official condemnation of organizations and individuals for perfectly honest opinions which happen to be stated also by Communists. The basic error of these sections is that they move in the direction of suppressing opinion and belief. This would be a very dangerous course to take . . . because any governmental stifling of the free expression of opinion is a long step toward totalitarianism."[33] Truman's veto, however, was roundly defeated by both chambers of Congress.

Not only did Congress override Truman's concerns, but innumerable writers and other voices forcefully drowned them out. One of the most outspoken was James F. O'Neil, who headed the American Legion for nearly thirty years. Writing in the *American Legion Magazine,* O'Neil beseeched his readers, "Never forget the fact that Communists operating in our midst are in effect a secret battalion of spies and saboteurs parachuted by a foreign foe inside our lines at night and operating as American citizens under a variety of disguises." And while these disguises could take many forms, some veneers were more common than others: "Hence Communists always appear before the public as 'progressives.' Yesterday they were 20th century Americans, last week 'defenders of all civil liberties,' tonight they may be 'honest, simple trades unionists. . . . These artful dodges and ingenious dissimulations obviously make it difficult for the average trusting citizen to keep up with every new Communist swindle and con game."[34] The paranoid suspicion that anyone could be a Communist in disguise was also expressed by the head of the FBI, J. Edgar Hoover, who claimed,

"The open, avowed Communist who carries a card and pays dues is no different from a security standpoint than the person who does the party's work but pays no dues, carries no card, and is on the party rolls. In fact, the latter is a greater menace because of his opportunity to work in stealth."[35]

Even though Truman seemed more concerned than Congress about some of the potential abuses of the McCarran Act, two of his executive orders helped set many of these developments in motion. The first, Executive Order 9835, set forth in 1947, established a federal loyalty oath program and called for extensive background checks of all government employees. It also allowed the FBI to further investigate an individual if an initial background check seemed inconclusive. And while the initial order permitted investigation if "reasonable grounds" existed for suspecting disloyalty, Executive Order 10241, passed in April 1951, replaced "reasonable grounds" with "reasonable doubt." Thus, the reformed version of the loyalty program put even more of the burden on the individual to prove innocence, rather than the panel to prove guilt. These programs were not limited to the state department. As Ellen Schrecker has explained, the procedures developed under these executive orders "became standard within other federal agencies, state and local governments, and private institutions," reflecting "both the legitimating power of the federal government and the fundamental assumptions that all these programs shared." This presumption of guilt, however, resulted in 500 people out of the first 7,667 who were investigated being included as a result of mistaken information related to someone else. As Schrecker has pointed out, mistaken identity was just one issue that created complications; pleading the Fifth Amendment also became "automatic grounds for dismissal within the federal government and . . . major corporations." Moreover, "non-Communists and even anti-Communists could lose their jobs if they seemed too feisty and individualistic." As one attorney recalled, "you couldn't say 'I did these things because I thought they were right and I still think they're right.' Because if you did that you'd be dead."[36]

In "The Monsters Are Due on Maple Street," the tide of suspicions, accusations, and presumption of guilt rather than innocence is clearly already setting in. Any unusual behaviors, such as Les's insomnia-driven star-gazing, are suddenly cause for major concern. But also already evident is the dangerous, simplistic completeness of Tommy's explanation, coupled with its uncritical acceptance by the neighborhood. That the explanation for the outage came from a comic book, yet not given much more thought by anyone, further symbolizes some of the troubling aspects of anti-Communist scapegoating— the way it arrested critical thinking. Despite the widely held belief expressed in Hoover's statement, "I . . . fear for the liberal and progressive who has been hoodwinked and duped into joining hands with the communists," Serling illustrates how the very opposite can likely happen: how paranoid, irresponsible accusations and the accusers behind them can be duped and subsequently jeopardize security, on both a local level and a national one.[37] The gullibility of Maple Street's residents is shown not in their subscription to progressive notions regarding the protection of human rights but rather in their unwavering belief that one of them has to be behind the power outage.

Although Truman supported and strengthened the federal loyalty program, his criticisms of the McCarran Act became increasingly relevant as the 1950s wore on and McCarthyism gripped the nation ever more tightly. Truman claimed that we "would make a mockery of the Bill of Rights and of our claims to stand for freedom in the world" and force people to avoid "saying anything that might be construed by someone as not deviating sufficiently from the current Communist propaganda line." And "since no one could be sure in advance what views were safe to express, the inevitable tendency would be to express no views on controversial subjects." Consequently, he foresaw one major result—the reduced "vigor and strength of our political life—an outcome that the Communists would happily welcome, but that free men should abhor." Truman concluded that we will "destroy all that we seek to preserve, if we sacrifice the liberties of our citizens in a misguided attempt to achieve national security."[38]

Throughout the episode, Charlie's unfounded eagerness to declare a guilty party not only reflected McCarthy's accusations, it also closely resembled the perspective of one of the most popular fictional characters of the day, Mickey Spillane's ruthless executor of justice, Mike Hammer. Somewhat like McCarthy, Hammer's character preferred to take matters into his own hands and implement justice his own way, rather than through established practice. As David Halberstam noted, Hammer was "the ultimate cold warrior, an Übermensch for frightened Americans who had heard tales of baby-eating Stalinists. Hammer's methods went beyond loyalty oaths, smears, and blacklisting. The evil of the Communists was battled with Hammer's only weapons: a blast from his forty-five, a kick that shattered bone on impact, and strangulation by Hammer's meaty hands."[39] With his fourth Mike Hammer novel, *One Lonely Night*, Spillane capitalized on stoking Communist fears. In it, Hammer confronts a gang of Communist thugs who plan to take over the United States, and in his typical chauvinistic fashion, the incorruptible hero monologues: "A Commie. She was a jerky Red. She owned all the trimmings and she was still a Red. What the hell was she hoping for, a government order to share it all with the masses? Yeah. . . . Sure it's great to be a Commie as long as you're top dog. Who the hell was supposed to be fooled by all the crap. . . . They're supposed to be clever, bright as hell. They were dumb as horse manure as far as I was concerned."[40] These statements shared striking similarity with some of McCarthy's: "If you want to be against McCarthy, boys, you've got to be a Communist or a cocksucker."[41] Without a doubt, however, the juvenile fantasies in Mickey Spillane's books as well as McCarthy's reckless views were achieving enormous success. While Spillane had sold thirty million copies of Mike Hammer novels, the head of the *Chicago Tribune*'s Washington bureau proclaimed, "McCarthy was a dream story. . . . I wasn't off page one for four years."[42] McCarthy, no doubt, appreciated the coverage.

While Charlie serves as an embodiment of McCarthy and Spillane, the deceased Pete Van Horn dramatically symbolizes the fate of hammer-wielding labor unionists. Already in the thirties and forties, unions were working to divulge Communists among their rank and file. By the late forties, however, unions were succumbing to increasingly popular practices by cracking down not just on Communist Party members but anyone who remotely aligned with the party's political stances. In the fall of 1949, under increasingly anti-Communist pressure, the Congress of Industrial Organizations moved to entirely expel its single largest union—the United Electrical, Radio, and Machine Workers of America (UE). Its November 1949 resolution decisively declared, "We can no longer tolerate within the family of CIO the Communist Party masquerading as a labor union. The time has come when the CIO must strip the mask from these false leaders whose only purpose is to deceive and betray the workers. . . . In the name of autonomy they seek to justify their blind and slavish willingness to act as puppets for the Soviet dictatorship." The resolution, however, did not cite any actual evidence of Communist infiltration or name any specific individuals who were instruments of the Communist Party. Instead, the accusations centered on a few abstract political deviations from the prevailing CIO stances. These deviances, which also incidentally coincided with the Soviet party line, included denouncement of the Marshall Plan and criticism of NATO as a "warmongering" institution. A third problem for the CIO was the UE's support for the Progressive Party and Henry Wallace in the 1948 election.[43] The CIO members, once victims of red-baiting, were now doing the red-baiting and, incidentally, foreshadowing the sharply declining influence and ever more prevalent image of unions as semi-communist institutions.

Apart from the thousands of Americans who lost their jobs, were black-listed, or were wrongfully accused during the Second Red Scare, the impact on political discourse and debate could not be confined to either *The Twilight Zone* or to the fifties. While President Eisenhower would publicly reprimand McCarthy and Congress would censure him in 1954, the same could not be said of his tactics, which clearly left a lasting imprint on American politics. Character assassinations, homophobic and sexual slander, and unfounded accusations *could* and *did* work, especially with the help of an uncritical popular press. George Kennan, the author of the famous long telegram and the original concept of containment, took account of these political changes in his memoir: "What the phenomenon of McCarthyism did . . . was to implant in my consciousness a lasting doubt as to the adequacy of our political system and public opinion . . . that could be so easily disoriented by this sort of challenge. . . . I could never recapture, after these experiences of the 1940s and 1950s, quite the same faith in the American system of government and in traditional American outlooks that I had had."[44] The paranoid associations constantly made in publicized HUAC hearings could rob a person of their individuality and human rights if they were associated with, among other things, the progressive dupe. This was perhaps most clearly and succinctly illustrated when McCarthy deliberately referred to Democratic prudential Nominee Adlai Stevenson as "Alger," alluding to Alger Hiss, who had recently been imprisoned after being accused of spying for the Soviets. If a politician could effectively associate a political opponent with treason, even if based only on the first letter of their first name, the tactic could prove highly effective with a national audience listening.

During the heart of the Second Red Scare, Associate Justice of the Supreme Court William O. Douglas tried to articulate what the political climate was quickly becoming in the nation where he served. In an article titled "The Black Silence of Fear," Douglas wrote,

> I think one has to leave the country, go into the back regions of the world, lose himself there, and become absorbed in the problems of the peoples of different civilizations. When he returns to America after a few months he probably will be shocked. He will be shocked not at the intentions or purposes or ideals of the American people. He will be shocked at the arrogance and intolerance of great segments of the American press, at the arrogance and intolerance of many leaders in public office. . . . He will find that thought is being standardized, that the permissible area for calm discussion is being

narrowed, that the range of ideas is being limited, that many minds are closed. . . . This is alarming to one who loves his country. It means that the philosophy of strength through free speech is being forsaken for the philosophy of fear through repression.

Douglas went on to lament how the Communist threat within the country has been "magnified and exalted far beyond its realities" and "irresponsible talk by irresponsible people has fanned the flames of fear" because of accusations being so carelessly made. In this postwar political climate, he went on, "character assassinations have become common" and "suspicion has taken the place of goodwill." Formerly, Douglas noted, we "could debate with impunity along a wide range of inquiry" and "could safely explore to the edges of a problem, challenge orthodoxy without qualms, and run the gamut of ideas in search of solutions to perplexing problems." In the past, "we had confidence in each other," but at present, "suspicion grows until the orthodox idea is the safe one" and "everyone who does not follow the military policymakers is suspect. Everyone who voices opposition to the trend . . . takes a chance. . . . Good and honest men are pilloried. Character is assassinated. Fear runs rampant. . . . This fear has stereotyped our thinking, narrowed the range of free public discussion, and driven many thoughtful people to despair." Douglas finally concluded, "Once we narrow the range of thought and discussion, we will surrender a great deal of our power. . . . Our weakness grows when we become intolerant of opposing ideas, depart from our standards of civil liberties, and borrow the policeman's philosophy from the enemy we detest."[45] Like the Stocktons in their shelter, millions of Americans risk banishing their minds and politics to the recesses of a dark cave out of fear.

Douglas's assessment of the political climate of postwar America bore striking resemblance to Serling's in "The Monsters Are Due on Maple Street." Ultimately, the nightmare that Americans needed to more actively consider was not a Communist takeover but how political debate was being increasingly overwhelmed by unfounded character assassinations, ad hominem attacks, and the cessation of critical, constructive thought. Although at the episode's conclusion, there were "monsters from outer space" seeking to manipulate life on Maple Street by causing the power outage, this was a result less of the outage and more of the neighborhood's reaction—an all-consuming fear and panic bringing about not just careless character assassinations but actual assassination. The most susceptible to deception were not, as the American Legion, John Birch Society, and J. Edgar Hoover repeatedly asserted, those willing and able to deviate slightly from the orthodox norm. Instead, the most vulnerable citizens were those who willingly, uncritically, and completely believed in the truth of the advertisement, the groundless political smear, and the children's comic book story. The more threatening deceptions included those who weaponized anti-Communism against the NAACP, Martin Luther King Jr. and the advancement of civil rights, others who used it against granting equal rights to women and the LGBTQIA+ community, those who used it against organized labor, and finally, those who used it to deny crucial political discussion about complex issues from ever having a chance to take place. These, in fact, were the harmful deceptions that endangered our communities, our political processes, our nation, and our minds, leading Ellen Schrecker to conclude, "McCarthyism did more damage to the Constitution than the American Communist Party ever did."[46]

Just as the morals of the neighborhood in "The Shelter" decline as the residents descend into the basement where the shelter is located, the growing paranoia on Maple Street is accentuated by the darkness that envelops the neighborhood. In each episode, the false security offered by fallout shelters or the scapegoating perpetrated by McCarthyism leaves a neighborhood worse off than it was before. By focusing solely on security and survival, the residents of each of these picturesque white American neighborhoods create an uncivil nightmare and leave behind the very American principles that are actually worth fighting for—self-expression, democracy, collective security, respect, and inclusiveness. In seeking to deal with particular symptoms, of, for example, Communist sympathies and radioactive fallout, both neighborhoods spread the diseases of fear, distrust, and greed, which have far more destructive consequences in the long run. Amid the anti-Communist fears of the postwar era, those working to achieve racial equality and address a variety of other social issues were constantly in danger of being considered un-American or a threat to national security, thus literally hurting their "neighbors." At the same time, proposing that personal shelters for the nuclear family were the solution to nuclear war benefitted white suburbs, while it disadvantaged the racially diverse cities that were more likely to be targeted in the first place. Many Americans, just like Bill in "The Shelter," wondered if their country could be the same again after fear-based tactics become the norm. Ultimately, the Cold War security popularly offered in social and political arenas proved profoundly deceptive, endangering racial minorities and even the white Americans they were supposed to protect the most, serving as yet another nightmare for postwar Americans living in and out of *The Twilight Zone*.

Cold War Childhood

Containment or Entanglement?

In her seminal study of the postwar return to domesticity, *Homeward Bound: American Families in the Cold War Era*, Elaine Tyler May convincingly argues how the nuclear family served as the quintessential form of domestic containment, enclosing a wide array of Cold War fears related to nuclear war, Communism, and sexuality: "In secure postwar homes with plenty of children, American women and men might be able to ward off their nightmares and live out their dreams. The family seemed to be the one place where people could control their destinies and perhaps even shape the future. Of course, nobody actually argued that stable family life could prevent nuclear annihilation. But the home represented a source of meaning and security in a world run amok. Marrying young and having lots of babies were ways for Americans to thumb their noses at doomsday predictions." Just as raising a family and owning a home in the suburbs represented the epitome of the American Dream, it also helped to ensure that American capitalistic priorities would take precedence among the populace. As developer William Levitt once remarked, "No man who owns his own house and lot can be a Communist. He has too much to do."[1]

Family life was at the heart of many marketing campaigns, which offered guarantees to housewives that postwar products, including home appliances, would free up their time and help them be more attentive mothers. The nuclear family was also *the* focal point for numerous popular television programs. Shows like *Father Knows Best* (1954–1960) and *Leave It to Beaver* (1957–1963) romantically depicted domestic life and traditional gender roles. They also generally showed that when problems did arise, they were easily resolved by everyone simply knowing and returning to one's proper place. Consistently, conflicts within television families were simplistic and lacked any complexity or ambiguity. Compromises were easily arranged, and order restored without too much trouble. In the *Father Knows Best* episode "Woman in the House," for example, Virge, the wife of one of Jim Anderson's old friends, comes to stay with the family (S2, e25). Her habits are quickly shown to be undesirable and unfeminine, as she smokes cigarettes, talks about Franz Kafka, and dresses in a semi-bohemian fashion. While tension mounts between her and the Andersons, particularly Margaret, Jim's wife, the feuding eventually dissipates when Virge embraces traditional feminine roles: helping to care for the children and making mashed potatoes.[2] Thus, family conflicts, as well as conflicts with others, were solved when everyone simply knew their role and cheerfully embraced it.

In a rapidly changing postwar world, however, with new middle-class values, white-collar jobs, suburban living, and childhood consumerism suddenly dominating American life, answers to problems did not come quite as easily as they did to the Andersons and Cleavers. Most married women, for example, soon found they could not simply stay at home and take care of their children but had to work as well. And even though the suburbs provided a family-friendly environment, the stresses that came from having to raise children according to middle-class values and provide them with entertainment, fun, and a rising tide of consumer goods, proved overwhelming for parents. Caught between these popular portrayals of idealized, traditional family life, and the actual complex world, having a family and raising children was perhaps not the clear-cut answer to contain Cold War issues but, rather, complicated them all the more. In fact, as parents soon found out, children learned to manipulate social and consumer pressures in a variety of ways, further complicating family life in unprecedented fashion. In short, parents quickly found out that returning to traditional values and "simpler times" was not feasible in the real world of postwar family life. In "It's a Good Life" and "Living Doll," *The Twilight Zone* captures, in horrifying fashion, the dual pressures parents felt regarding proper child-rearing etiquette and the burden of dealing with their children as increasingly influential consumers (S3, e8; S5, e6). As Grace and Fred Hechinger noted, "The permissive philosophy of child-rearing and the rushing of adolescent social development had opened the floodgates of material generosity" and in "a society which judges prestige very largely by outward appearance, what an adolescent owns automatically turns into a yardstick of the entire family's place in the sun."[3] And just as national containment policies throughout the world led to increasingly complex and seemingly irresolvable conflicts, family life, beset with pressures to live and attain the American Dream, frequently proved to be a dubious means to practice containment at home. Just as likely, raising children in the postwar era became an increasingly elaborate entanglement.

Growing Up Authoritarian

During its five-season run, *The Twilight Zone* included several episodes that portrayed some of the more challenging aspects of family life and childhood. Among these, Reginald Rose's "The Incredible World of Horace Ford" showed how inaccurate certain portrayals and memories of childhood can be (S4, e15). When toy designer Horace Ford visits the neighborhood where he grew up, he expects to be reminded of his idyllic childhood. Instead, he is transported back in time to his boyhood, where he is ridiculed, beaten up, and bullied. Eventually, when his wife comes and finds him, he is transformed back into an adult, but his perception of childhood has drastically altered: he realizes that his own childhood was not the time of simple innocence and joy he remembered. With "It's a Good Life," Serling similarly sought to show how childhood is not necessarily a time of idyllic innocence and purity but one often filled with anxiety, manipulation, power struggles, and mind games.[4]

Originally airing on the evening of November 3, 1961, the episode begins with Serling's announcement, "Tonight's story . . . is somewhat unique and calls for a different kind of introduction." He describes Peaksville, Ohio, as the only remaining town after the rest of world vanished mysteriously. Its relatively few inhabitants include Mr. and Mrs. Fremont, Aunt Amy, and a monster who bears the responsibility for the rest of the world's disappearance. As the camera cuts between shots of a rural village, showing farmhouses, barns, and broken-down cars, Serling states that the monster had taken away the automobiles, the electricity, and the machines simply "because they displeased him and . . . moved an entire community back into the dark ages—just by using his mind." Fearing the monster's displeasure and wrath, Peaksville's inhabitants are continually forced to "think happy thoughts and say happy things." If they do not, the monster might "wish them into a cornfield or change them into a grotesque, walking horror." Consequently, the camera shows two residents walking back through the town and abruptly smiling after realizing the monster's proximity. Finally, Serling introduces the audience to the monster himself: "His name is Anthony Fremont," as the camera cuts to a red-haired, freckle-faced six-year-old boy in overalls, playing on a fence. Serling warns his viewers, however, that although he has "blue, guileless eyes . . . the mind behind them is absolutely in charge. This is *The Twilight Zone,*" and the screen fades to black.

"When those eyes look at you, you better start thinking happy thoughts." Anthony Fremont, the child-tyrant of "It's a Good Life." Still from "It's a Good Life" (2:25)

The episode begins with a young man named Bill riding up to the Fremont house to deliver groceries on his bike, a reminder that Anthony has eradicated the automobile. As he gets off his bike, he greets Aunt Amy, who sits on the front porch, and Anthony, who is playing in the front yard. Bill makes a point to comment how good it is to see Anthony and how much "we all love you" and adds what a good day it is. When Aunt Amy states that it is in fact a "terrible, hot day," Anthony makes a sour face and only smiles again when Bill insists, "I wouldn't say that, no sir! It's just fine . . . it's a real good day!" When Bill asks Anthony what he's doing, emphasizing, "it's real good whatever it is," Anthony replies, "I made a gopher with three heads." After Bill praises his efforts, Anthony says that he's through playing with the animal he created and decides to kill it, displaying his severe sadistic tendencies for the first time as he yells, "Gopher, you be dead!" Bill again merely praises his actions and smiles. Inside the house, Bill unloads the groceries for Mrs. Fremont, Anthony's mother, and mentions how they no longer have any soap, undoubtedly the result of Anthony's dislike for soap and wishing it out of existence. Mrs. Fremont, clearly exhausted, begins to confess with quivering lips that she once hoped that an animal with sharp teeth Anthony created would have bitten her son when he was outside, but before she can finish expressing her disquieting thought, Bill cuts her off and says he needs to get going.

In the following scene, Anthony's sadistic side is conveyed even more. While Mr. Fremont is shaving and getting dressed, Anthony walks into the bedroom. Sprawling on his parents' bed, he laments that no kids came to play with him. His father replies, "Well, you remember the last time some kids came over to play, the little Fredericks boy and his sister?" Anthony says he had a good time with them, while his father responds: "It's good you have a good time. . . . It's just that . . . well Anthony, you, uh, you wished them away into the cornfield, and their mommy and daddy were real upset." Soon thereafter, a dog can be heard barking in the distance. "That's Bill Soams's collie," Anthony says. When his father says that there are not many dogs around anymore because Anthony wished them away, his son replies: "I don't like them—they didn't like me. I hate anybody like that. I hate anybody that doesn't like me." After his father reassures him that everyone loves him, Anthony recalls an episode when he heard someone say he "shouldn't wish away all the automobiles and things and electricity. They said it wasn't good that I did that. . . . He shouldn't have thought those bad thoughts. That's why I made him go on fire." Anthony gets up from the bed, stands by the window, and says that the dog outside does not like him and is a "bad dog." As Anthony's eyes open wide, the dog can be heard whimpering then falling silent. The father somberly realizes his son just killed another dog, and he drops his head. He changes his demeanor quickly, however, when his distressed wife comes into the room. He tells her, "Isn't it a real good thing that he done that, honey?" His wife, trying to resist weeping, embraces him and concurs, "It's a real good thing."

The following scene shows everyone gathered for the birthday of Dan Hollis, a friend of the Fremonts. Before they celebrate, however, the focus is on Anthony and what he wants. The Fremonts and all their friends are gathered around the television for TV night. Not surprisingly, Anthony dictates what the group watches—a violent bloody battle between two triceratops. Although the town has no electricity, Anthony can turn it on when he wants to—in this case, to watch TV. He sits in the front, right up close to the TV while everyone else is gathered behind him. As the camera pans among the faces, people look either disgusted or distressed as they watch the battling dinosaurs. When the program ends, Anthony declares, "That's all the television there is!" and the guests praise his entertainment choice. Mrs. Fremont proceeds to tell Dan's

"Happy birthday to me!" Dan Hollis is transformed into a jack-in-box during his birthday party after he thinks "bad thoughts" about Anthony. Still from "It's a Good Life" (21:20)

wife, Ethel, to give Dan his birthday surprise. The guests expectantly watch Dan tear away the wrapping paper, revealing a Perry Como record. Excited, Dan announces that he has not heard Perry Como in years and would love to hear some new music. Anthony, however, despises singing and does not want the record to be played. Several of the guests, including Dan, say that it is in fact a good thing he cannot listen to his birthday present.

Afterward, Mrs. Fremont asks their friend Pat Riley to play piano for everyone. Pat begins to play but nervously says to Anthony, "It would be good if you told me what to play." Anthony responds, "Play anything." As Pat anxiously plays "Moon Glow," Dan sits on the couch drinking the peach brandy he received as another gift. Realizing that Dan might be getting slightly drunk, Ethel implores, "Please, for the love of heaven, don't say anything." Dan calmly responds, "I'm not saying anything," but a moment later he thinks out loud that there are only five bottles of liquor left in the town. His frustration builds until he cries out that he cannot even play his Perry Como record, and he throws his glass and shatters it in the fireplace.

Finally finding some more courage, Dan walks over to the piano and says, "Don't play that Pat. That's not what I want you to play. Play this." And he starts to sing "Happy birthday to me, happy birthday to me, happy birthday dear Danny . . ." The guests beg him to stop, knowing the consequences if he persists. Dan, however, only gets more audacious and begins, "You Are My Sunshine." With years of dammed up anger and frustration making Dan crack, the living room soon bursts with pent-up adult rage. Dan points at Anthony, calling him a "dirty little monster" and a "murderer." He then dares Anthony: "You think about me. Go ahead Anthony. You think bad thoughts about me. And maybe some man in this room, some man with guts, somebody who's so sick to death of living in this kind of place and willing to take a chance will sneak up behind you and lay something heavy across your skull and end this once and for all!" Anthony points right back at Dan Hollis, yelling, "You're a bad man! You're a very bad man!" While Dan begs someone to take a lamp or a bottle to Anthony's head, to no avail, Anthony performs the anticipated deed, transforming Dan into a jack-in-the-box, with his head bouncing back and forth on a toy spring. To finish this latest expression of unbridled power, he threatens Dan's new widow: if she thinks bad thoughts about him, he will do the same to her. Serling finally offers his closing thoughts: "No comment here, no comment at all. We only wanted to introduce you to one of our very special citizens, little Anthony Fremont, age six, who lives in a village called Peaksville in a place that used to be Ohio. And if by some strange chance you should run across him, you had best think only good thoughts. Anything less than that is handled at your own risk, because if you do meet Anthony, you can be sure of one thing: you have entered *The Twilight Zone*."

In customary fashion, this episode features a monster rather unlike the fantastic depictions seen in *Godzilla*, *The Creature from the Black Lagoon*, and other science fiction classics. Rather, the monster is one of us, one of our species, and what's more, it is depicted as the most innocent and uncorrupted of humans—a young child. The episode's themes of family dynamics, childhood, and the anxiety of child-rearing was likewise the focus of millions of Americans in the mid-twentieth century. And while child development certainly proves to be a concern for every generation, because the United States experienced the highest birth rate in its history during the 1950s and 1960s, it was especially critical during that period.

From the opening scenes, "It's a Good Life" plays on the idea that a more traditional, pastoral environment is desirable for families, a common theme of shows like *The Andy Griffith Show*, as it depicts Peaksville as a town that has returned to almost premodern conditions. This more natural and bucolic sensibility is represented to an extreme in Peaksville, with its lack of modern industry and technology, as the episode unromantically shows the unique challenges of family life in a premodern setting. *The Twilight Zone* shows how Peaksville's remote location and more primitive surroundings are highly undesirable, especially for the parents. Adults lack the ability to travel or drive cars, they lack modern forms of entertainment, and they have minimal food options. Anthony's ability to make his own schedule and force the adults to cater to his whims cripples his parents and the entire town. By discarding elements of modernity, Anthony effectively gains more tyrannical power over his family and everyone else in the village.

Right away, the dynamics between the six-year-old Anthony and the community residents are clearly established. Everyone, including his own family and the local delivery boy, must unwaveringly accommodate Anthony's wishes and constantly shower him with praise for his choices, no matter how cruel, destructive, or unreasonable. Everyone lives in constant fear of upsetting him, and as a result, his parents and neighbors withhold reproach at all costs. It is an authoritarian family environment in reverse, with the adults submitting to Anthony's every whim. "It's a Good Life" captures what served as a preoccupation for childhood experts and Americans alike—the potential threat of tyranny. For both professionals and lay people, the conditions of childhood and the family were crucial to ensure that tyrants did not sprout on American soil. To this end, *The Authoritarian Personality,* a 1950 work cowritten by Theodor W. Adorno, Else Frenkel-Brunswik, Daniel Levinson, and Nevitt Sanford, sought to unearth what led individuals to have more fascist and prejudiced worldviews. The results of their numerous surveys strongly suggested that children who were raised in families with strict, threatening authority figures, harsh discipline, black-and-white thinking, and inflexible traditions frequently were predisposed to fascist-leaning views later in life. They describe children from such families as much like the adults' behavior in this episode: "On the surface theirs is a stereotyped, rigid glorification of the parents, with strong resentment and feelings of victimization occasionally breaking through on the overt level in the interview material."[5] While *The Authoritarian Personality* revealed a predictable yet resentment-filled glorification of authority among certain children, in this episode, the adults are the ones forced to have respect for a tyrannical child while they carry loads of resentment, buried just beneath the surface. The authoritarian personality, with all its destructiveness, is the focus of "It's a Good Life."

During this same period, Dr. Benjamin Spock's guide for parents, *The Common Sense Book of Baby and Child Care*, first published in 1946, became a consistent bestseller, turning Dr. Spock into an international celebrity. The significance and impact of Spock's work is hard to overstate. In the generation prior, psychologists had advised parents to be firm, stoic, and even unaffectionate to their children. For example, Lena and William Sadler advised parents, "Handle the baby as little as possible. Turn it occasionally from side to side, feed it, change it, keep it warm, and let it alone; crying is absolutely essential to the development of good strong lungs. A baby should cry vigorously several times each day."[6] Several years later, John B. Watson instructed parents, "Let your behavior always be objective and kindly firm. Never hug and kiss them, never let them sit in your lap. If you must, kiss them once on the forehead when they say good night. Shake hands with them in the morning. Give them a pat on the head if they have made an extraordinarily good job of a difficult task."[7] In direct contrast to his predecessors, Spock encouraged a more flexible approach to parenting and highlighted the importance of physical affection. Despite, or perhaps because of, his more humane approach and his book's tremendous success, Spock became the target of disillusioned parents and politicians, who looked for someone or something to blame for unruly youth culture.

The enormous popularity of Spock's work reflects the reality of a rapidly increasing national birth rate as well as the psychological preoccupation and worry that came along with it. To put it simply, children took up not only an unprecedented amount of physical space in postwar American homes but an unequalled amount of mental and psychological space as well. The burgeoning field of childhood psychology and the general population's fascination with it shared similar roots with the birth rate: economic affluence and a general rise in income. These developments meant not only the financial ability to support children but also that families had to worry less about basic needs and sustenance and more about nebulous concerns for their children, such as providing fun and fostering emotional stability. Martha Wolfenstein explained this phenomenon of the postwar era: "A recent development in American culture is the emergence of what we might call 'fun morality.' Here, fun, from having been suspect if not taboo, has tended to become obligatory. Instead of feeling guilty for having too much fun, one is inclined to feel ashamed if one does not have enough."[8] As parents sought to uphold the new standards of middle-class living and fun morality, they increasingly sought guidance from experts like Spock, whose book, resting on millions of American bookshelves and coffee tables, symbolized the psychological unrest in the hearts and minds of young parents and the search for a resolution to their anxieties.

While Spock helped to ease the minds of many young parents, not all his readers had their confusion and worry over child-rearing so easily dispelled. Many readers struggled to know just how to apply Spock's principles. While his book arrived at a time when strict and severe discipline would soon be outmoded, Spock believed parents had taken certain instruction to an extreme and out of context, so much so that he updated and revised his book several times. In his second edition, published in 1957, Spock implores in a somewhat defensive tone, undoubtedly stemming from a decade of parents' letters and criticisms: "The most important thing I have to say is that you should not take too literally what is said in this book. Every child is different, every parent is different. . . . Remember that you know a lot about your child and that I don't know anything about him." He explains that when he first wrote *Common Sense,* general attitudes were much more "inflexible" and "strict." In the ensuing years, however, the general consensus on child-rearing shifted dramatically, with great help from Spock himself. He states in his 1957 edition: "Nowadays there seems to be more chance of a conscientious parent's getting into trouble with permissiveness than with strictness. So, I have tried to give a more balanced view." He declares, "If you are an old reader of this book, you'll see a lot has been added and changed, especially about discipline, spoiling, and the parents' part." While Spock maintained his stance on many things, such as showing a child plenty of affection, many of the revisions in the 1957 edition carefully qualify certain instructions about discipline and reward.[9] In this way, the largest increase in the US birth rate in history not only inspired *The Twilight Zone's* "It's a Good Life" but also shaped the increased psychological anxiety over childcare, along with the reading and misreading of Doctor Spock.

While many parents eventually blamed a strawman version of Spock's advice for creating spoiled, rebellious children, Spock's intentions and actual advice were quite different. Many critical parents and pundits characterized Spock as encouraging leniency and license, some even placing the blame for the sixties' youth rebellion and failure in Vietnam on his parenting advice. Norman Vincent Peale famously criticized Spock's philosophy: "Feed 'em whatever they want, don't let them cry, instant gratification of needs." Nowhere in Spock's writing, however, did he call for such instant gratification or over-permissiveness, and by the late sixties, it became obvious to those who seriously looked into his work that criticisms such as Peale's were wholly unjustified and grossly misguided. But Spock was a convenient scapegoat who caused, according to President Richard Nixon, a "fog of permissiveness" to set in on America's youth.[10] Nixon, however, failed to seriously consider that, along with marketers, he, not Dr. Spock, had actually encouraged and idealized American consumerism and indulgence on many occasions, such as the 1959 Moscow Kitchen Debate. While Spock did call for mothers to avoid "cross-looks and scoldings," he also continually stressed the importance of discipline and rituals, encouraged mothers to be like a "friendly boss," and also never completely ruled out the possibility of spanking a child, although countless Americans accused him of doing so.[11] In the end, outspoken critics like Peale and Nixon, unable to bend the nation to their will, seemed to exude more of the childlike frustration Spock helped parents to manage among their progeny.

In his work on Spock, William Graebner convincingly shows how the turmoil of the Great Depression, the rise of totalitarianism in Europe, and the trauma of World War II greatly shaped Spock's psychological views and those of his contemporaries. More than anything else, the evil of tyranny, which ostensibly caused World War II, needed to be expunged at home and abroad, "at home" taking on a very immediate, literal meaning for Spock and parents. Simply put, the family needed to be made "safe for democracy"; not to the point that children ran the roost, but to the point that cooperation, conformity, and mutuality could thrive. As Graebner explains: "At the center of this unstable world was an unstable infant and child—fearful, frustrated, insecure, and potentially destructive in his aggressive tendencies." Inspired by these growing concerns, Spock's book can be seen as a clear attempt to rid the nation of potential tyrants while they are yet toddlers. To do this, as Graebner states, Spock "sought to create a society that was more cooperative, more consensus-oriented, more group-conscious, and a society that was more knowable, more consistent, and more comforting."[12]

In "It's a Good Life," Anthony clearly does not exude the qualities either trumpeted by Spock or reflected in David Riesman's concept of being other-directed, which includes cooperation, compromise, and empathy.[13] Simply stated, Anthony is the antithesis of "the organization man." "It's a Good Life" taps into the fears of tyranny and the cravings for conformity that inspired Spock's decision to write *The Common Sense Book of Baby and Child Care* in the first place, not to mention the decision millions of Americans made to purchase and regularly refer to the book. After years as a pediatrician, Spock knew parents needed as much reassurance as instruction, evidenced by his famous opening supplication: "Trust yourself. You know more than you think you do." For many of his readers, however, the tendency was, rather, to question oneself and take certain instructions to an extreme. Tapping into the fear and anxiety over how much permissiveness is too much, Serling's episode converts the possibilities into a parental nightmare. Not only does Anthony have power over his family and neighbors, but he can bend reality itself to his wishes when it presents obstacles to his immediate pleasure and instant gratification. Equipped with fantastical powers, Anthony can alter the world around him.

Another element in this episode is that, in order to preserve Anthony's smile, everyone else must interpret reality, no matter what it is, as invariably positive. No one can even express differences of opinion or taste, as Aunt Amy illustrates when she states that the day is "hot" and "terrible" but is quickly corrected. A consensus affirming the simple positivity of everything must be maintained, including something as basic as the weather, even if it means risking heat stroke or hypothermia. This fact is reiterated when Bill runs to the window in the last scene, only to find that it is now snowing. Mr. Fremont asks Anthony if he made it snow. After his son responds affirmatively, Mr. Fremont gets panicked, saying that the crops will be ruined, but then stops this line of thinking and instead praises Anthony for making it snow: "It's good you're making it snow. Real good. And tomorrow's going to be a real good day." As Anthony alters reality to his liking, the results must be discussed only in smiling, affirming ways. Consequently, the residents of Peaksville behave much like postwar marketers—willing to say and do anything to appease Anthony's anxieties and desires. As Hannah Arendt had argued years earlier, the "ideal subject of totalitarian rule is . . . people for whom the distinction between fact and fiction . . . no longer exists."[14] In the way Anthony demands everyone and everything cater to his dreams and desires, even if it means denying reality, curbing freedom of speech, harming others, or permanently removing disagreeable people, he serves as the perfect embodiment of the origins of totalitarianism.

Throughout the episode, Anthony's utter incapability of playing and getting along with other children, adults, and even animals is frighteningly apparent. As Spock pointed out,

> the spoiled child is not a happy creature even in his own home. Then, when he gets out into the world, whether it's at 2 or 4 or 6, he is in for a rude shock. He finds that nobody is willing to kowtow to him; in fact, everybody dislikes him for his selfishness. . . . What

makes him stop grabbing toys from other children as he grows older? Not the slaps that he might get from the other child or his parent.... The thing that changes him is learning to love his regular playmates and discovering the fun of playing *with* them.[15]

Gerald H. J. Pearson, who also authored several mid-twentieth-century works on psychoanalysis and childhood, discussed what can happen when children are continually gratified: "These children have not learned to tolerate any anxiety, particularly that which arises when the immediate gratification of an instinctual desire is prevented by reality.... It reverses the whole parent-child relationship."[16] This reversal is clearly depicted in Anthony's relationship with his parents, who go out of their way to avoid the possibility of Anthony having to deal with any kind of anxiety. Relatedly, as sociologist Edgar Z. Friedenberg articulated, children's experience of conflicts in life does not have to mean outright warfare, and "it need not even involve hostile action.... There need be no intent to wound, castrate, or destroy on either side." In fact, conflict that occurs between a child and the outside world helps them grow into adulthood. But any hint of conflict or disagreement is instantly annihilated for—or by—Anthony. Friedenberg continues, "Some of the experiences of adolescence which turn out to be most beneficial to growth are, it is true, painful at the time. Looking for your first job . . . getting soundly beaten in your first statewide track meet when you are used to being the fastest runner in town—none of this is fun. But such experiences are not sickening, heartbreaking, or terrifying because, even at the time, they can be felt as bringing you in closer touch with reality."[17] By putting Anthony's comfort above reality itself, the entire town plays an extremely destructive game.

Childhood psychologist Erik Erikson similarly pointed out how important it is for parents to differentiate between their children's fear and anxiety. While fears are based on real, recognizable dangers that can be dealt with rationally, anxieties are "diffuse states of tension which magnify and even cause the illusion of an outer danger, without pointing to appropriate avenues of defense or mastery." The anxiety that comes with the possibility that another child, or even a dog, does not like him is unbearable for Anthony, resulting in their immediate destruction. In this regard, Erikson continued by paraphrasing FDR,

We have nothing to fear but anxiety. For it is not the fear of danger, but the fear of the associated state of aimless anxiety which drives us into irrational action, irrational flight—or, indeed, irrational denial of danger. When threatened with such anxiety we either magnify a danger which we have no reason to fear excessively—or we ignore a danger which we have every reason to fear. To be able to be aware of fear, then, without giving in to anxiety; to train our fear in the face of anxiety to remain an accurate measure and warning of that which man must fear—this is a necessary condition for a judicious frame of mind.[18]

In many ways, the characters in "It's a Good Life" obsessively try to stamp out all causes of anxiety, while ignoring or downplaying those things that should be properly feared—Anthony's tyrannical and destructive habits that endanger people's essential needs, such as crops and food. Because the adults around him allow Anthony's unfounded and unpredictable anxieties to control the entire family, real destruction occurs freely and ruthlessly.

In Spock's second edition, he seems to have taken notice of this stress and emotional self-neglect among parents, as he adds a section simply titled "Parents Are Human." Spock, undoubtedly somewhat surprised that he needed to state explicitly that parents "have needs," explains that "books about child care, like this one, put so much emphasis on all the needs that children have . . . that parents sometimes feel physically and emotionally exhausted. . . . They get the impression that they are meant to have no needs themselves. . . . It would be only fair if this book had an equal number of pages about the genuine needs of parents, the frustrations they constantly meet not only in the home but outside it."[19] Unwittingly, Spock may have helped to reveal a profitable market for self-help books for adults, having realized that adults need to be reminded of their basic emotional and psychological needs as well.

One of these needs is that of leisure and entertainment, a fact illustrated in the episode by Dan distinctly wanting to listen to Perry Como. Not only does Anthony insist on his own preferences, but he prohibits others from meeting their own needs. Spock implored parents, however: "Balance is achieved by . . . keeping for yourselves such other interests and pleasures as won't hurt him at all."[20] That Anthony keeps Dan from his entertainment preferences speaks to another significant phenomenon of the postwar period, namely the widening gap between adult and children's entertainment, most clearly seen in music. Perry Como became a popular choice of the older generation, which was raised on big-band vocalists such as Frank Sinatra and

Rosemary Clooney. By shunning their own harmless enjoyment of Perry Como, the adults descend further into a state of futile martyrdom while also failing to teach Anthony a vital life skill: to tolerate others and their different opinions and tastes. In an environment Anthony runs, the adults are forced to wonder whether they have what they need to live a mentally healthy life. In Dan's case, the answer is clearly negative, and he resorts to a childlike tantrum, from which he is relegated to utter powerlessness. Dan's transformation from an adult who simply wants to listen to Perry Como to a child throwing a tantrum to finally morphing into a kid's plaything confirms that he has literally become what the adults have figuratively been the whole time: a child's toy.

While this episode does not propose specific child-rearing techniques or necessarily present an obvious pro- or anti-Spock message, it dramatizes the anxieties and worries of parents across America. Spock, along with countless other Americans, was distressed by the industrial age and the demands it placed on parents and children alike. By encouraging parents to take a less authoritative approach to parenting and behave more like "friendly bosses," Spock arguably was trying to help them foster qualities such as other-direction and cooperation, which were becoming increasingly necessary in the postwar world and economy. Just as Spock, Pearson, and Erikson all cautioned parents to not allow their lives, behavior, and outlook be controlled by the anxieties of postwar life, "It's a Good Life" horrifyingly shows why parents were being offered such advice. Misreading such advice and seeing family life and a child's happiness as the solutions to Cold War fears, however, was similar to misreading foreign entanglements—they could result in complicating, rather than containing, the tensions of postwar American life.

Frightening Dolls, Scarier Parents

While "It's a Good Life" dramatizes new concerns over discipline and parent-child dynamics, "Living Doll" shows the psychological complexity as well as the consumer pressures involved with postwar parenting. A related episode, "Nightmare as a Child," tells the story of Helen Foley, a teacher who returns to her apartment to find a young girl named Markie waiting for her (S1, e29). As they begin to talk, it soon becomes clear that Markie is actually Helen's younger self and is there to remind her of her mother's traumatic murder, which she witnessed as a child. Having re-exposed this repressed traumatic experience, Helen is soon able to identify the murderer (S1, e29). In "Living

Doll" the traumatic elements of childhood and the pressures on parents to provide for their children are simultaneously explored. Airing on November 1, 1963, the episode depicts a doll named "Talky Tina," based on the Mattel Corporation's "Chatty Cathy," the first mass-marketed pull-string talking doll, released in 1960.

The episode begins with a young mother, Annabelle, and her daughter, Christie, pulling up to their suburban home in a station wagon after a shopping excursion. As they get out of the car with several packages, Annabelle instructs Christie to go right upstairs with her doll, as she does not want Erich, Christie's stepfather, to see it. As they enter the house, Erich is sitting at a desk balancing a checkbook and immediately enquires about their trip. He discovers, to his dismay, that Annabelle bought Christie another doll, which he believes she does not need. Undeterred, Christie opens the box and reveals the doll, exclaiming "She's alive, Daddy, and her name is Talky Tina!" Erich disgustedly remarks how costly a doll like that must have been, but Annabelle tries to reassure him: she put it on the charge account. Meanwhile, Christie demonstrates all the doll can do: "She moves and she can talk and I just love her already!" After she winds up the doll, Talky Tina suddenly comes to life, moving her hands, shaking her head, and saying, "My name is Talky Tina, and I love you very much!"

Erich, unimpressed, prods Annabelle about the price again. After she states that she does not think it is the price that is bothering him, Erich sardonically replies, "Now we'll get more of that Freudian gibberish you've been getting from her doctor, huh?" Annabelle firmly responds, "It isn't Doctor Lubin's fault that she feels rejected," referring to Christie's therapist. After Erich yells at Christie to "shut that thing off," Christie leaves the doll, still in motion, on the sofa and runs up to her room in tears. Alone with the doll, Erich winds it up to see it for himself. To his surprise, Talky Tina strikes a very different tone, moving her arms and head while she ominously says: "My name is Talky Tina, and I don't think I like you." Erich, puzzled now, is accompanied by Rod Serling's opening narration: "Talky Tina, the doll that does everything, a lifelike creation of plastic and springs and painted smile. . . . To Erich Streator, she is a most unwelcome addition to his household. But without her, he'd never enter *The Twilight Zone*."

As the episode continues, the doll's maliciousness and Erich's anxieties become increasingly evident. Erich winds the doll one more time, and she announces, "My name is Talky Tina, and I think I could even hate you." In disgust, he flings the doll across the room, smashing her against the wall

"Tina does everything!" Christie enthusiastically welcomes her new companion, Talky Tina. Still from "Living Doll" (1:43)

before she falls to the floor. As Tina lies on her back, her eyes spring eerily open and she strikes an even more threatening tone, one unprompted by any winding: "My name is Talky Tina, and you'll be sorry." Immediately thereafter, Annabelle descends the stairs, after tending to her upset daughter, and sees the doll laying on the floor. Realizing her husband has just thrown the toy across the room, Annabelle looks at him with worried, confused eyes. "Why, Erich?" He simply responds that he didn't like what it said. Erich picks up the toy, wanting to prove its maliciousness, but the doll only says, "I love you." After Annabelle confesses that she may no longer be able to tolerate Erich's anger toward Christie, Erich merely mocks Annabelle's love for her daughter, stating that he is only her stepfather and is "incapable of loving children because we can't have any of our own," revealing his impotence. Annabelle responds in a hopeful tone that he could love Christie if he only gave her a chance.

In the following scene, the family sits down to dinner while Christie pretends to feed her doll. After Annabelle states that Tina will be a good playmate for Christie, Erich retorts, "Mm hmm. Lacking a brother or sister is that what you mean? That's why you bought the doll, isn't it? Sort of a reminder?" Annabelle despairingly looks down and says, "It hadn't occurred to me, but if that's what you want to think." After the family finishes dinner, Christie leaves to play with a friend and Annabelle cleans up, again leaving Erich alone with the doll. Tina comes alive once more and tells Erich that she is beginning to hate him. Erich, wiping mashed potatoes from her plastic mouth, tells the doll he is going to get rid of her. The doll looks back at him and quips, "You wouldn't dare." After Erich props the doll up on the table, Tina says that Annabelle and Christie would both hate him if he attempted to get rid of her. Unbothered, Erich puts a cigarette in his mouth, lights a match, bringing it close into Tina's face. He is surprised when Tina says, "Ow." When he asks, "So you have feelings?" Tina explains that everything has feelings. After Erich asks if she can feel pain, Tina responds, "Not really, but I could hurt you." He laughs and remarks: "Threats from a doll!" When Annabelle comes back into the room, Erich accuses her of tricking him by placing a walkie-talkie inside the doll and voicing it herself, which Annabelle dismisses as absurd. Now more determined than ever to bring his tormenter to justice, Erich throws Tina in the garage garbage can, firmly closing the lid. He turns off the garage light and heads back into the house, seemingly triumphant.

As Erich sits on the couch, Christie asks if he has seen her doll, and he pleads ignorance. While Christie and her mom both go to search for Tina, Erich relaxes, satisfied with his clandestine efforts. Suddenly, the telephone rings. When Erich picks up the phone, he immediately hears a voice: "My name is Talky Tina, and I'm going to kill you." He returns to the garage only to find that Tina is no longer in the garbage can. Now in a state of panic, he asks Annabelle what she did with the doll, thinking she found her in the garbage and hid her somewhere. Annabelle, confused, says she did no such thing but finds it "dreadful" that Erich put her in the garbage. Finally, somewhat convinced of his wife's innocence, he nervously describes the phone call with Tina threatening to murder him. Annabelle, baffled by all that she is hearing, can only tell him that she doesn't know what to say. Erich walks up the stairs to Christie's room, where he finds Tina tucked into bed with Christie, then snatches her, leaving Christie in tears. He proceeds straight to the garage, this time determined to end the feud by taking Talky Tina on a torture-filled tour of his workshop.

Their first stop is the vise. Erich places Tina between the metal slabs and twists the lever until her tiny plastic head is squeezed tight. Surprised that the doll is not writhing in pain, he says, "I thought you said you have feelings."

"Erich, what are you doing?!" Annabelle looks on in disbelief as her husband attempts to cut through Christie's doll with a table saw. Still from "Living Doll" (17:32)

Tina only giggles and mockingly replies, "I can stand it if you can." Realizing that the vise alone will not kill this doll, Erich brings out a blow torch, attempting to light her on fire. But each time he lights the torch and pulls it close to her face, Tina simply blows out the flame. Increasingly frustrated, he loosens the doll from the vise and brings her to her next stop—the table saw. He flips the switch on and brings the whirring saw to her neck. Sparks fly as the blade makes contact, but Erich cannot cut through the doll after repeated attempts. In the midst of this, Annabelle comes into the garage and asks Erich what he is doing. With the visual evidence proving sufficient to answer her question, she begs him to stop, but he shoves her away, and Annabelle has little choice except to run off, in a frightened state. Erich finally reaches for a burlap bag and shoves the doll inside, securing the top with a rope. He then throws the bag into the garbage can, placing bricks on the lid for added security, finally feeling successful.

Erich heads back upstairs, only to find his wife packing her things. After he tries once more to convince her that the doll really has been tormenting him, Annabelle can only tell him that he has become "a sick, neurotic stranger . . . filled with blind, unreasonable hate," adding, "You better see a good psychiatrist." Erich sits down, slowly, on the edge of the bed, saying softly, "I couldn't have imagined it." Picking up where she left off, Annabelle says, "Tell him you tried to kill a doll." Realizing his relationship is on the brink of collapse, Erich tries to make amends by offering to give the doll back to Christie, and he heads back down to the garage to free Tina from her garbage can captivity. As he lifts her out of the bag, Tina says, "My name is Talky Tina, and I don't forgive you." Erich can only plead, "Please shut up!" and he turns off the lights, heading back upstairs to give the doll to Christie.

With everyone in bed now, Erich lays on his back with his eyes open as he hears the doll's mechanical movements in the hallway. He gets up to look for Tina, checking Christie's room before proceeding down the stairs. Suddenly, he trips on the doll, which causes him to somersault several times on his neck down the stairs, killing him instantly. Frightened by all the commotion, Annabelle screams and rushes to see what happened to Erich, then finds him and the doll at the bottom of the stairs. As she picks up the doll, Tina says her last words, "My name is Talky Tina, and you better be nice to me." In shock, Annabelle drops the doll, and Serling's closing narration comes in: "Of course, we know dolls can't really talk and they certainly can't commit murder. But to a child caught in the middle of turmoil and conflict, a doll can become many things—friend, defender, guardian—especially a doll like Talky Tina, who did talk and did commit murder in the misty region of *The Twilight Zone.*"

The "Living Doll" episode captures several important developments: the burgeoning market for children's consumer goods, the increasing availability of credit, and the ever-expanding prominence of Freudian psychology in American minds. The dramatic rise in the birth rate during the decades following World War II, as well as Americans' growing ability to purchase consumer goods, meant that manufacturers' efforts to churn out children's toys had enormous profit potential. Americans spent a total of $5.78 billion on toys and sporting goods in 1950, and by the end of the 1960s, this figure had ballooned to $15.24 billion.[21] Just as women's fashion, automobiles, and home furnishings went through changes to encourage Americans to buy or replace products more frequently, so too did toys. But if toys could be a boon for marketers and provide companionship and fun for children, they could also prove to be a financial burden and terror for adults, illustrated in fantastically horrifying ways in "Living Doll." Faced with these market changes and their children's growing consumeristic sensibilities, parents sought assistance from new lines of credit and psychoanalysis to help them achieve fiscal and psychological balance. These supposed reliefs, however, could complicate the wallet, the mind, and the family, potentially forming the kind of nightmare seen in this episode of *The Twilight Zone.*

"Living Doll" was based on not only an expanding children's consumer market but a rapidly changing one as well. In generations past, toy manufacturers had often appealed to parents even more than children, knowing they had to convince parents that their products were worth purchasing. However, during the late fifties and early sixties, with the advent of television, toy companies discovered they could market directly to children. No longer having to make educational ("This will help your child's brain develop!") or nostalgic appeals to parents ("Remember when you played with _____?"), companies such as Mattel were increasingly empowered by television to communicate directly with children. Mattel was the first major toy manufacturer to see and take full advantage of television's marketing power.

In 1955, Ruth and Elliot Handler, Mattel's owners, sponsored a segment of Walt Disney's *Mickey Mouse Club* on ABC. The contract, which was for a full year, cost the Handlers $500,000, their company's entire net worth at the time. In previous generations, toy manufacturers typically only advertised around the holidays and counted on individual retailers to demonstrate and sell their products. With this new contract, Mattel became the first toy manufacturer to invest money in TV advertising year-round.[22] With its slogan, "You can tell it's Mattel, it's swell," the company increased its television presence. In 1959, Mattel began sponsoring *Matty's Funday Funnies,* which featured boy mascot Matty Mattel and allowed the company to promote its latest toys both during the show and during commercial breaks. Mattel now saw its success explode with the release of Barbie in 1959 and Chatty Cathy in 1960. These new toys, along with the secure TV spots that immediately introduced them to children, made Mattel's sales figures soar to $100 million by 1965. While radio programs in the 1930s and 1940s featured ads for different products aimed at children, the ability to demonstrate toys in action and to show children playing with them made TV a nearly irresistible marketing force.

In a classic case of manufacturing desire, television brought new toys into the home before they were ever purchased and, as a result, transformed America's youth into unpaid in-home salespeople. This is demonstrated by Annabelle's statement that Talky Tina is a toy Christie had "her eye on for months." Due to repetitive TV adds, manufacturers like Mattel could now count on children to close their sales.[23] As marketing researcher Eugene Gilbert explained, "An advertiser who touches a responsive chord in youth can generally count on the parent to finally succumb to purchasing the product. . . . Parents generally have little resistance or protection against youth's bombardments. . . . A parent subjected to requests from the youngster who thinks he is in dire need of an item, witnessed on television, may find it easier to 'give in' rather than dispute rationally with a highly emotionalized child."[24] Mattel, perhaps more than any other toy manufacturer at the time, reaped massive benefits with these tactics.

Just as marketing expanded and changed, so too did toys. Although dolls had been around for centuries, companionate dolls that could interact with children emerged in the 1960s. Chatty Cathy was the first in a series of successful talking dolls manufactured by Mattel. One of the several Chatty Cathy advertisements Mattel ran in 1961 promoted not only the doll's unique ability to interact with kids but also its ability to model seasonal fashions, just like a real boy or girl. One of Chatty Cathy's eleven utterances was "Please change my dress," and a 1961 Mattel advertisement promoted most of all this fashion-consuming aspect of the doll: "We can change her dresses, now goodness knows—now we got a wardrobe full of pretty clothes! For nursery school, you're crisp and cool, for summer there's a play time set. In winter, burrrr, your collar fur in the coldest season she can get!"[25] The lifelike doll became a friend who could not only play and speak with a young child but even follow fashion trends with them. In a different promotional piece, a newspaper ad struck an unintentional ominous tone, one fitting *The Twilight Zone*, when it proudly proclaimed: "You never know what adorable Chatty Cathy will say."[26]

Throughout "Living Doll," Erich's inability to procreate is mirrored by his powerlessness regarding the toys his stepdaughter Christie brings home. And although Annabelle took her to get the doll, the sale was largely performed by the marketers who advertised the product to Christie and the creditors who financed the exchange. Purchases like this one partially reflected the vision of advertising agent Charles H. Brower, who exhorted creditors: "If we are to break the present economic log jam, you installment-credit bankers and we in advertising must do it by working together." If television advertisements made marketing a talking doll much easier, the increased availability of credit made selling much easier and more lucrative than ever before. Credit not only freed consumers' abilities to purchase items when they wanted but also temporarily relieved them of the psychological pressure and stress that can come with exchanging actual money. As one marketing researcher pointed out, credit "removes the air of finality inherent in a cash transaction. In a sense, the credit buyer makes up his mind to buy while he is still paying for the item."[27] In other words, credit helps to delay both the actual purchase and the deliberate mental choice to do so. The mental stress and conclusiveness of a cash transaction is exchanged for peace of mind via deferred payment, but it comes at a cost, with interest. That price, however, also remains more concealed, reflected in the fact that Annabelle never says how much the doll actually cost but repeatedly says she merely "put it on the account." Just as the doll offers Christie psychological comfort, so too does purchasing on credit for Annabelle, just as it did real American consumers.

And although Christie and her mom seem happy about their trip to the department store, Erich's discomfort and anxiety become readily apparent as he demands to know how much the doll cost. Despite the comfort and flexibility credit offered young families, this spousal exchange illustrates how credit simultaneously added a new layer of complexity to personal finances and married life. And the driving force behind these changes in credit were actually department stores, as retailers learned that selling their products on revolving credit meant customers bought even more. Not only did department stores sell more items when they made credit available, but their ability to charge interest on customers' unpaid balances meant that stores could pursue credit expansion as an end in itself, in order to increase profit margins. Original price tags now only represented a fraction of what retailers would make from selling a product: a doll that retailed for twenty dollars might cost thirty dollars or more by the time it was actually paid off.

To be sure, credit was not new. Since the 1920s, consumers had been offered thirty-day credit accounts. These accounts, however, obligated customers to make a payment within the month before they could make another purchase. Typically, these accounts were also only available at higher-end stores.[28] Revolving credit, however, was controlled by a credit manager who set credit limits based on each individual's finances and allowed customers more flexibility in making payments by charging them somewhere around 1 percent interest on their unpaid balance. Beginning in the late fifties, however, option accounts began to replace both these thirty-day credit accounts and the strictly budgeted revolving accounts. Option accounts at department stores set no individuated credit limits and therefore did not require account holders to meet with credit managers either—any customer could use these new option accounts. Consequently, managing debt and credit became the sole responsibility of the consumer. This shift in credit options also enabled women, particularly, to renegotiate their roles in financial decisions, freed from both the dictates of a department store credit manager and their husbands' monetary inclinations. One credit controller explained the impact option accounts would have on customers in deliberately gendered terms: now "*she* becomes her own credit manager."[29] So, credit could either help to renegotiate traditional gender roles when it came to personal finance, or, as in the case of Erich and Annabelle, it could create another source of tension.

In the nervous exchanges between Erich and Annabelle, it becomes increasingly clear that finances are not the only issue plaguing their relationship. Neurosis and even psychosis are deeply affecting Erich. Freudian psychologists would interpret his neurotic symptoms as serving "the purpose of sexual gratification for the patient" and being a "substitute for satisfactions which he does not obtain in reality." Erich, with the satisfaction of procreation lacking, is deluded to the point of thinking that his wife, his stepdaughter, and the recently purchased doll are all coconspirators, there to humiliate and emasculate him. Erich's antagonistic stance toward everyone, even Christie's new doll, might remind the viewer of Freudian thinking regarding neurotic sufferers of expectant dread, who "always anticipate the worst of all possible outcomes, interpret every chance happening as an evil omen, and exploit every uncertainty to mean the worst." To Erich, his wife's use of department store credit is a deliberate emasculating slight, and her choice to purchase a doll for Christie was a purposeful mockery of his impotence. He does not question these neurotic thoughts but accepts them as the truth. For Freudian psychologists, though, someone who readily accepts their neurosis without inspecting the underlying causes "has made a bad bargain," having "paid too heavily for the solution of the conflict; the sufferings entailed by the symptoms are perhaps as bad as those of the conflict they replace, and they may quite probably be very much worse."[30] Erich soon found out how much worse it could get.

While Erich indiscriminately dismisses psychology as "Freudian gibberish," his wife discounts his fantasies and considers them merely another expression of his anger toward Christie. Freudian thinking, however, theorizes that to reach a cure or resolution of neurosis, one must first "equate fantasy and reality and not begin with whether the . . . experiences under examination are the one or the other. . . . This is clearly the only correct attitude to adopt toward these mental productions." Indeed, "they too possess a reality of a sort. It remains a fact that the patient has created these fantasies for himself, and this fact is of scarcely less importance for this neurosis than if he had really experienced what the fantasies contain. The fantasies possess *psychical* as contrasted with *material* reality, and we gradually learn to understand that *in the world of the neuroses* it is *psychical reality which is the decisive kind.*" Erich and Annabelle would both need to accept the apparently absurd, but psychically real phenomenon that a scheming, malicious child's doll is in fact threatening Erich. After Erich's various failed attempts to destroy his stepdaughter's toy, his neurosis reflects the Freudian conjecture that once "the disease has persisted for a considerable time it seems finally to acquire the character of an independent entity; it displays something like a self-preservative instinct; it forms a kind of pact . . . with the other forces in mental life, even with those fundamentally hostile to it."[31] Tina's self-preservation reflects the preservative fortitude of Erich's neuroses. And just as the tools of the traditionally masculine environment of his workshop prove ineffective in his fight against Tina, Erich's attempts to assert traditional male authority over his family only worsen his psychological state and his relationship with his wife and stepdaughter. Moreover, for Annabelle and Christie, a single-parent home emerges as safer and more desirable than one that includes an abusive father figure.

While Talky Tina represents Erich's neurosis, the final scene embodies Annabelle's feeble strength against the forces of childhood marketing and consumerism. And while the doll, as Serling put it, served as a kind of "friend" and "guardian" to Christie, the fact that a consumer good, and not her own family or friends, provided her with companionship and security, presents another dilemma to the home audience: if one allows consumer goods to fill voids that should be met by people, what are the ultimate costs for parents and children? Just as children could learn to depend on a doll or other consumer good for their companionship, parents could become overly dependent on the world of toys and gadgets to fill voids in their children's lives. In much the same way, it was up to everyday Americans to figure out whether consumer goods and toys were truly what they needed.

In both of these episodes, the idea that the white nuclear family was the best place to contain Cold War tensions and uphold American values is thrown into serious doubt. The worlds of millions of Americans who opted to raise families arguably became more complex and disorienting, not less. Burdened with having to adapt to suburban life, middle-class parenting values, the pervasive influence of television, and unprecedented levels of marketing and consumerism geared specifically toward children, parents could find that in choosing to start families they increased the complicated aspects of postwar life. The attempt to fall in line with these white consumer ideals was even more challenging for nonwhite families, as they faced continual discrimination in employment, housing, and access to lines of credit. By dramatically depicting the potential nightmares of childhood and family life, rather than simply showing another overly simplistic, unreal domestic fantasy, Serling sought to raise his viewers' ability to think critically and realistically about important domestic issues. Should the aspirations of white American domestic life be the objective or envy of millions? A simple return to tradition would not necessarily smooth family problems out, just as constant, even toxic, positivity would not create tranquility for children and home life. Similarly, turning to the world of consumer goods and children's toys would not resolve profoundly damaging emotional neglect and abuse. Thus, *The Twilight Zone* again left complex problems somewhat unresolved, for the viewing audience to consider for themselves, their children, and their families.

White-Collar Weariness

Postwar Work and Leisure Transformed

While manual laborers found pink slips in their mailboxes with increasing frequency during the postwar period, the promises of white-collar positions served to entice millions of Americans who wanted the best chance at achieving the American Dream for themselves and their families. A 1956 census revealed that more people were employed in white-collar work than manual labor for the first time in American history.[1] While not all such jobs represented a rise in one's standard of living, most Americans who took white-collar jobs were making more money than their blue-collar counterparts and were able to buy suburban homes, new automobiles, and a host of other modern consumer goods. Without a doubt, white-collar work made the good life possible for millions of Americans. Although postwar Americans enjoyed more income and the ability to consume more goods, it soon became evident to workers and social critics alike that the nature of most white-collar work was alienating, dull, monotonous, and bureaucratic and did not provide the sense of satisfaction that working in production did or the sense of community that farming and other manual jobs once had. Instead of giving people a sense of their own craftsmanship or service to other community members, many white-collar jobs came with the primary benefit of increasing an employee's purchasing power. White-collar work did not necessarily expand a person's sense of self or sense of community but worked primarily to increase one's ability to consume more goods.

In this context, Sloan Wilson's protagonist in the 1955 bestselling novel *The Man in the Gray Flannel Suit* remarked, "I really don't know what I was looking for when I got back from the war, but it seemed as though all I could see was a lot of bright young men in gray flannel suits rushing around New York in a frantic parade to nowhere. They seemed to me to be pursuing neither ideals nor happiness—they were pursuing a routine. For a long while I thought I was on the sidelines watching that parade, and it was quite a shock to glance down and see that I too was wearing a gray flannel suit."[2] White-collar culture seemed to sweep over America and took it overnight, leading many critics, such as C. Wright Mills, to reflect on what it all meant for the United States. Mills articulated in no uncertain terms, "By examining white-collar life, it is possible to learn something about what is becoming more typically 'American' than the frontier character ever was. What must be grasped is the picture of society as a great salesroom, an enormous file, an incorporated brain, a new universe of management and manipulation. By understanding these diverse white-collar worlds, one can also understand better the shape and meaning of modern society as a whole, as well as the simple hopes and complex anxieties that grip all the people who are sweating it out in the middle of the twentieth century."[3] As one of the most significant features of the postwar period, the fast-moving, pill-popping, paperwork-filled world of white-collar work necessarily found a place of residence in *The Twilight Zone.*

Rising to the Top of Anxiety

The Twilight Zone episode "A Stop at Willoughby" first aired on May 6, 1960 (S1, e30). Along with it, "Nightmare at 20,000 Feet," starring William Shatner as protagonist Robert Wilson, also explored how white-collar work can lead to compromised psychological heath (S5, e3). Having already suffered one nervous breakdown, Wilson is traveling on an airplane with his wife when he begins to suffer another. Thinking he sees a gremlin on the plane's wing, Wilson tries to warn his wife and the flight crew, but they merely think he is seeing things and give him a sedative to help calm him down. After the plane lands, damage wrought by the gremlin is clearly shown, as Wilson's supposed hallucinations are confirmed to be reality. The main premise of the show and the disbelief of Wilson's wife and flight attendants, however, works effectively because Wilson is a stressed-out salesman: his visions are easily dismissed by so many because of the psychologically demanding nature of his work.

In a similar way, "A Stop at Willoughby" dramatized white-collar neuroses, beginning with an office meeting in a New York City high rise, overlooking the city's skyline. Seven white men in designer suits sit around a conference table, waiting for another colleague, Jacob Ross. These are ad men, figuratively and literally positioned high above the city's nearly 8 million residents. The head of the advertising agency, Mr. Oliver Misrell, puffs on a cigar while the episode's main character, Gart Williams, nervously taps a pencil on his hand. After waiting over a half-hour for Ross, one of the secretaries comes into the meeting room, notifying the men of Ross's sudden resignation. Misrell erupts in anger as Ross's departure means his firm is losing a lucrative advertising account with an automobile company. He blames the setback on Williams, who had placed Ross in charge of the account. Too furious to remain seated, Misrell stands up, snatches the cigar out of his mouth, and articulates in a not-so-subtle way how aggressive and belligerent their work is: "Get with it, boy. . . . This is a push business, Williams . . . a push, push, push business. . . . You don't delegate responsibilities to little boys. . . . It's push, push, push all the way, all the time, right on down the line!" After listening meekly to his boss's verbal lashing, Williams retorts, "Fat boy, why don't you shut your mouth?!" and storms out of the room. As he shuts the door behind him, Gart grabs his stomach; he is evidently suffering from some kind of stress related ulcer. Helen, Gart's secretary, asks if there is anything she can bring him. He replies cynically, "Yeah, a sharp razor and a chart of the human anatomy showing where all the arteries are." He enters his office, closes the door, and turns off the lights, sitting down at his desk in film noir–like darkness. Serling's opening narration introduces the home viewers to the dejected main character as he sits motionless at his desk:

> This is Gart Williams, age thirty-eight, a man protected by a suit of armor all held together by one bolt. Just a moment ago, someone removed the bolt, and Mr. Williams' protection fell away from him and left him a naked target. He's been cannonaded this afternoon by all the enemies of his life. His insecurity has shelled him, his sensitivity has straddled him with humiliation, his deep-rooted disquiet about his own worth has zeroed in on him, landed on target, and blown him apart. Mr. Gart Williams, ad agency exec, who in just a moment will move into *The Twilight Zone* in a desperate search for survival.

The screen fades to black.

The episode continues with Gart commuting back home on a Connecticut-bound MTA train, nodding off to sleep and dreaming of another life. In his dream, he finds himself on a vacated, antique train. He opens his window, revealing a small, charming village filled with horse-drawn carriages, children walking back from a fishing trip, and a man riding around on a penny

"It's a push, push, push business!" Oliver Misrell dresses down Gart Williams during a boardroom meeting. Still from "A Stop at Willoughby" (2:08)

farthing bicycle. The conductor walks down the train car, announcing, "Willoughby! This stop is Willoughby!" This only adds to Gart's confusion. After he asks the conductor about Willoughby, he is further puzzled when the man also mentions the date—the summer of 1888, mid-July. The smiling conductor describes the exotic location as a really lovely little village: "You ought to try it sometime—peaceful, restful, where a man can slow down to a walk and live his life full measure." Gart attempts to get off the train but is startled and wakes up, finding himself back on a mid-twentieth-century commuter train bound for his Connecticut suburb.

When Gart finally arrives at home after a long day of ridicule and commuting, he immediately pours himself a highball. As he takes his first drink, his wife, Jane, slowly comes down the stairs with a look of disgust and asks if he plans to spend his evening getting "quietly plastered?" Having heard about Gart's outburst during the day's meeting, she unsympathetically tells him to spare her his "little homilies" and asks if he wrecked his career, concerned more for her husband's employment status than his mental health. Gart responds sardonically that his boss "found it in that great, oversized heart of

"Will you spare me your little homilies?" Jane unsympathetically interrogates Gart on his employment status. Still from "A Stop at Willoughby" (10:20)

his to forgive. The somewhat obese, gracious gentleman will allow me to continue in his employ because he is such a human-type fella . . . with a small, insignificant, parenthetic additional reason that if I were to go to a competitive agency, I might possibly take a lot of business with me," emphasizing that he is valued only for the profits he generates and not for who he is as an employee. After Gart desperately confesses to Jane that he is "tired and sick," she quickly responds that she is "sick and tired of a husband who lives in a kind of permanent self-pity. A husband with a heart-bleeding sensitivity that he unfurls like a flag whenever he decides the competition is a little too rough for him." Gart sadly looks up from his drink, earnestly explaining, "Some people aren't built for competition, Janie. Or big, pretentious houses they can't afford, or rich communities they don't feel comfortable in, or country clubs they wear around their neck like a badge of status." After Jane asks what he would prefer to his current life and occupation, he adamantly replies, "Any job at all where I can be myself!"

The underlying marital tension becomes increasingly apparent when Gart goes on to describe himself as an average guy with a wife who "has an appetite." When Jane coolly asks where he would be if it was not for her appetite, her husband sits down on the stairs and explains that he knows where he would prefer to be, telling her about his dream of Willoughby. With a rare smile, Gart describes the town as a "Currier and Ives painting" filled with bicycles, bandstands, wagons, and serenity. Jane, however, is repulsed by her husband's simple, romantic dream: "You know what the trouble with you is, Gart? You were just born too late because you know you're the kind of a guy that could be satisfied with a summer afternoon or an ice wagon being drawn by a horse! So, it's my mistake, pal, my error, my miserable tragic error to get married to a man whose big dream in life is to be Huckleberry Finn!" Jane walks upstairs while her husband only shrugs and says to himself, "Yeah, maybe."

When Gart rides the train home next, he again dreams of Willoughby, this time almost stepping off the train to walk into town. But just as he heads toward the exit, the train starts moving again. When Gart wakes up, he vows that the next time he finds himself dreaming of Willoughby, he will most definitely get off the train. Back in his office, Misrell can be heard barking orders through the telephone at Gart, demanding he come up with new advertising ideas for television. While Gart swallows several tablets of medication, his boss demands, "What we need here, Williams, is a show with zazz, an entertainer with moxie! We've got to take the audience by the ears and give them a yank, jar 'em, rock 'em, give them the old push, push, push!" These demands illustrate how sponsors affected not just the advertising on television, but the actual programs: "Tomorrow morning I want at least a preliminary idea for the show. You know what I want—just a rough format with a few details as to how we integrate the commercials within the body of the show." Following this one-way conversation, Gart takes several other calls, one regarding a sponsor's frustration over the low ratings of a particular show and another from a disgruntled client who received scratched negatives from the office. As he juggles several phone calls, his secretary, Helen, adds to the chaos, repeatedly imploring him to speak with Misrell, who wants to discuss an urgent matter. With an incessantly muttering telephone in each of his hands and Helen demanding what remains of his thinly spread attention, Gart gets up from his desk and stumbles into his bathroom, on the verge of a panic attack.

He leans against the sink and looks up in the mirror, seeing several haunting likenesses of his boss, each admonishing him: "Push, push, push Williams! Push, push, push! Get with it boy!" Having had enough of the incessant cacophony that repeatedly plays in his own mind, Gart smashes the mirror with his fist, the cracked glass reflecting a very cracked ad executive.

"Plenty of room and lots of fish!" Gart dreams of the small, slow-paced town of Willoughby. Still from "A Stop at Willoughby" (21:55)

He stumbles back into his office, where he telephones Jane: "I've had it, understand? I've had it. I just can't take this another day. Not another hour. This is it right now. I've got to get out of here. . . . Janie, will you help me, please? Will you please help me?" No words can be heard on the other end, only the click of Jane hanging up her phone, further emphasizing the disconnect between husband and wife.

When Gart rides the train home, he again falls asleep on the train. As expected, he begins to dream of Willoughby, but this time, he successfully gets off the train. As he walks into the village, he is kindly greeted by some boys who just went fishing and then is warmly welcomed by a mustachioed local. As he continues toward town, the camera cuts back to the present day, showing Gart's dead body lying in a snowy ditch near the train tracks. The conductor explains to the medical crew that he jumped off the train and "shouted something about Willoughby, then ran out to the platform and that was the last I saw him. Doctor says he must have died instantly." As the ambulance drivers carry his body to the car, they shut the door, revealing the name of a funeral parlor: "Willoughby and Son." Serling offers his closing remarks: "Willoughby? Maybe it's wishful thinking nestled in a hidden part of a man's mind, or maybe it's the last stop in the vast design of things—or perhaps, for a man like Gart Williams, who climbed on a world that went by too fast, it's a place around the bend where he could jump off. Willoughby? Whatever it is, it comes with sunlight and serenity, and is a part of *The Twilight Zone.*"

"A Stop at Willoughby" clearly captures two of the most significant and enduring changes of the 1950s—the massive migration to the suburbs and the dramatically expanding job market for white-collar work, particularly in advertising. Just as white-collar jobs surpassed blue-collar jobs during the 1950s for the first time in US history, by the end of the 1960s, the suburbs housed the majority of American residents. This now mostly white-collar and suburban America, saturated with advertising, spoke to the nearly unprecedented affluence and social mobility afforded to Americans during the postwar era. And while the suburban white-collar lifestyle was touted as the embodiment of the American Dream and embraced by millions across the country, *The Twilight Zone*'s "A Stop at Willoughby" exposes how this dream could be more akin to a nightmare for those who realized what they were having to give up to enjoy modern amenities and enhanced social status. In particular, the paper pushing, product selling, and daily commuting could prove more of a hindrance than a help when it came to fostering a sense of individuality and community.

In this regard, Serling engages a subject discussed by several contemporary critical works, among them William Whyte's *The Organization Man,* Betty Friedan's *The Feminine Mystique,* and David Riesman's *The Lonely Crowd.* These works, much like "A Stop at Willoughby," raised concerns over how self-expression, identity, and community were often requisite sacrifices for one to partake of postwar American affluence. Social mobility was not necessarily an inherently or entirely beneficial thing, as "the individual, driven by the belief that he should never rest content in his existing station and knowing that society demands advancement by him as proof of his merit, often feels stress and insecurity and is left with no sense of belonging either in the station to which he advances or in the one from which he set out."[4] In *Twilight Zone* fashion, Serling encouraged his audience to consider the costs and rewards involved in the postwar American Dream.

Throughout the episode, Gart clearly believes he is caught in a social trap, one that William Whyte also described in his seminal work, *The Organization Man.* Whyte lamented: "Few things are more calculated to rob the individual of his defenses than the idea that his interests and those of society can be wholly compatible. The good society is the one in which they are most compatible, but they never can be completely so, and one who lets The Organization be the judge ultimately sacrifices himself. . . . It is hard enough to learn to live with our inadequacies, and we need not make ourselves more miserable by a spurious ideal of middle class adjustment."[5] Between his work and his home life, Gart cannot express any kind of individuality. The middle-class adjustment is total—work, wife, home, and even his leisure time is dictated by a kind of all-encompassing and all-demanding middle-class package.

The central elements of the episode, including Gart's experiences at work, his commute, and his dream on the train, also dramatize issues raised in David Riesman's best-selling 1950 study, *The Lonely Crowd.* Dividing the evolution of the American character into different "directions," Riesman characterized the nineteenth century, here allegorized by Willoughby, as "inner-directed" because of community values and tradition. In contrast, the postwar United States was increasingly "other-directed" because of the pressure to work within bureaucracies and adapt among different social groups. Riesman argued that while other-direction incentivized positive qualities such as empathy and adaptability, it sometimes meant losing the sense of self and community that inner-directed America offered. Gart clearly despises many of the features that make up his contemporary world of other-direction and literally dreams of living back in the nineteenth century, when inner-direction reigned. Riesman explained that in inner-direction, "the source of the direction is 'inner' in the sense that it is implanted early in life by the elders and directed toward generalized but nonetheless inescapably destined goals."[6] It created a strong sense of identity but one that was largely crafted by one's family, community members, and religious leaders. Riesman termed this internalized view of the world a *gyroscope,* meaning that one interpreted people and experiences from a kind of fixed axis or reference point.

Riesman explained that the majority of postwar Americans, who were other-directed, developed their characters from a wider variety of sources, not just family and local community. Rather than internalizing a set of ideals early on from ancestors and community members, Americans in the fifties needed to "be able to receive signals from far and near; the sources are many, the changes are rapid. What can be internalized, then, is not a code of behavior but the elaborate equipment needed to attend to such messages."[7] Riesman referred to this social equipment as a "radar," serving as the means to socially scan the wants and needs of others. As an advertising executive, Gart not only has to have this essential social radar to function bureaucratically, but his very job in marketing and advertising speaks to the demands placed on him to read and anticipate others, crafting advertisements that suit the perceived desires of the American public. His very existence and livelihood are based on Riesman's concept of an other-directed radar.

Compared with nineteenth-century inner-directed individuals, the postwar other-directed Americans, as Riesman discusses them, also carried many gendered implications. And just as there was considerable tension between Gart and Jane, the perceived worlds of the nineteenth and twentieth centuries seemed to involve fundamental concerns over gender roles as well. David Potter's 1962 article "American Women and the American Character" pointed out how Riesman's generalizations, among those of many other scholars, were put "mostly in masculine terms." Compounding this was that the pressure to socially conform historically has usually been greater regarding women, who largely lacked the social access to a life of individual entrepreneurialism in the inner-directed nineteenth century.[8] More recently, James Gilbert has explained how Riesman's *Lonely Crowd* "depicted the contemporary world— other-direction—as a situation that particularly threatened masculinity. His lonely crowd was principally an assembly of vulnerable men described in words that launched a signal of distress over the feminizing changes in modern culture."[9] And although the United States in 1888 also included congested urban centers and corporations, the romanticized individuality and community of Gart's nineteenth-century dream spoke to the longing for the days when men had to be less socially conformist and adaptable—when they employed internal gyroscopes instead of radars.

Throughout the episode, Jane and Gart's heated exchanges about the costs involved with obtaining middle-class rewards cast doubt on the pursuit of the American Dream as an end in itself. The mere fact that white-collar status, suburban living, and consumer spending were the supposed key components to achieving a dream life belies the reality that not everyone's dreams are the same or even should be. In postwar America, rewards were boasted everywhere and costs frequently muted, leading critics such as David Potter to explain that if "the social pressures upon the individual to enter the competitive contest are, in some cases, literally intolerable, resulting in neurosis, is not this because society itself regards the rewards as irresistible and is determined to compel everyone to strive for them? It is a commonplace of gambling that the intentness of the players is in proportion to the size of the stakes, and the stakes of the American game have certainly contributed something toward giving it a greater tenseness than some participants can bear."[10] The middle-class dream, while largely accessible to Gart and other white men in their thirties, may lead only to a wealthy form of depravity if it means giving up too much of one's self.

The discussions between Jane and Gart further illustrate the gendered tension of postwar life in the United States and, specifically, how women were frequently and unjustly seen as the main cause for the ills of excessive consumerism and suburban comfort. However, Jane does not appear entirely happy, either; she displays a dissatisfaction that seems to go beyond a single interaction with her husband. As to the source of her frustration, one could easily point to Gart's anachronistic tendencies and a marital mismatch. But on an even more fundamental level, the consumer culture and pressures to keep up a middle-class lifestyle emerge as likely culprits for Jane's discontent as well. The economic anxieties to work and to consume sow the seeds of dissatisfaction in both Jane and Gart, alienating them from themselves and one another, despite their dependence on each other.

This spousal alienation reflects, among many things, one psychiatrist's conclusions regarding vicarious living, a common feature of living in a consumer society where desires are not necessarily one's own but represent what one is pressured to desire:

> The most frequent manifestation of vicarious living is a particularly structured dependence on another person, which is often mistaken for love. Such extremely intense and tenacious attachments, however, lack all the essentials of genuine love—devotion, intuitive understanding, and delight in the being of the other person in his own right and in his own way. On the contrary, these attachments are extremely possessive and tend to deprive the partner of a life of his own. . . . The other person is needed not as someone to relate oneself to; he is needed for filling out one's inner emptiness, one's nothingness.[11]

Clearly, Jane and Gart lack this delight and fulfillment in each other and even themselves, foreshadowing many of the critiques Betty Friedan raised three years later when she stated, "The suburban house is not a concentration camp, nor are American housewives on their way to the gas chamber. But they are in a trap, and to escape they must . . . exercise their human freedom, and recapture their sense of self. They must refuse to be nameless, depersonalized, manipulated, and live their own lives again according to a self-chosen purpose. They must begin to grow."[12] The work-consuming cycle that permeates Jane's and Gart's lives leaves them little room to express and expand their senses of individuality, and as a result, limits their capabilities to love and support each other.

While this episode illustrates some aspects of the discontent housewife, it also alludes to how women were frequently and unjustly blamed as if they had themselves created the modern consumer culture of postwar America and thereby increased their husbands' stress levels. In popular print culture, particularly in women's magazines, such as *Good Housekeeping, Coronet,* and *Ladies' Home Journal,* wives were persistently singled out as the guilty parties for their husbands' excessive stress and maladaptation to middle-class life. Throughout the many discussions of this phenomenon emerged the trope of the "nagging wife." Mrs. Dale Carnegie wrote an article, "How to Help Your Husband Get Ahead," whose title she also gave a book she later wrote. Carnegie informed her readers that "wives have been trying to influence husbands by nagging since the days of the caveman. . . . To date, it hasn't worked—except in reverse." Citing one particular case, Carnegie explained how an "old friend of our family told us that his career was almost wrecked by a wife who belittled every job he ever had. . . . His wife would greet him by saying: 'Well, how's the boy genius? Did you bring home any commissions or just a lecture from the sales manager? I suppose you know the rent is due next week?'" In the same piece, Carnegie called wifely nagging "an emotional disease" and advised women to simply ask their husbands about it, and "if he should tell you that you are a nag, don't react by violent denial—that only proves he is right."[13]

Another article, featured in *Good Housekeeping,* warned women that they were the key difference in their husbands' careers: "We employers realize how often the wrong wife can break the right man. This doesn't mean that the wife is necessarily wrong for the man but that she is wrong for the job. On the other hand, more often than is realized the wife is the chief factor in the husband's success in his career. . . . If a man has a peevish, nagging wife, if she is jealous and possessive, if she is lazy or overambitious or extravagant, that man is going to be unhappy. And his unhappiness will interfere with his concentration." The article lists several desirable and undesirable qualities of a professional man's wife: "A good wife is friendly . . . smiles easily and she is pleasant to be with." Her primary interests are her husband and home, and although the author claims it is difficult to immediately determine a "good wife," the "real troublemakers are fairly easy to spot." These include "the complaining woman," who "can toss a cloud over the brightest of days—and the brightest of men." Other undesirable types include "the dominating woman," who "knows it all—from what a man should eat to how he should run his business" and the "wife-in-a-rut" who is "a pathetic little creature . . . out of her element."[14] Articles like these consistently placed the responsibilities of middle-class adjustment, including new and challenging forms of white-collar work and unprecedented levels of suburban living and commuting, squarely on a married woman's shoulders. And while men understandably struggled in this modern living arrangement, women's emotional and psychological burdens were more frequently and unmercifully seen as character flaws and in clear violation of marital obligations, not a byproduct of adjusting to new roles and expectations, just like their husbands. These popular articles contained hardly any real practical advice for wives and couples; they offered only condemnatory commentary while holding up impossibly perfect ideals for marital relations.

Collectively, these popular magazine articles emphasized that a wife's duty was to serve both her husband and, indirectly, the company for which he worked. In this episode, however, instead of a lack of marital support for career advancement representing the problem, it could be that the unrelenting pressures related to professional advancement and the pursuit of wealth were the crux of dissatisfaction for the individual and the relationship. William Whyte, for example, noted the inherent conflict of interest between the corporate or business world and that of marriage and family. He mockingly noted that "unlike the Catholic Church, the corporation cannot require celibacy, and because its members are subject to the diversions of family ties, the corporation does fall short of complete effectiveness . . . and if it officially praises the hearth and family, it is because it can afford the mild hypocrisy."[15] Thus, Jane and Gart's apparent lack of intimacy was not so much due to Gart's lack of status, wealth, and a career, but actually *because* he possessed all those things. Even though Whyte's famous study on corporate culture illuminated the marital and familial tensions that almost inevitably arose when one tried to attain the American middle-class dream, popular stereotypes of the nagging and spend-happy wife perpetually shifted attention and responsibility from businesses and employers for the psychological, emotional, and marital difficulties that they helped to generate.[16]

As far as struggling wives were concerned, they would mostly have to wait for Friedan and other second-wave feminists to give popular voice to their shared "problem that has no name." Like many writers of popular magazine articles, Friedan also saw a kind of illness taking root in American women, but rather than frame it as a likely internal character flaw, she pointed to profoundly misguided gender roles and expectations. She explained, "It is not an exaggeration to call the stagnating state of millions of American housewives a sickness, a disease in the shape of a progressively weaker core of human self . . . at a time when the dehumanizing aspects of modern mass culture make it necessary for men and women to have a strong core of self, strong enough to retain human individuality through the frightening, unpredictable pressures of our changing environment. The strength of women is not the cause, but the cure for this sickness."[17] For marriage to be a healthy and enduring enterprise, women did not need to be even more docile and subservient to their husbands; rather, they needed exactly what the men they married did—a sense of self and the ability to invest in their own growth.

"A Stop at Willoughby" illustrates how other-direction affected not just white-collar workers and suburban families but television content as well. As an ad executive, not a television writer, Gart is asked to come up with creative ideas for a show, demonstrating how the advertising industry was increasingly dominating television programming. John E. Hasty, a film and television producer, matter-of-factly expressed this point of view, undoubtedly shared by countless sponsors: "TV viewers cannot be regarded as an audience to be entertained. . . . They are prospects . . . for what the sponsor has to sell. This fact constitutes the show's reason for being. . . . In a TV production the selling motive stands as the dominant factor."[18] It is not only a possibility that the creative aspects of television be used for selling, but an outright imperative of the medium, represented clearly in the dialogue between Gart and Misrell. Just as Gart's work in advertising did not offer much in the way of self-expression, it also limited the self-expression of television writers. Moreover, the simplistic depictions of family life on television only deepened the gulf between consumer imagery and lived realities. Watching serene families consuming modern products and amenities, television viewers were left to think commodities would solve their complex problems, not least of which was work-life balance.

Given his limited options and people to turn to, Gart's reliance on medication to deal with work-related anxiety speaks to the drastically increasing usage and mass-marketing of psychotropic drugs during the postwar era. As Andrea Tone's work has recently shown, pharmaceutical companies sought to fill the psychological needs created by this "pathology of success." And before drugs like valium were popularly considered "mother's little helpers," they were most frequently marketed to, and associated with, successful and stressed-out men—athletes, executives, and independent bachelors.[19] Calling attention to the price of success and achievement, ads emphasized how highly achieving men courted psychological stress, which prescription drugs could partially assuage. In 1968, one of the largest producers of psycho-pharmaceuticals, Roche Laboratories, published a manual, *Aspects of Anxiety,* which outlined some of the social issues that necessitated the use of their drugs. Like much of the marketing for many psychotropic drugs, Roche's manual emphasized a gendered treatment of stress and success: "Like women, men are under particularly heavy stress during periods of major adaptive efforts. For adult males, these typically include leaving the parental home, serving in the armed forces, marrying, becoming a father, getting ahead in business, growing older, and retiring. Men's problems, however, are com-pounded by an unspoken obligation to live up to society's concept of ideal masculinity. . . . Men—according to one point of view—dam up their feelings and develop ulcers and high blood pressure."[20] Gart, trapped in the social demands of marketing, reaches out for yet another mass-marketed consumer good—pharmaceuticals.

Although Gart finally escaped to Willoughby in his dream, the real-life consequences, seen in his actual death, illustrate the dangers of escapism. Attempting to escape to the romanticized, inner-directed world of the nine-teenth century proved impossible and a death sentence for Gart and postwar Americans alike. And while nostalgic and escapist portrayals of a bygone era abounded on television, as in consistently top-rating programs such as *Bonanza, Gunsmoke,* and *The Andy Griffith Show,* Serling reminds his audi-ence that it is gravely misguided to view such romanticized portrayals as actual escapes. *The Andy Griffith Show,* set in an oversimplified past, featured episodes such as "Andy's Rich Girlfriend," which grossly simplified the challenges associated with relationships and modern living (S3, e2). Much like Gart in *The Twilight Zone,* Andy yearns for the simple pleasures in life, while his girlfriend, Peg, comes from wealth and enjoys the finer things, such as fine dining, cocktails, and international travel. When Andy becomes con-vinced that they are incompatible because of these differences, he goes to a nearby lake to clear his head and skip rocks. To his surprise, he finds Peg there doing the exact same thing, and the two are reunited over the simple joy of skipping rocks.

Episodes like these romanticize the past, with its seemingly simple, wholesome lifestyles, and depict that life as a kind of "answer" to postwar anxieties. But the mere fact that these were television programs, necessitating modern technology to illustrate the days before TV as inherently better, only exacerbated the tensions of postwar living. That, coupled with the fact that all these programs promoted consumer goods via advertising as "the answers" to modern dilemmas, only deepened these socially pervasive cognitive dissonances. Caught between two dominant, discordant messages, viewers could find themselves filled with a great deal of confusion and tension. On the one hand, happiness meant modern amenities, suburban housing, and consumption; on the other, it actually meant returning to the simple unbought pleasures that characterized the days of yore. Americans could find themselves in a condition very similar to Gart's—working and living for the modern American Dream but fantasizing about a mythologized past and carrying a deep desire to escape, with no practical resolution in sight. This enormous gap between complex modern living and all-too-simple nostalgic prescriptions was filled mainly by pill-popping and pencil-tapping anxiety. Serling dramatically distilled this tension-packed psychological middle ground in "A Stop at Willoughby."

Rather than hold up an overly simplified past or a glorified present as the resolution for postwar Americans, Serling illustrated how pursuing either dream as an end in itself means sacrificing those abilities that enable people to experience fulfillment in real life—compromise and choice. As William Whyte stated:

> whatever kind of future suburbia may foreshadow, it will show that at least we have the choices to make. The organization man . . . must fight The Organization. Not stupidly, or selfishly, for the defects of individual self-regard are no more to be venerated than the defects of co-operation. . . . It is wretched, dispiriting advice to hold before him the dream that ideally there need be no conflict between him and society. There always is; there always must be. Ideology cannot wish it away; the peace of mind offered by organization remains a surrender, and no less so for being offered in benevolence. That is the problem.[21]

The problem that has no name, the problem of other-direction, the problem of the organization man, could only be realistically dealt with by making personal, relational, and social growth and expression more essential than pursuing or escaping to any commodified fantasy, past or present.

Life in Retail: "Ever So Much Fun"

Relatedly, the potential dangers of work serving as the means to purchase more consumer goods, rather than to achieve self-actualization, is explored in a number of other *Twilight Zone* episodes. "What You Need" tells the story of small-time crook Fred Renard and an elderly peddler named Pedott, who seems to know what people "need" before they do (S1, e12). Seeing Pedott's special abilities, Renard desperately pursues him. Ultimately, Pedott gives Renard a pair of slippery shoes, which he puts on, only to slip and fall in front of an oncoming car, showing that no matter what Pedott has, Pedott, as a vendor, is always going to be more concerned with his own gains more than Renard's or anyone else's. Here, the world of peddling on the street resembles the white-collar world of consumption, as marketers and manufacturers ultimately have their own interests in mind, even when they supposedly have what consumers and workers "need."

One of the most memorable episodes to deal with this topic was "The After Hours," first airing on Friday June 10, 1960 (S1, e34). It begins as many other *Twilight Zone* episodes, in an ordinary setting that television viewers undoubtedly could identify with: a department store. The show opens with a young, well-dressed woman named Marsha White, played by Anne Francis, perusing different items on the first floor of the store. After not finding anything, Marsha waits at the elevator along with several other shoppers. When one of the elevator doors opens, the operator looks at her and announces, "Going up, ma'am." Marsha steps on to the elevator and tells him what she is looking for—a gold thimble. He replies, "That would be specialties, ma'am. The ninth floor." As the elevator doors shut, the camera focuses on the numbered dial indicating the store's floor numbers. The elevator ascends, and the dial moves from the left to the right, but here the viewer notices a problem: the numbers only go up to eight, not nine. As the camera returns inside the elevator, Marsha somewhat bashfully states, "I'm not accustomed to such service. . . . Well, there were a whole lot of people waiting for the elevator. I seem to have a private one." The operator nonchalantly responds, "This is an express elevator to the ninth floor." The doors open, and Marsha steps out but is troubled to find nothing but bare display cases on a dark, empty floor. As she turns back toward the elevator, telling the attendant there must be some mistake, the doors are already closing. The worried look on her face is accompanied by the sound of eerie woodwinds and strings, along with Rod Serling's opening narration: "Express elevator to the ninth floor of a department

"I'm not accustomed to such service!" Marsha White ascends an express elevator to the ninth floor. Still from "The After Hours" (2:14)

store, carrying Miss Marsha White on a most prosaic, ordinary, run-of-the-mill errand. Miss Marsha White on the ninth floor, specialty department, looking for a gold thimble. The odds are that she'll find it—but there are even better odds that she'll find something else, because this isn't just a department store. This happens to be *The Twilight Zone*."

Now on the ninth floor, Marsha wanders past the empty display cases as a saleswoman asks, "Can I show you something?" After Marsha explains she is looking for a gold thimble, the saleswoman walks her over to a display case that holds only a single gold thimble. After paying for it, Marsha stops in her tracks and declares, "Now that's odd . . . you haven't any merchandise here at all except the thimble. Except the very thing I needed. . . . Well you may be a little more sophisticated than I am, but this I call odd." However, she finds not just this feature of her shopping excursion odd, but the entire interaction with the saleswoman. After the store representative calls Marsha by her name, unnerving her further, she proceeds to ask if she is happy. "I beg your pardon? . . . Am . . . am I what? Am I happy? Well you'll forgive me, but that's

"I think we have something you'd like." The saleswoman shows Marsha the only piece of merchandise on the ninth floor: a gold thimble. Still from "The After Hours" (4:07)

really none of your business." The saleswoman laughingly replies, "Well suit yourself; it's none of my business!"

Disoriented, Marsha steps onto the elevator, only to find that the thimble is scratched. After the elevator operator tells Marsha where she can return it, she goes to speak with the store's managers. When they instruct her to return the item to the gifts department, which sells thimbles, Marsha retorts, "I did not purchase this in the gift department. I was taken up to the ninth floor." The manager replies, "That's what makes it so difficult to understand. You see, we don't have a ninth floor." When they ask if she has a receipt, she realizes she did not get one during the hurried, nervous exchange. As she looks across the storeroom, she notices the saleswoman who waited on her. The only problem is—she is a mannequin, and this causes Marsha to instantly faint from shock.

Having collapsed, Marsha falls asleep on the sofa in the manager's office. When she comes to, the store is closed and every customer and employee has left. Frightened all the more, Marsha frantically looks for an escape. She heads toward one of the doors, walking uncomfortably in her heels as the camera focuses in on her wobbly legs and feet. She bangs repeatedly on the obscure glass of one of the doors and cries out for help, but there is no reply. She soon becomes spooked to tears after she hears voices, apparently coming from the store's many mannequins, calling her name over and over. The camera quickly cuts among the many mannequin faces as they say, "Marsha. You remember Marsha, Marsha, climb off it. Come on, dear. Marsha, Marsha. Come on, dear. We know who you are. Marsha, Marsha. Climb off it." Overwhelmed and frightened by this barrage of voices, Marsha retreats into the elevator, which takes her back up to the ninth floor.

When the elevator doors open, the saleswoman mannequin who had waited on her earlier is waiting for her, which frightens her to tears. As the mannequin suddenly comes to life and approaches to console her, she states: "You'll forgive an observation, but you're acting like a silly child." She takes the whimpering Marsha by the hand, walking her slowly back into the ninth floor, with mannequins all around. As the two women walk across the room, each of the other mannequins slowly comes to life and follows them, forming a circle around Marsha and the saleswoman. The salesclerk tells her, "Think now. Concentrate. Remember now? All of us will help you. Coming back to you?" Marsha, whose tears now have subsided, thinks for a moment, "I'm a mannequin!" The saleswoman explains that each mannequin has a month off for leisure time and that this had been Marsha's month, and it ended yesterday. As the saleslady walks toward the elevator for her own month off one of the other mannequins turns to Marsha and asks, "Did you enjoy yourself, Marsha? Was it fun?" She looks forlornly down at her hands, locking them into a mannequin pose, "Ever so much. Ever so much fun." As the camera zooms out, Serling closes his episode with an appeal to viewers to question the seemingly normal and predictable nature of postwar American life: "Marsha White, in her normal and natural state—a wooden lady with a painted face, who one month out of the year takes on the characteristics of someone as normal and flesh and blood as you and I. But it makes you wonder, doesn't it, just how normal are we? Just who are the people we nod our hellos to as we pass on the street. A rather good question to ask, particularly in *The Twilight Zone*."

In unforgettable fashion, "The After Hours" dramatizes many peculiarities of postwar retail work, consumption, and merchandising. That the episode primarily revolves around Marsha's interest in finding a gold thimble is particularly instructive. The mere fact that she is looking not just for a basic, functional thimble but one that is gold, a soft but expensive metal, illustrates that this is a luxury good, not one born out of basic necessity. And while

"Remember now? Coming back to you?" After being trapped in the store, Marsha reunites with her fellow mannequins. Still from "The After Hours" (20:09)

luxury items were nothing new, the mass market for luxury goods and the ability for an ever-increasing middle class to purchase them, indicated in Serling's description of the errand as prosaic, was largely unprecedented. The thimble's luxury, rather than utility, is further emphasized when Marsha takes the elevator back down and discovers a cosmetic scratch on the thimble and states she can no longer send it to her mother. What ultimately matters is the item's luxurious appearance, not its usefulness. Louis Cheskin, a prominent marketing researcher, captured this essential aspect of postwar consumerism: "In earlier years, consumption was mainly of a biological and material nature; in our present society of abundance, consumption is largely psychological. Eating . . . fills a biological need. Steak provides psychological satisfaction."[22] The gold thimble proves even more luxurious than steak, as one gains no physical sustenance from it, only psychological satisfaction. One of the psychological satisfactions for Marsha is ostensibly to show herself to be a loving, thoughtful daughter, something that consumer products, particularly of the luxury sort, promised to do. As one department store report claimed, in regard to selling products to housewives: "Take every opportunity to explain how your store will help her fulfill her most cherished roles in life."[23] The thimble also represents perfectly something marketers frequently tapped into, namely that "people readily accept something new about the old."[24] The thimble, which has been around for centuries, symbolizes tradition and history, on the one hand, and a mass modern consumer culture, on the other, as it is available at large department stores. Furthermore, it represents a task once performed by hand, sewing, that is now an artifact of the past.

If the shopping excursion embodied the ubiquity of mass luxury and the fact that consumerism offered a means for a woman to prove her affection to her loved ones, another crucial aspect of Marsha White's errand is its eerie predetermined or fatalistic nature. The elevator she boards is exclusively for the ninth floor, a fact she was unaware of initially. The bizarre realization that the operator knew where Marsha wanted to go before she even said anything to him is built up by her mentioning an advertisement for the thimble. Her destination and errand seem first shaped by the advertisement and then by the elevator operator, who knew already that the gold thimble must be what she wants. Finally, when Marsha arrives on the ninth floor, the journey reeking of consumerist predestination intensifies as the only object on the entire floor is a single gold thimble. Marsha's entire journey from the advertisement to the elevator to the checkout counter seemed too preordained for her liking, and she felt perhaps what Vance Packard lamented in *The Hidden Persuaders,* that marketing manipulation invaded the privacy of one's own mind.[25] Marsha's mind, her desires, and even her choice to spend her day shopping appeared not under her own control but merely results of sly marketing and salesmanship. As the marketing researcher Ernest Dichter explained, many people are "more afraid of what to do with the four empty leisure days than . . . three workdays."[26] Through advertisements and sales, marketers happily assuaged this fear for millions of Americans just like Marsha.

Marsha, descending toward the ground floor, discovers that the thimble she purchased is scratched: capturing another feature of postwar consumerism, the faulty thimble shows how the planned obsolescence of quality shaped the manufacturing and selling of home goods. Acknowledging that durable, high-quality products will not bring American shoppers back to the stores, many companies deliberately set "death dates" for their wares, making their repair or replacement an inevitability. While the fashion and automobile industries had already implemented such tactics, home goods proved slightly more challenging to market in this way, as manufacturers found that their customers expected their housewares to be more permanent than a lot of other consumer goods. Among the many iterations of this concept, the business journal *Dun's Review and Modern Industry* ran an article in its February 1959 issue titled "Planned Obsolescence: Rx for Tired Markets?" Its author, Martin Mayer, wrote: "The more durable the item, the more slowly it will be consumed. . . . It is clear that a pattern of successful style of obsolescence must eventually be reinforced by a decrease in the durability of the product." When defective products were returned, they were often repaired and resold on clearance or during special sales.[27]

While marketers wanted to appeal to consumers through emotionally charged advertisements, Marsha's act of consumption exemplifies the opposite of what Dichter expressed about advertising: "When writing a communication, whether on safety or on products, or when preparing a television commercial, it is very important the most pregnant moment be chosen in illustrating the action and the drama of possession."[28] For Marsha, the "drama of possession" proves to actually be deflating and disappointing, running counter also to Louis Cheskin's thoughts: "Why make handles on cups so that they won't break off? Who wants to pay ten percent more for dishes so that dishes will last a lifetime? Most housewives want or welcome an excuse to buy a new set of dishes every year or so. . . . Furniture, clothes, dishes can all be made to last longer at very little additional cost. But neither the maker nor the consumer is interested in this."[29] Marsha, though, is interested in giving her mother a decent gift, but the drama of possession and planned obsolescence will not just frustrate her ability to do this, it will even deny her the possibility of leaving the store.

When Marsha asks the elevator operator to look at the faulty product, he apathetically responds that complaints are on the third floor. Here, Serling exposes another defect of postwar consumerism: its increasingly impersonal bureaucratization. Marsha purchases the thimble from a saleswoman who did not make the item and arguably did not even really sell it to her, as the advertisement and the anonymous individuals who created the flyers performed that task. Marsha then has to attempt to return it to another representative on an entirely different floor. She rides an elevator operated by a listless gentleman whose singular and extremely limited cog-in-the-wheel role is unmistakable due to his hat and jacket, which both simply read, "Elevator." So Marsha is disturbed by not just her faulty item but all of her exchanges with the store's staff, illustrating the psychological divide between consumer and seller.

This division is made more evident as one of the floor managers proclaims, "Tell her to come back tomorrow, and we'll get her a replacement of her merchandise or refund or anything else she wants. What I'd like to give her is a bus ticket. A one-way bus ticket to any department store west of Cleveland, preferably Chicago or Los Angeles or Honolulu!" Retail workers who are obligated to cater to customers all day feel not actual affection toward those customers but resentfulness and bitterness, which becomes evident in exchanges like the floor manager's. While consumer goods and department stores promise happiness, there is no real interest in achieving it, except to ensure that the customer believes that the store really is interested in their satisfaction, in the hopes of them coming back again for more. "Please come again, anytime," the clerk says. In fact, a purchased product that proves unsatisfactory or unfulfilling can very likely bring a customer back in the store again in search of something adequate. Just three years after this episode aired, these ideas were articulated in Friedan's *The Feminine Mystique,* which cited a department store report that pronounced its purpose "was not only to sell the housewife but to satisfy . . . the yearning she has . . . to feel herself a part of the changing world. The store will sell her more . . . if it will understand that the real need she is trying to fill by shopping is not anything she can buy there."[30] For Marsha White, satisfaction seems ever elusive.

The eerie turning point of "The After Hours" features a saleswoman who turns out to be a mannequin, serving as a metaphor for the dehumanizing and self-alienating nature of white-collar, wage-labor work, as well as the consumer experience. The sales lady represents to a large degree what C. Wright Mills described in his 1951 book *White Collar:* "One knows the salesclerk not as a person but as a commercial mask, a stereotyped greeting and appreciation for patronage . . . with anonymous sincerity the successful person makes an instrument of his [or her] own appearance and personality."[31] This is illustrated most clearly in the saleslady's exchange with Marsha, as the saleslady knows Marsha but Marsha does not know her. Throughout the entire episode, the audience never learns the name of either the saleswoman or the elevator operator, further illustrating the anonymity and lack of individuality department store workers have.

Moreover, the attributes of the saleswoman—her sophisticated clothing, speech, and mannerisms—all become part of the sale of products and business of the store. Her attire, physique, and demeanor are no longer her own, but they now belong to the store in which she is employed and to her work toward making her commission. As Mills writes: "the one area of her occupational life in which she might be free to act, the area of her own personality must now also be managed" and becomes the "instrument by which goods are distributed."[32] Skill and experience become secondary to the importance of appearance and the ability to perform superficial, predictable social niceties with customers as a retail worker. The department store employee is unable to authentically connect with customers because they are forbidden to be themselves and instead must become only nameless representatives of sophisticated consumerism ready to verbalize polite clichés. The focus on personality, charm, and beauty consequently creates tension-filled interactions where a remnant of distrust is always present. Marsha, even though she finds what she was looking for, is left with an unsettling feeling about her purchase and exchange with the saleswoman.

The focus on appearance and the marketability of the self along with the product became a chief component of both sales and even politics in postwar America, which several historians have recognized. Perhaps less self-evident, however, is the way these tactics undermine the gospel of American ingenuity and hard work. A nation increasingly dominated by marketing and salesmanship ethics is one that undervalues hard-won experience and even basic knowledge of products and business practices. Vice President Richard Nixon perhaps most clearly and publicly embodied this in his 1959 Kitchen Debate with Nikita Khrushchev, as he married consumer chic, female opportunity, and American politics. Just as Nixon promoted color televisions and washing machines in Moscow, the best merchants of shirts were no longer tailors or even designers but people completely divorced from the processes of making the product they sold.

However, far from being an amateurish, naive way of doing business or promoting the American way of life, this tactic was firmly grounded in marketing through motivational research. Throughout the 1950s and 1960s, psychologists such as Ernest Dichter and Louis Cheskin were busily uncovering the great extent to which consumers purchase products not out of rational calculation but for subconscious and emotional reasons. Their research helped formulate innumerable ad campaigns, including Marlboro cigarettes and Ford Mustangs, which appealed not to function but to displays of virility. Thus, the salesrooms and employees of department stores, not to mention diplomatic visits to the USSR, began embodying the psychological depth approach marketers had been employing. The appeals made not to a product's efficacy, durability, technicality, and reliability but to its promise of fulfilling a psychological need or weakness had begun to pervade ads, in-store discussions, and political debate. In other words, a saleslady, just like an ad in a magazine, needed to sell the more dreamlike qualities of sophistication, elegance, and luxury, not the thimble, for these are customers' true desires. "It's quite distinctive looking, I think. Don't you?" she says to Marsha. Just as the best salespeople sell a dream and not a product, they also become dreamlike, nebulous mixtures of warm, comforting personalities and appealing physiques. As Henri Bergson claimed: "The greater part of our time we live outside ourselves, hardly perceiving anything of ourselves but our own ghost, a colorless shadow. . . . We live for the external world rather than for ourselves; we speak rather than think; we are acted rather than act ourselves."[33] The world of consumption both in and out of *The Twilight Zone* was one filled with hazy persons.

When Marsha eventually finds herself alone in a department store, concealed behind the obscure glass, the audience can only come to one conclusion: she is indeed trapped. She is confined behind the glass of a department store, a confinement that eerily resembles the encasement of a Barbie Doll behind clear plastic. Not more than one year before the episode aired, in fact, Barbie was released in the United States and promoted by an ad that crooned the lyrics, "Barbie, you're beautiful, you make me feel . . . my Barbie Doll is really real." Marsha, even physically resembles Barbie, and she shares another feature with the doll: it became one of the first toys that was a consumer itself—Barbie could be dressed in a variety of different outfits and accessorized with jewelry pieces. Marsha White's confinement was complete. From her destabilizing high-heeled shoes to her idealized beauty, she was trapped inside the store that helps to promote all these constricting ideals within the restraining world of manufactured consumer desire.

In the end, Marsha's small glimpse into being something more than just a mannequin laborer proved only a tease, as, with little struggle, she returns to her spot on the floor as a display model. In many ways, her character embodies Theodor Adorno's declaration that the "repetitiveness, the selfsameness, and the ubiquity of modern mass culture tend to make for automatized reactions and to weaken the forces of individual resistance."[34] Marsha, like so many television viewers, glimpses a world beyond, only to return to her routinized life. Here again, "The After Hours" employs fantasy to comment on how wage-labor work, not to mention salaried work, involves the granting of vacation time to employees. For Marsha White it is no different, as she works as a store mannequin and is allotted a certain amount of free time. In this life, a kind of self-alienation can take place, however, as C. Wright Mills explains: "Each day men sell little pieces of themselves in order to try to buy them back each night and week end with the coin of fun. With amusement, with love, with movies, with vicarious intimacy, they pull themselves into some sort of whole again. . . . Thus the cycle of work and leisure gives rise to two quite different images of the self: the everyday image, based upon work, and the holiday image, based upon leisure."[35] For Mills, the work-leisure cycle creates two distinct personalities. Marsha White forgets her work self, consumed by her leisure time and mindset. For Serling, the work-consumer cycle blurs the lines between these two identities, as a number of department store employees, many of them middle-class men and women, worked for a supplementary income, not out of sheer necessity but for the ability to consume more products. *The Twilight Zone* takes this one step further, as an advertisement drew Marsha back to the very store where she works. Through *Twilight Zone* fantasy, Serling blurs the lines between mannequin and human just as the lines between work and consumption were in consumer America. We work to buy, and we buy where we work.

As consumers and worker-objects in a rapidly expanding economy, Americans became part of an increasingly blurry world of power relations and marketing. While Serling does not offer a clear solution or sales pitch, mass-marketing that depicted misleadingly clear and simple solutions was a fundamental part of the problem in the first place. The sense of self and community, frequently sacrificed for white-collar positions that promised to, above all, enhance one's ability to consume, were depicted as not necessarily worth surrendering. While Gart and Marsha felt dehumanizing pressure to fit into their respective molds, nonwhite Americans would be pressured to give up that much more of their authentic selves and identities—needing to conform to white ideals of personality, behavior, fashion, and professionalism in the workplace. White-collar employment was significantly less racially diverse than other lines of work—including agricultural jobs, domestic work, and various forms of manual labor—and the professional standards set in white-collar spaces were just that: white. While the loneliness and self-alienation experienced by so many white-collar workers was largely justified by the increased amount of purchasing power and the ability to consume, the commodities one gained by sacrificing one's sense of self and community were frequently remnants of nostalgic remorse. Like Marsha and Gart, Americans could use their leisure time to locate pieces of a lost world full of abandoned identities—a gold thimble, a coonskin cap, or a television show that romantically portrayed the simple lifestyles of a bygone era. Perhaps viewers of *The Twilight Zone* could retain something more than a mass-marketed trinket that at once played on a collective nostalgia for the past and continually alienated people from the possibilities of the present. Maybe the white-collar nightmares of *The Twilight Zone* could restore the possibilities of self-expression, identity, and community to those still living, and perhaps a few would even conclude that the idealistic dreams of white-collar employ were not what they wanted for themselves.

Consuming Conformity

The Planned Obsolescence of Selfhood in Postwar America's Marketplace

Arguably no element was as vital to the postwar American Dream as consumer culture. In Lizabeth Cohen's words, which also served as her book title, postwar America was, foremost, a consumer's republic. Cohen's work demonstrates how after World War II "the purchaser as citizen" emerged as one who "simultaneously fulfilled personal desire and civic obligation by consuming."[1] Following the war, several pieces of policy helped lay the groundwork for this dominant trend, beginning with the Servicemen's Readjustment Act of 1944 (the GI Bill). This bill helped to transform veterans into suburban residents who commuted to work in newly purchased automobiles in the morning and returned to homes full of consumer goods at night. In unprecedented ways, the American economy was tied to consumerism, as policies such as the Employment Act of 1946 prioritized and enhanced Americans' purchasing power in the decades to come. In addition, the Federal Housing Administration's postwar mortgage financing program granted increasingly affordable loans for millions of Americans to purchase houses in the suburbs, just as the Federal Highway Act of 1956 boosted, and all but guaranteed, the essential role automobiles would continue to play in the lives of Americans. In a myriad of ways, postwar public policy consistently lined up with the thinking in *Brides* magazine, that "what you buy and how you buy . . . is very vital in your new life—and to our whole American way of living."[2] The inarguable point was the imperative need for both the individual and society to define one's life through consumption. And as consumer culture became more inextricably connected to the American way of life than ever before, Vice President Richard Nixon sought to impress his Soviet audience in the 1959 Kitchen Debate the best way he knew how: with color televisions and household appliances.

While Nixon's performance at the debate emphasized the superiority of the American way of life because of the availability of consumer goods and purchasing power, Serling encouraged his viewers to be more critical of these dominant assumptions; he specifically illustrated how consumer purchases actually blurred, not asserted, individual power. Just as money was exchanged for goods, control was being exchanged as well, and because this power exchange was largely subconscious, it was perfectly suited for *The Twilight Zone*. The oft-used term alone, "purchasing power," intrinsically connected, and even equated, the ability to purchase with power. In several different episodes, though, Serling illustrated how postwar consumer comforts could in reality disempower individuals and limit human agency and health. Just as Ernest Dichter claimed objects had souls and humanlike qualities, humans, conversely, could be increasingly objectlike in both physical and grammatical senses of the word—they were not just being increasingly objectified but were also the reactive and/or passive objects, playing a secondary role to consumer trends and marketing tactics. As Serling demonstrates, consumer products frequently tapped into human minds more effectively than human minds could manage the unprecedented flood of consumer goods.

By looking at the pieces of the American Dream one supposedly needed the most—consumer goods, suburban living, beauty products, et cetera—Serling critically showed how these things all came at a cost that was perhaps not always worth paying for both the individual and society. Although touted as such, the elements that made up the American Dream were not the simplistic panaceas their popular portrayals made them appear to be. Instead, the power and insidious pressure to purchase could actually rob a person of their sense of individuality, not provide it. And while marketers like Dichter thrived in this hazy world that made it increasingly difficult to distinguish power relations between goods and people, Serling showed the social costs Americans needed to consider.

Handsome, Pretty, and Happy

On January 24, 1964, *The Twilight Zone*'s "Number 12 Looks Just Like You" aired on CBS (S5, e17). This episode dealt with the superficiality and conformity promoted by the marketplace, particularly with regard to definitions of beauty and was far from the only episode to explore such subject matter. "Eye of the Beholder" flips the concept of beauty on its head: at the end of the episode a woman forced to undergo cosmetic surgery is revealed to be healthy and physically attractive (S2, e6). Meanwhile, the faces of the doctors and nurses performing the procedure, which remained hidden throughout most of the episode, are revealed to be piglike. The episode concludes with the woman's banishment from society because she cannot physically conform. Similarly, "The Masks," which takes place in New Orleans during Mardi Gras, features family members visiting their ailing grandfather (S5, e25). Knowing his relatives are largely there not to offer him love and support but to take his money, he forces them to all wear masks he has designed, which they do reluctantly. After he dies, and the family members are free to take off their uncomfortable masks, their faces are permanently deformed, physical reflections of their shallowness and distorted priorities. Finally, "The Trade-Ins" tells the story of an elderly couple looking to be young again (S3, e31). When they realize they only have enough money for one of them to undergo a procedure that will allow them to do so, they decide to remain their elderly selves, electing not to restore their bodies but the youth-giving love they have shared. In these episodes, *The Twilight Zone* consistently illustrates that human beauty is achieved not through materialism or by physically conforming to the standards promoted by consumer culture but in embracing individuality, aging, and imperfection.

"Number 12 Looks Just Like You" begins with a mother and daughter sitting in a large waiting room. Above them hang two large portraits of models simply labeled "12" and "8," with the mother bearing striking resemblance to "12." Clearly, this is not an average waiting room for a family doctor; rather, it is at an institute that performs complete physical transformations. And instead of magazines to peruse, awaiting patients are surrounded by large pictures of models, possible options for one's new face and body. As the daughter sits looking at an old photo album, the mother, whose nametag identifies her as "Lana," says, "I can't decide. Eight or twelve. I think twelve might suit you better. What do you think, Marilyn?" Her daughter, however, is immersed in the photo album. Lana, confused by Marilyn's apparent lack of interest, says most girls "are thrilled to death when it comes time to pick a pattern," recalling how she was so excited she could not even sleep for several nights prior to her transformation. Walking over to Marilyn, Lana sees that the old family photo album has a picture of Lana before the operation. Ashamed of her old self, Lana says, "I was a sight, wasn't I?" Marilyn explains that she thinks her mother was beautiful. When she bashfully asks her mom, "Am I very homely now?" Lana tells her that after the operation she will be "beautiful." Marilyn's apprehension becomes more apparent as she asks if she would still have to undergo the operation if she really does not want it. Lana

"I finally chose number twelve. . . . It's everybody's favorite." Lana fondly recalls undergoing the transformation while her daughter, Marilyn, shows more interest in an old photo album. Still from "Number 12 Looks Just Like You" (0:35)

tries to quiet her doubts, exclaiming that the "transformation is the most wonderful thing that could happen to a person!" Detecting her daughter's anxiety, she says, "Don't worry darling, you're just nervous. What you need is a glass of instant smile!" After she rings a buzzer, a maid arrives, and Lana requests two glasses of "instant smile." While they wait for their drinks, Lana asks, "What's so terrible about being beautiful? After all, isn't everybody?" As Lana admires the models' pictures, Marilyn forlornly gazes at her mother, and Rod Serling introduces the episode: "Given the chance, what young girl wouldn't happily exchange a plain face for a lovely one? What girl could refuse the opportunity to be beautiful? For want of a better estimate, let's call it the year 2000. At any rate, imagine a time in the future when science has developed a means of giving everyone the face and body he dreams of. It may not happen tomorrow, but it happens now . . . in *The Twilight Zone.*"

As the episode returns, Marilyn's uncle Rick, who bears striking resemblance to a Ken Doll, arrives to discuss the transformation. Marilyn tells him, "I don't want to be transformed. I want to stay ugly," with a defiant smirk. Rick responds that he does not think she is ugly but just "different." They sit down as Rick reminisces about how Marilyn's deceased father once went through the operation. "Number seventeen, just like you," she responds, referring to the model he chose. Rick proudly claims that it is "a very popular number these days" and her father "wouldn't have settled for anything less." Marilyn remains unconvinced, though and earnestly asks, "Yes, but is that good? Being like everybody? I mean, isn't that the same as being nobody?" Rick takes a deep breath and asks where she is getting these "radical ideas." But when she begins to talk about her dad again, he quickly interjects, "Your dad was a handsome man!" While Marilyn politely agrees, she adds that he also thought about things and read books, telling her uncle, "We talked a lot. Just the two of us . . . about real things. Not just about electronic baseball or super soccer, and where to buy your clothes, or how to fix your hair . . . there's got to be more to life than just that." Unmoved by her warm memories, Rick says, "You know what I think? You don't feel very well. What you need is a nice cup of instant smile." His niece roundly objects and explains how she does not feel like smiling all the time but sometimes wants to cry or frown. In response, Rick tenderly places his hands on her shoulders and says, "Marilyn, you are a very sick girl."

In the next scene, one of Marilyn's friends, Val, who has already undergone transformation, tries to assuage her nerves: "Don't you think you're being awfully silly? . . . it isn't as if it hurts or anything. When I did mine, I didn't feel a thing. . . . You like the way I look don't you? It's like getting a new hairstyle or new clothes or something. You just look better." Marilyn, says that she will merely look like "one of those drawings the bureau sends over" and no one will see her or know her for who she really is. Despite concerted efforts by her mother, uncle, and friend to convince her to undergo the operation, Marilyn remains firm in her convictions.

At a loss as to what to do for her daughter, Lana takes Marilyn to see the doctor. His name, Rex, reflects his ominous social power. Initially, he assumes the eighteen-year-old Marilyn is eager and wants to have the operation even sooner than the normal age, which is nineteen. Holding his pinky toward his mouth, the doctor explains, "Marilyn is just like the rest of them nowadays. . . . You see she looks at you, Lana, and all the women around her at the pictures, and then she looks at herself in the mirror. . . . From pure perfection of body, face, limb, pigmentation, stance, carriage, she looks at herself and she's horrified. . . . The child says to herself, 'Why should I be so hideous, so awkward, oversized, unbalanced . . . ?' In short, Lana, our Marilyn is tired of being a monster." After Rex finishes pontificating, Lana finally has a chance to tell him

"Don't you think you're being awfully silly?" Val ridicules Marilyn for being resistant to the transformation. Still from "Number 12 Looks Just Like You" (6:25)

the real reason for their visit—Marilyn actually does not want the operation at all. When Rex says the operation is merely "part of growing up" and a "sign of maturity," Marilyn asks: "What? Being like everyone else?" Intrigued by her resistance, Rex asks her if he can take a brain scan. Sitting back down at his desk, he asks Marilyn about her father: "Did he ever say to you that the transformation was bad?" "No, . . . he thought it was tragic," she replies. Lana explains to the doctor that while her husband had some "non-conformist ideas . . . it was just talk." After Marilyn asks if she could be forced to undergo the operation against her will, Rex explains that no one who did not want the operation has been forced to go through it. He adds, however, that the "problem is simply to discover why you don't want it, and then to make the necessary corrections." Recognizing the sinister meaning behind these words, Marilyn is left speechless, as the sound of timpani signals the unyielding march of fate for Marilyn.

To discover just what is ailing her, making her want to remain "ugly," Marilyn visits another doctor, "Sigmund Friend," an obvious allusion to the father of psychoanalysis. Referring to himself as Professor Sig, he tells Marilyn that he needs to find out what is at the root of her fear. He then describes the noble origins of the socially prescribed transformation, which also seems to have deep racial implications: "Many years ago, wiser men than I decided to try and eliminate the reasons for inequality and injustice in this world of ours. They saw in physical unattractiveness one of the factors which made men hate. So, they charged the finest scientific minds with the task of eliminating ugliness in mankind." Marilyn, who also lacks "ideal" beauty, humbly responds that while she may not be pretty, she is not ugly either, causing Professor Sig to laugh and explain that she is ugly to everyone who has had the operation. "Not to people who love me," Marilyn retorts. Sig expounds on the benefits of the operation as not just beautifying people but also prolonging their lives. He says Marilyn's mother, for example, would already be showing signs of aging and wrinkling, had she not undergone transformation many years ago. After Marilyn declares once more that she does not want the operation, Sig gives up for the moment and finally asks her why. "Have you ever read Shakespeare . . . or Keats or Shelley?" Marilyn asks. Puzzled, the professor says how those authors were banned long ago and asks where she found them. She explains that her father gave their works to her, along with those of Aristotle, Socrates, and Dostoevsky: "Did you know that Dostoevsky was an epileptic? He was ugly, he was deformed, but he wrote about beauty, about real beauty. . . . These men wrote about life and about the dignity of the individual human spirit and about love!" Having heard enough from his unruly patient, Sig demands Marilyn to cease: "The introduction of smut into this interview will not help your case . . . not at all!" After she asks to leave, Marilyn discovers she has to stay overnight in a special room reserved just for her.

The next day, when Lana and Val come to visit her, the doctor explains that Marilyn was "quite upset" the previous night and he opted to give her "a mild sedative" to help her relax. Once he leaves the room, Marilyn says she knows the doctor is going to force her to undergo the operation. Her mother, however, still confused by her daughter's resistance, says, "I just don't see why you're so unhappy when all they want to do is make you pretty." Her daughter responds that the procedure is less about making everyone beautiful and more about making everyone the same. As Lana leaves the room, Val stays behind and asks Marilyn why she puts so much weight on her father's words and memory: "I don't see why you're so concerned about him. He's dead. I mean, surely, you've had other fathers. My mother's been married eleven times and, personally, I've liked the stepfathers better anyway. . . . I know

"And the nicest part of all, Val, I look just like you!" Marilyn admires her transformed self in the mirror as the others look on approvingly. Still from "Number 12 Looks Just Like You" (23:54)

you've had nine fathers since the first one. Everybody marries everybody these days. . . . I just don't see how anybody can stay married to the same husband for a hundred years. And besides, I've heard your father was pretty dull." Infuriated, Marilyn gets out of bed and orders Val to stop talking about him: "Can't anybody understand? I loved him! I cared about him! He was good, and he was kind, and he cared about me, not what I wore, not the way I looked, but what I thought, what I felt. And what's more important, he cared about himself and his dignity as a human being. Valerie, he didn't die in the Ganymede incident. My father killed himself because when they took away his identity he had no reason to go on living. . . . Valerie, can't you feel anything?" But her friend only responds that she feels good, always feels good, and that "life is pretty, life is fun, I am all, and all is one!" Exhaling in disbelief, Marilyn breaks into tears, exclaiming hysterically, "They can't understand! They can't understand! They can't understand!" Disturbed by Marilyn's display of emotion, Val dismisses herself and leaves Marilyn to cry on her own.

In the next scene, Marilyn attempts to escape. Running down the sterile, gray hallway, she backs into one of the rooms, only to find Doctor Rex and his assistant waiting for her: "We've been expecting you. . . . Sooner or later everyone wants to be beautiful. . . . She's chosen number eight! Excellent!" The three of them approach the operating table, Marilyn's worst fears now painfully coming to pass. When the procedure is completed, Marilyn emerges to meet her mother and Val. Completely transformed and bubbling with excitement, Marilyn rushes over to the mirror to look at herself: "The nicest part of all, Val, I look just like you!" As she stands, admiring her new, beautiful body and face in the looking glass, Serling makes his closing remarks: "Portrait of a young lady in love . . . with herself. Improbable? Perhaps. But in an age of plastic surgery, body-building, and an infinity of cosmetics, let us hesitate to say impossible. These and other strange blessings may be waiting in the future, which, after all, is *The Twilight Zone.*"

"Number 12 Looks Just Like You" captures several important developments in postwar America, including the burgeoning market for cosmetics and pharmaceuticals and the increasing popularity of cosmetic surgery. On the surface, it seemed that science, technology, and consumerism all now offered the public unprecedented access to ideals of beauty. Nature and genetics no longer had the final word, but a market increasingly filled with products to make one beautiful seemingly was "democratizing" physical beauty. This episode also captures the fact that the market for cosmetic beauty products and ideals was no longer strictly for women—they were being increasingly marketed to men as well. The emphasis on artificial physical beauty and fake smiles as the keys to achieving happiness fit comfortably within the postwar consumer economy, which was always looking for something new to sell and promise potential customers. As Vance Packard pointed out in his exposé of the ad industry, *Hidden Persuaders,* cosmetic companies knew they could make even more money off cosmetic products such as creams and lotions than they could off of soap because these products promised beauty, not just cleanliness.[3] The socially constructed and consumer-driven promise that physical beauty would bring individual happiness is inspected in this episode to form yet another *Twilight Zone* nightmare for postwar Americans.

In the opening scene, as Marilyn expresses her apprehension about the operation, her mother recommends a glass of "instant smile," a clear metaphor for psychotropic medication. During the fifties and sixties, a wide variety of psychotropics began to flood the marketplace, beginning with the introduction of Miltown. This new pill quickly gained popularity among celebrities who used it to calm their nerves and relax during their stress-filled schedules. As one Hollywood insider mentioned, "If there's anything this movie business needs, it's a little tranquility. . . . Once you're big enough to be 'somebody' in filmtown, you've just got to be knee-deep in tension and mental and emotional stress. The anxiety of trying to make it to the top is replaced by the anxiety of wondering if you're going to stay there. So, big names and little alike have been loading their trusty pillboxes with this little wonder tablet."[4] Miltown, or the "don't-give-a-darn pill," was used and openly praised by the likes of Judy Garland, Milton Berle, Tennessee Williams, Jimmy Durante, Aldous Huxley, Jerry Lewis, and Norman Mailer, among countless others. As historian Andrea Tone has noted, "Hollywood entertainment culture transformed a pharmaceutical concoction into a celebrity fetish, a coveted commodity of the fad-prone glamour set."[5]

The drug's booming popularity, however, actually troubled Frank Berger, one of its chief creators, as well as many other doctors. In response, in December 1956, the New York Academy of Medicine's Subcommittee on Tranquilizing Drugs issued a report that stated, "Anxiety and tension seem to abound in our modern culture and the current trend is to escape the unpleasantness of its impact. . . . But when has life ever been exempt from stress? In the long run is it desirable that a population be ever free from tension? Should there be a pill for every mood or occasion?"[6] These growing concerns over popular obsession with these new antianxiety drugs were further justified when Marilyn Monroe was found dead with lethal levels of barbiturates in her blood on August 4, 1962, in her home in Brentwood, California. Barbiturates, once given to American soldiers in the Pacific and described by the *New York Times* as "more of a menace to society than heroin or morphine," were designated as a controlled substance under the Controlled Substances Act of 1970.[7]

In the 1960s, however, another drug overshadowed Miltown and barbiturates: benzodiazepines. Among the most popular forms of the drug were Hoffman-Laroche Laboratory's Librium and Valium, which became known as "mother's little helpers" because by the late sixties housewives had become their popularized users. While these pills were not nearly as hazardous as barbiturates, consumers were mostly left to discover the potential side effects for themselves, including impotence, addiction, and severe withdrawal symptoms.[8] In 1975, Valium was classified as a controlled substance, and patients were limited to five refills before having to again consult a physician. However, as Andrea Tone has pointed out, "tranquilizer users were no less at the mercy of manufacturers' claims and doctors' ignorance than they had been for decades." That education regarding the drugs was still not sufficiently provided for the drug-taking public under these new regulations somewhat guaranteed the continued ignorance of users. There followed a psychotropic flood, coupled with a public education famine.

This relative lack of education regarding psychotropic drugs was just part of the general public's illiteracy regarding health. In a variety of ways, dominant messages in popular culture and advertising dovetailed to encourage hypercritical, perpetual dissatisfaction with one's own body. The result—an increasingly dominant, yet relatively unexamined belief, that beauty is a commodity one purchases on the market—carried tremendous profit potential. The supposedly ideal images of beauty typically carried racial and ethnic components as well. The early-twentieth-century African American entrepreneur Madam C. J. Walker illustrated how one could make a fortune from beauty and hair products which helped "remove or modify Negroid characteristics." And as E. Franklin Frazier explained, such products were featured in ads that explicitly promised consumers that "the Negro can rid himself of his black or dark complexion" and "straighten his hair."[9] That postwar marketers were selling to a public who by and large lacked proper education regarding their bodies made selling this assumption, and the products that came with it, a significantly less challenging enterprise than it otherwise might have been. Simply put, countless Americans were learning to dislike their bodies before they even knew much about these bodies.

As a result of this ever-expanding gap between self-knowledge and self-loathing, the Boston Women's Health Book Collective formed in 1969. Its contributors frequently criticized the detrimental impact of the beauty industry, particularly on women: "We are encouraged to blend together and hide our differences. We are discouraged from appreciating our uniqueness."[10] With its 1970 publication, *Our Bodies, Ourselves,* the organization sought to partially alleviate this growing crisis involving medicine, health, and the beauty industry. This guidebook, which has sold almost 4 million copies in twelve languages, helped people to educate themselves regarding miscarriage, birth control, menstruation, and a variety of other health issues that were woefully and unnecessarily shrouded in mystery. Similarly, the National Women's Health Network formed in 1975 to better educate women about drug use and medical practices.[11] As Phyllis Chesler, who in 1972 authored *Women and Madness,* declared, "if women take their bodies seriously—and ideally we should—then its *full* expression, in terms of pleasure, maternity, and physical strength, seems to fare better when *women* control the means of production and reproduction."[12] The underlying issue of all these efforts was clear: women were being actively alienated from their bodies: "Our bodies are the physical bases from which we move into the world; ignorance, uncertainty—even, at worst, shame—about our physical selves create in us an alienation from ourselves that keeps us from being the whole people that we could be."[13]

This alienation was to a great extent also perpetrated by industries that supposedly had women's health interests in mind: medicine, psychiatry, and pharmacology. The exchanges between Marilyn and her uncle reflect a trend in both popular culture and psychiatry: viewing health as the equivalent to happiness. Television's consistent and largely exclusive depiction of life in idealistic and positive form was also reflected in bestselling books, such as Norman Vincent Peale's runaway bestseller, *The Power of Positive Thinking.* As Peale encouraged his readers to visualize success and replace negative thoughts with positive ones, many critics considered such admonitions akin to a destructive self-hypnosis. Peale, they argued, encouraged delusional thinking at the same as time he deterred readers from critical thinking and deepening self-awareness.[14]

The association of happiness and positivity with well-being was not just relegated to popular culture and mass-marketed books, though. Throughout the postwar period, psychiatrists were increasingly diagnosing human sadness as a mental illness, a direct result of new symptom-based approaches to diagnostics. Recently, Allan V. Horwitz and Jerome C. Wakefield have pointed out this twentieth-century phenomenon in their work, *The Loss of Sadness: How Psychiatry Transformed Normal Sorrow into Depressive Disorder,* where they track the rise in pathologizing common forms of human sadness. Horwitz and Wakefield show how empirical psychiatric studies between 1920 and 1970 "relied on measuring only symptom presentations at a single point in time" and as a result, "largely set aside issues of course, duration, and especially, the situational context of symptoms."[15] Consequently, patients who showed certain symptoms in isolated instances were erroneously diagnosed with medical disorders. And while sadness and anger proved to be a "starting point for creative change and growth" for the authors of *Our Bodies, Ourselves* and many of its readers, those emotional states were at the same time being increasingly considered medical disorders.[16] Instead of a starting point for change, emotions could prove just as likely to be the ending point. The way psychiatric diagnoses and pharmaceutical drugs worked in tandem could potentially arrest a person's development. Author Jacqueline Susann succinctly and popularly allegorized this growth-stunting in her 1966 bestselling classic

Valley of the Dolls, referring to pills as "dolls": "They're beautiful little red dolls that take all your cares away."[17] These pills did not always improve mental health but could psychologically infantilize users and keep them in perpetual states of childlike dependence.

To be sure, psychiatrists prior to the twentieth century almost universally distinguished between normal sadness, grief, and bereavement and melancholia, a medical disorder requiring professional help. Psychiatrists commonly asserted that not respecting this distinction could be potentially dangerous for the patient. Emil Kraepelin, a German psychiatrist and Freud's contemporary, was among those who drew this important line. Additionally, by the late nineteenth century, Kraepelin developed an innovative diagnostic approach that would also profoundly influence psychiatric diagnostics and then the formation of the DSM in the second half of the twentieth century. Using symptoms as the principal basis to create distinct categories of mental illness, Kraepelin's work, for example, helped to differentiate between what psychiatrists now refer to as bipolar disorder and schizophrenia. Kraepelin, like so many others before him, found it important to separate normal human sadness and what was termed *morbidity.* To distinguish the two, practitioners looked at two main criteria: the presence or absence of an assignable cause and the trajectory and pattern of a patient's symptoms over time. Thus, sadness that had no clear cause and/or only increased in severity over time was likely to be diagnosed as a serious medical condition.[18] Shorter periods of sadness and/or grief were not pathologized but deemed a vital part of mental health.

As Horwitz and Wakefield have shown, however, mid-twentieth-century researchers who sought to create a more reliable and predictable model for psychiatric diagnoses employed this symptom-based approach with one complicating modification—they decontextualized it: "These researchers claimed to emulate Kraepelin, but their approach in fact sharply diverged from his" because the "researchers who relied on statistical techniques to isolate symptom patterns simply assumed, quite reasonably, that all the symptoms they entered into their models were manifestations of disorders in the sampled populations." As psychiatric researchers undertook an "urgent quest for reliability," their criteria "inadvertently rejected the previous 2,500 years of clinical diagnostic tradition that explored the context and meaning of symptoms in deciding whether someone is suffering from intense normal sadness or a depressive disorder." The unwitting result of this effort . . . was to be a massive pathologization of normal sadness that, ironically, can be argued to have made depressive diagnosis less rather than more scientifically valid."[19] So the immediate diagnosis of Marilyn as a "very sick girl" reflects how popular culture and psychiatry suppressed the expression of a broad spectrum of healthy human emotions. In varying degrees and for different reasons, popular culture products and diagnostic methods in psychiatry increasingly equated a clean bill of mental health with redundant expressions of simplistic cheerfulness, or as Herbert Marcuse once sardonically described it, "euphoria in unhappiness."[20]

In a psychiatric climate that somewhat inadvertently helped pathologize sadness and a popular culture that practically banished it, patients sought the simplest, most convenient and cost-effective relief: prescription drugs. And as Thomas Whiteside succinctly wrote in the *New Yorker*, an "age in which nations threaten each other with guided missiles and hydrogen bombs is one that can use any calm it can get, and calm is what the American pharmaceutical industry now abundantly offers."[21] One family doctor explained, "Patients are far from passive recipients of these drugs" but arrive "requesting, and even demanding medication to relieve their anxiety . . . as if we are holding back this wonderful panacea."[22] While psychoanalysis was relatively expensive, mass-marketed drugs like Miltown and Valium were reasonably affordable for almost every middle-class family. As Andrea Tone has explained, these medications "meshed easily with the convenience mentality of the 1950s, the therapeutic ethos that sanctioned changing oneself rather than the world."[23]

As Marilyn's consultation progresses, the doctor's false assumptions regarding her eagerness to undergo the operation reflect how being comfortable in one's body was commonly seen as abnormal. The authors of *Our Bodies, Ourselves*, giving voice to this phenomenon, stated, "Our feelings about our physical selves have been negative. Our hair is too straight or too curly, our noses too small or too large, our breasts too big or too small. . . . We are always making some comparison, we're never okay the way we are. . . . The ideal woman in America is something very specific. . . . Unfortunately, this is not *our* ideal, not what *we* created."[24] Here again, nonwhite Americans would feel the weight of these pressures and assumptions even more intensely as they experienced incessant demands to conform to white ideals of beauty that also undoubtedly had profound emotional and psychological side effects. As a direct response to social standards that idealized whiteness and white beauty standards, renowned photographer Kwame Brathwaite cofounded two influential organizations in the late fifties and early sixties—the African

Jazz Arts Society and Studios and the Grandassa Models. These organizations celebrated Black culture, music, style, and traditions and were instrumental in popularizing the Black is Beautiful movement. In 1962 Harlem, the Grandassa Models showcased African beauty in an event titled "Naturally, '62: The Original African Coiffure and Fashion Extravaganza Designed to Restore Our Racial Pride and Standards." Headlined by jazz artists Abbey Lincoln and Max Roach, the show was a massive success and helped to promote natural Black beauty, which stood in stark contrast to dominant white cultural ideals. As history professor Tanisha C. Ford has pointed out, "the Grandassa Models were not simply countering the images of pale and frail British models such as Twiggy and Jean Shrimpton who appeared in mainstream U.S. publications. They were also challenging the ubiquitous presence of lighter-complexioned, straight-haired Black models in Black-owned publications such as *Ebony*." Brathwaite's photography celebrating natural Black features and beauty would appear on the covers of Blue Note jazz albums throughout the decade. Meanwhile, artists such as Nina Simone, would embrace the movement's most influential designers and stylists in their hair, clothing, and music fashions.[25]

In the context of racialized consumerism as well as white male–centered medicine and psychology, celebrating one's natural self might be seen as a form of mental illness. As the episode continues, specialist Professor Sig determines that Marilyn's comfort with her natural body and her intellect both indicate pathologies. From the Freudian perspective, a "normal" woman should desire, above all, to be beautiful, so Marilyn's comfort in her own skin and her prioritization of the ability to think for herself suggest neurotic desires. In this way, Freud explained that women who desire "the capacity to pursue an intellectual career" were simply repressed and neurotic.[26] From the Freudian perspective, Marilyn's comfort with her body and intellect represented a double pathology.

In this scene, the obvious allusions to Freud and psychoanalysis emerge as yet another source of Marilyn's oppression. As Betty Friedan and Freud biographer Ernest Jones have noted, Freud's personal views of sexuality, not to mention those of Victorian Europe, greatly informed his theories. That Freud's sexuality was also "exceptionally puritanical and chaste," even by Victorian standards, was evidenced in his many personal letters, which further reveal an infantile view of women and sex.[27] In "Number 12 Looks Just Like You," this extremely narrow view of women and sexuality is shown in the idealization not only of feminine beauty but of youth as well. In a letter in which

Freud criticized John Stuart Mill's ideas of female emancipation, he wrote, "If . . . I imagined my gentle sweet girl as a competitor, it would only end in my telling her . . . that I am fond of her and that I implore her to withdraw from the strife into the calm, uncompetitive activity of my home. It is possible that changes in upbringing may suppress all a woman's tender attributes . . . and . . . the most delightful thing the world can offer us—our ideal of womanhood." He succinctly concluded, "Nature has determined woman's destiny through beauty, charm, and sweetness."[28] Regarding their intellectual capabilities, Freud explained that young women "frequently stagger us by . . . psychological rigidity and unchangeability" and concluded that in such cases, there are "no paths open to her for further development."[29] Freud's letters foreshadowed common feature of postwar American cultural cognitive dissonance: the constrictive idealization of youth and beauty and the disparagement of the forced results, which were stunted psychological, emotional, and intellectual growth. Just as Freudian thinking dismissed women's ambitions to pursue careers or engage in intellectual activity as a sign of neurosis, the professor here dismisses Marilyn's treasured philosophy and literature as "smut."

Friedan, however, argued that Freudian psychological theory further enshrined the restrictive feminine mystique. She explained how "girls . . . were told by the most advanced thinkers of our time to go back and live their lives . . . restricted to the doll's house by Victorian prejudice. And their own respect and awe for the authority of science—anthropology, sociology, psychology share that authority now—kept them from questioning the feminine mystique." And just as Marilyn's knowledge was scorned, countless articles from professionals and popular writers also derided the idea of women pursuing further education. Friedan explained, "The feminine mystique has made higher education for women seem suspect, unnecessary, and even dangerous. . . . But . . . I discovered that the critics were half-right; education was dangerous and frustrating—but only when women did not use it." That the professor claims classic philosophical and literary books have been banned not just for women but for everyone also reflects what Richard Hofstadter famously referred to as "anti-intellectualism" in America. He defined this anti-intellectual phenomenon as "resentment and suspicion of the life of the mind and of those who are considered to represent it; and a disposition constantly to minimize the value of that life."[30] Banning books meant that neither women nor men would be likely to question or challenge the new frightening status quo. And although Marilyn's struggles are entrusted to doctors, Friedan argued that these deeper "problems cannot be solved by medicine, or even by psychotherapy." Instead, postwar America needed "a drastic reshaping" that would enable all people "to reach maturity, identity, completeness of self."[31] Marilyn was confronting every one of these dilemmas at once.

In his 1964 *One-Dimensional Man,* Herbert Marcuse distinguished between real needs, such as shelter, food, and water, and false needs, such as the need to perpetually chase after commodified ideals of beauty or success. These false needs, represented by the beauty and cosmetic industry, were socially superimposed by advertisements and media, squashing individual development and expression. In exchange for completely succumbing to these false needs, Marilyn, like so many postwar Americans, sacrificed her identity and health. Marcuse states, "No matter how much such needs have become the individual's own" or how much one "identifies . . . with them . . . they continue to be what they were from the beginning—products of a society whose dominant interest demands repression."[32] This episode throws into serious doubt the enthusiastically promoted notion that the procedures, products, and pills available to postwar Americans were keys to self-expression and fulfillment. Indeed, these alluring offerings represented some of the most formidable obstacles to meeting one's real needs of authenticity, individuality, community, and connection. Marilyn could not resist getting caught up in the tide of chemically induced white smiles, perpetually youthful bodies, and an utter lack of individuality. Perhaps viewers of "Number 12 Looks Just Like You" could consider not succumbing to these false needs.

Giving Comfort to the Comforted

"The Lateness of the Hour," *The Twilight Zone*'s first production on videotape, aired on December 2, 1960 (S2, e8). This episode illustrates how the priorities of comfort, predictability, relaxation, and convenience can have nightmarish consequences. In a related way, "A Nice Place to Visit" tells the story of Rocky Valentine, a burglar who, shot and killed by the police, appears to go to heaven (S1, e28). As he gambles at a casino, he continually wins and is surrounded by admiring women. Eventually, however, Rocky gets bored with the ease and predictability of his heavenly existence and demands to go to the "other place." He finds out, though, that he *is* in hell. His luxurious comforts and predictable winning are actually his eternal punishments. "The Lateness of the Hour" explores how making the world excessively comfortable, predictable, and controlled can have dehumanizing effects.

The episode begins in a large mansion, during a thunderstorm. Inside, a young woman named Jana stands by a window, watching the storm and looking at a photo album. Meanwhile, Mrs. Loren, her mother, can be heard moaning in an almost orgasmic way from the other side of the room. As the camera pans across the room, it becomes apparent that the Lorens are an affluent family, as their home is filled with classical art, an extensive library, and antique furniture. The husband reads a book, while his wife continues to moan as she gets a back massage from Nelda, one of their maids. Jana approaches her father, Dr. William Loren, and enquires about one of the pictures in the album. Her parents, though, seem uninterested; William responds that he cannot remember when it was taken, while an irritated Mrs. Loren adds, "It seems like that's all you do lately is look at that album." When she shows the photograph to her mother, Jana comments suspiciously that Nelda does not look any different now than in the picture. When Jana walks to the bookshelf to put the album back, her father says that Nelda can do it. "That's all right father. I'd like to put it away myself," she replies. After Jana walks over to the fireplace, her mother asks, "You're not chilly are you, Jana, dear? Shouldn't be. Seventy-two degrees in here. Isn't it, William? Isn't it seventy-two degrees?" He confidently responds, "Exactly. The optimum temperature." Jana, however, seems somewhat uneasy amid all the luxury and replies sardonically, "Of course. The optimum temperature. And the fireplace designed for perfect heat radiation. The chair, for maximum comfort. And the windows, for the most efficient light and proper ventilation. Oh, yes, and the ceilings, for the most desirable acoustical qualities. Everything built to perfection, father. Everything designed for a perfect life."

Disgusted by the excessive comfort in her home and the continual groans of her mother, Jana wears a pained look and takes several deep breaths. Finally giving way to the inner tension, she exclaims, "Haven't you had enough of that, Mother?!" But Mrs. Loren simply replies that the massage helps build her appetite. Clearly feeling oppressed by her family's routine, Jana suggests they eat dinner a little earlier or later or perhaps go to a restaurant. Stunned, her father says, "Why in the world would we go out to eat in a restaurant . . . ? We'd walk through the rain and get ourselves sopping wet. Then we'd eat some greasy, unpalatable food served off of dirty, unwashed plates, and after that it would be a moot question whether we'd succumb to ptomaine or pneumonia"; then he kisses Jana gently on the cheek. She indignantly responds, "Outside there must be the clean beautiful sound of rain, and in here, those constant animal grunts of pleasure!" After her father scolds her, Jana eggs him

"Oh father, we're atrophying in here!" Jana expresses disgust with the dull and predictable life her family leads. Still from "The Lateness of the Hour" (3:02)

on, "Yell at me, father. Please, yell at me. I can't tell you how delighted I am to hear you yell at me. Why, it proves to me that you've got lungs. . . . Oh, father, we're atrophying in here. We sit here day after day and year after year, while that clock just turns and turns. And we decay with every minute of the time, while Nelda, the maid, and Robert, the butler, and Gretchen, the cook, and Jensen, the handyman . . . this army of domestics do everything but our breathing for us!" Jana then storms up the winding, elegant staircase. When one of the maids says that she sounds jealous, Jana finally snaps and pushes the maid down the stairs, but the servant merely smiles, apparently unharmed. Serling introduces his audience to the setting: "The residence of Dr. William Loren, which is in reality a menagerie for machines. We're about to discover that sometimes the product of man's talent and genius can walk amongst us untouched by the normal ravages of time. These are Dr. Loren's robots, built to functional as well as artistic perfection. But in a moment, Dr. Loren, wife, and daughter, will discover that perfection is relative, that even robots have to be paid for. And very shortly will be shown exactly what is the bill."

As the episode continues, Robert, one of the butlers, tends to William, who requests his evening pipe. During their exchange, Jana simultaneously mouths every single word; she clearly knows everything the two men will say, reflecting the monotony of their lives. William asks her if they should discuss her "sudden" and "inexplicable" unhappiness and her increasingly rebellious attitude. Defending their lifestyle, he says, "I explained to you a long time ago why I did what I did. Why I retired from the world, why I built these people." Jana, now finding her footing, responds, "What you've done to yourselves is an atrocity, but what you've done to me is even worse. You've turned me into a freak. An unsocial, unworldly, insulated freak!" Her father, putting his hands on her shoulders, reassuringly states that he has also protected her from harm and disease and that insulation from the twentieth-century world is a gift: "You've never had to look into the face of war or the face of poverty or preju-dice. . . . What you think of as imprisonment just happens to be asylum and security, yes, and survival." Jana, unconvinced, retorts, "Asylum in a hothouse? Security in a mausoleum? Survival as a vegetable survives. What you're becom-ing and what you're making me become—a vegetable!" Jana cries that they are being controlled by their machines because of their utter dependence on them and demands the machines be destroyed. William explains that the servants are not mere machinery, however, but products of scientific precision with implanted memories and even a certain amount of free will. He dramatically pronounces, "Jana, you're not asking me to destroy machines, you're asking me to destroy that which has life!" But she remains indignant, calling them "com-plicated toys" and their house a "playroom." Jana finally offers her parents an ultimatum, either they get rid of the machines, or she will leave. As she storms up the stairs again, one of the robots beseeches her to respect her parents and to act more appropriately. But in response, Jana ominously warns her father that the machines may be indestructible, but he is not.

Hoping he can smooth out his daughter's frustrations, William enters her bedroom but notices that she has already begun packing her things. When he asks her if she really wants to leave home, Jana responds, "I want you to open the windows and let the air in. I want you to let the world in." After thinking for a moment, William tells Jana that he agrees to her demands and will get rid of the machines immediately. He descends the staircase and takes out a remote control from his jacket pocket and turns the knob. Soon thereafter, all the machine-servants gather around him, and he orders them to the basement. After a brief moment of resistance, all of the robots retire as commanded. Having successfully discharged his machines, William explains

Committed to comfort, the Lorens transform their defiant daughter into a personal maid, ensuring their secluded life of bliss remains undisturbed. Still from "The Lateness of the Hour" (23:41)

to his wife that it will be just the two of them along with their daughter from now on. Jana excitedly descends the stairs and searches all the rooms for any robots. When she does not find a single one, she delightedly says they can all live normal lives now and make friends, have parties, and maybe she could even meet a man and have children someday. Mrs. Loren, however, appears troubled when Jana mentions having kids, but William, trying to save Jana's positive mood, reassures her that it is just a shock for her mother to hear that for the first time. Jana is unconvinced, however, and insists that something is amiss. Returning to the photo album, she asks why there are no pictures of her as a little girl—just her parents and the robots. Her parents, stunned into silence, have no reply. "What am I?!" Jana cries. Her father reluctantly begins to explain how he and Mrs. Loren were childless and wanted someone to share their lives with. "You built a daughter!" Jana screams. Her parents try to comfort her and explain that although she is a machine, they love her like a real daughter. But Jana only becomes increasingly hysterical and bangs her hand repeatedly on the railing, screaming, "No pain! No pain at all! No pain!

No love. I can't even feel love." After a moment of deliberation, William, who does not want to live without Jana, seems poised to make another decision.

As the final scene begins, Mrs. Loren's groans of pleasure can be heard again. This time, however, the maid massaging her back is Jana, who has been transformed into a servant and renamed Nelda. The Lorens have reprogrammed their daughter to serve them as a maid. Before the final credits, Serling offers one final remark, "Let this be the postscript: should you be worn out by the rigors of competing in a very competitive world, if you're distraught from having to share your existence with the noises and neuroses of the twentieth century, if you crave serenity but want it full time and with no strings attached, get yourself a workroom in a basement and then drop a note to Dr. and Mrs. William Loren. They're a childless couple who made comfort a life's work, and maybe there are a few do-it-yourself pamphlets still available—in *The Twilight Zone*."

"The Lateness of the Hour" features several key developments in postwar America—the exodus from inner cities to suburban landscapes, the rapidly increasing rate of mechanization and automation of the home, and the subsequent impacts these changes were exacting on the lives and habits of individuals and families. The Lorens' obsession with cleanliness reflects, for instance, one of the primary driving factors of suburbanization during the postwar period, namely people's desire to live in cleaner, healthier neighborhoods. Among Cleveland suburbanites, for example, 61 percent said they relocated to live in a clean neighborhood, while 48 percent did so for better schools or to be homeowners, and 28 percent cited having a garden or yard as their primary motivation.[33] But amid this mass migration, in his aptly titled 1962 work, Michael Harrington attempted to remind Americans that there was indeed an other America. Harrington wrote, "The poor are increasingly slipping out of the very experience and consciousness of the nation. If the middle class never did like ugliness and poverty, it was at least aware of them." However, as a result of the seemingly laudable transformations taking place in postwar America, the poor had been rendered "increasingly isolated from contact with, or sight of, anybody else." While middle-class white Americans retreated to the suburbs, the ever-increasing invisibility of poor Americans loomed as an ominous, if largely hidden, problem, only to suddenly reemerge when inner-city riots grabbed national headlines and attention. Harrington's work, for example, estimated that one quarter of the population (40–50 million) in the United States lived in poverty, in households with less than $3,000 in annual income.[34] By defining suburbanization as the solution to urban and rural problems, Americans left social and racial inequalities in their wake, rendering them all the more dangerous with the physical distance now separating impoverished racially diverse inner cities and middle-class, mostly white suburban cul-de-sacs.

William Loren reflects many of the ideas and perspective of city planners that critics like Jane Jacobs sharply criticized in her influential 1961 book, *The Death and Life of Great American Cities*. Jacobs criticized the profoundly influential "Decentrist" principles of planners, such as Ebenezer Howard, who idealized small-scale planned communities. Jacobs explains that "Howard looked at the living conditions of the poor . . . and justifiably did not like what he smelled, saw, or heard. He not only hated the wrongs and mistakes of the city, he hated the city and thought it an outright evil and an affront to nature that so many people should get themselves into an agglomeration. His prescription for saving people was to do the city in." Howard went to work on designs seemingly infused with logic, balance, and rationality, which allotted a certain amount of space for residences, agriculture, and industry in what became known as the garden city movement. Jacobs, however, critiques this overplanned and curated type of living as robbing communities of the diversity, vibrancy, spontaneity, and color that makes them interesting and attractive in the first place. She writes, "His aim was the creation of self-sufficient . . . very nice towns if you were docile and had no plans of your own and did not mind spending your life among others with no plans of their own." Much like Dr. Loren, these principles, which supposedly offered comfort and security to all, mostly reflected the planners' self-serving biases with very little effort to consider the residents' varied desires: "As in all Utopias, the right to have plans of any significance belonged only to the planners in charge"—an assessment that sounds like it came directly from William Loren. Jacobs writes how these champions of "Decentrism" purposefully endangered human interactivity by prioritizing privacy: "The presence of many other people is, at best, a necessary evil, and good city planning must aim for at least an illusion of isolation and suburban privacy." Just as William is astonished at Jana's frustration over her isolation and interest in the outside world, Jacobs noted, "that the sight of people attracts still other people, is something that city planners and city architectural designers seem to find incomprehensible. They operate on the premise that city people seek the sight of emptiness, obvious order and quiet. Nothing could be less true."[35] What was desirable for Decentrist planners and William Loren was a nightmare for residents like Jana.

The Lorens seem the epitome of the Decentrist, comfortably distanced American Dream: "The planned community must be islanded off as a self-contained unit, that it must resist future change, and that every significant detail must be controlled by the planners." As white politicians, investors, businesses, and residents increasingly abandoned urban areas to invest in and retreat to the suburbs, they left America's city streets emptier, more dangerous, volatile, and violent. The insecurity American urban residents increasingly experienced was not a coincidence. "It does not take many incidents of violence on a city street . . . to make people fear the streets. And as they fear them, they use them less, which makes the streets still more unsafe." Jacobs notes that the "first thing to understand is that the public peace—the sidewalk and street peace—of cities is not kept primarily by the police, necessary as police are. It is kept primarily by an intricate, almost unconscious, network of voluntary controls and standards among the people themselves, and enforced by the people themselves. . . . No amount of police can enforce civilization where the normal, casual enforcement of it has broken down." Instead of committing to humane policies that understand, support, and sustain the needs of civilization in urban areas, we "let those unfortunate enough to be stuck with it take the consequences." Ultimately, "the problem of insecurity cannot be solved by spreading people out more thinly."[36] Defining safety as something mostly achieved in the private sphere renders it a kind of luxury commodity available if the price is right, while guaranteeing that the public sphere will be insecure and hazardous.

In the years that followed Harrington's work on the structured invisibility of poverty and Jacobs's book on the impacts of modern urban planning, Americans were reminded of the American Dream's deadly side effects. After race riots broke out in cities across the country, the presidentially appointed Kerner Commission was set to task to uncover the root causes for a great deal of urban unrest. After visiting cities across the country, the commission concluded in its report, published in 1968: "Our nation is moving toward two societies, one black, one white—separate and unequal." The report continued, "What white Americans have never fully understood . . . is that the white society is deeply implicated in the ghetto. White institutions created it, white institutions maintain it, and white society condones it." It also criticized the media's woeful lack of diversity: "The press has too long basked in a white world." The commission recommended prioritizing integrated, affordable housing, employment opportunities, social services, and opening segregated suburban enclaves to nonwhite residents. The report noted that in many communities "the police have come to symbolize white power, white racism, and white repression" and also documented that in several cities policing was the number one grievance—above even unemployment and housing issues.[37] The Johnson administration largely ignored the commission's findings on housing, health, and jobs, and subsequent administrations have done the exact opposite of what residents victimized by urban instability recommended by expanding and militarizing city police forces rather than reforming them. At the same time, one of the most successful children's programs in television history emerged in 1969, asking, "Can you tell me how to get to Sesame Street?" The show's prioritization of inner-city representation, education, and creativity also tapped into a legitimate human desire for community engagement with the diverse outside world that had clearly been lacking in the Loren household and in many actual residences across America. Meanwhile, the supposedly comfortable all-white suburban dream epitomized by the Lorens was leaving gaping wounds on abandoned streets and neighborhoods across the country, creating and perpetuating two separate "Americas," one being increasingly policed and criminalized, the other isolated, unfulfilled, and socially disengaged.

While the Lorens appear to be an established upper-middle-class family and not a nouveau-riche or recently transformed middle-class one, the fact that their desires and habits reflected the aspirations of millions of Americans who had unprecedented access to clean, comfortable suburban living made the episode that much more poignant. Here was a family who had distanced itself from the city and the headaches of modernity in an idealized form. But as Lewis Mumford explained, "the cost of this detachment in space from other men is out of all proportion to its supposed benefits. The end product is an encapsulated life. . . . Every part of this life, indeed, will come through official channels and be under supervision. Untouched by human hand at one end: untouched by human spirit at the other."[38] This episode shows how an encapsulated life, one untouched by the human hand and spirit, can have costly effects on human development. Serling's statement that the Lorens' residence is, in reality, a "menagerie for machines," dramatizes the ways suburban living was perhaps better suited for machines and consumer goods than for humanity. The immediately obvious obsession with predictability, order, and routine in the Loren household alludes to how humans in this type of environment were likely to mimic and take their cues from machines, not the other way around. The Lorens' lifestyle appears just as robotic as the machine-maids that serve them.

Another clear aspect of the Lorens' lifestyle is the mastery over their physiological needs through modern technology. All their physical needs are taken care of, even the desire for sensual pleasure is fulfilled not by a human but by one of the robots, who induces groans of ecstasy from Mrs. Loren. At the time this episode aired, one of the most influential psychological theories was Abraham Maslow's hierarchy of needs. Maslow first developed this theory, which placed human needs in a pyramid, at various levels, in a 1943 article and featured it in his 1954 book, *Motivation and Personality*. According to Maslow, physiological needs, which include air, water, food, clothing, shelter, and reproduction, are the most fundamental necessities of human beings and fill up the bottom of the pyramid. Maslow theorized the need for safety and security was the next essential component, followed by love, belonging and relationships in a third grouping, esteem in a fourth, and, finally, at the pyramid's apex, self-actualization as the pinnacle need of human beings.[39] Maslow later added another level: self-transcendence, which consisted of altruistic and spiritual pursuits.[40]

William Loren, the episode's patriarch, has clearly succeeded in seeing that many of his family's most fundamental needs are met. However, he also clearly exhibits an almost neurotic concern with predictability, sanitation, and orderliness. Maslow referred to this kind of fixation as "compulsive-obsessive neurosis." He explained:

> Compulsive-obsessives try frantically to order and stabilize the world so that no unmanageable, unexpected or unfamiliar dangers will ever appear. . . . They hedge themselves about with all sorts of ceremonials, rules and formulas so that every possible contingency may be provided for and so that no new contingencies may appear. They . . . manage to maintain their equilibrium by avoiding everything unfamiliar and strange and by ordering their restricted world in such a neat, disciplined, orderly fashion that everything in the world can be counted upon. . . . Anything unexpected (dangers) cannot possibly occur. If . . . something unexpected does occur, they go into a panic reaction as if this unexpected occurrence constituted a grave danger. What we can see only as a none-too-strong preference in the healthy person, e.g., preference for the familiar, becomes a life-and-death necessity in abnormal cases.[41]

William Loren perfectly characterizes this obsessiveness. When Jana proposes going out to dinner, or even just having a dinner at a different time, he rebuffs her idea in a melodramatic, life-or-death fashion, claiming they would be all but guaranteed to succumb to the ravages of a fatal disease.

While the suburban lifestyle was rapidly becoming the dominant norm in the United States, many postwar critics pointed out that seclusion in a suburb was not necessarily the ideal it was popularly portrayed as. And while many families, like the Lorens, were concerned with meeting their basic needs of health and safety, several writers reminded Americans that physiological needs did not constitute the whole of existence. Much like Maslow, who posited a hierarchy of needs, critics such as Betty Friedan and Lewis Mumford sought to raise their readers' awareness that an isolated life in the suburbs could actually stunt personal development, internal satisfaction, and social awareness. Mumford explained, "As an attempt to recover what was missing in the city, the suburban exodus could be amply justified, for it was concerned with primary human needs. But there was another side: the temptation to retreat from unpleasant realities, to shirk public duties, and to find the whole meaning of life in the most elemental social group, the family, or even in the still more isolated and self-centered individual. What was properly treated a beginning was treated as an end."[42] And amid a flurry of messages that defined women's fulfillment as raising a family in the suburbs, Friedan pronounced, "There is only one way for women to reach full human potential—by participating in the mainstream of society, by exercising their own voice in all the decisions shaping that society."[43] *The Twilight Zone*'s "The Lateness of the Hour" dramatizes how when one treats suburban security and comfort as ends in themselves, it can stunt psychological and social maturity and even make certain human qualities atrophy over time.

This suburban life, though, was not merely idealized inside the home through advertisements and television programming like *The Adventures of Ozzie and Harriet* (1952–1966), *Father Knows Best* (1954–1960), *Leave It to Beaver* (1957–1963), and *The Donna Reed Show* (1958–1966), it was also promulgated in schools. A flood of educational films that covered proper etiquette and life habits instructed students how their families could live proper middle-class lives. These films included titles such as *A Date with Your Family* (Simmel-Meservey, 1950), *Let's Be Clean and Neat* (Coronet, 1957), *Let's Be Safe at Home* (Portafilms, 1948), *Let's Give a Tea* (Simmel-Meservey, 1946), *Mealtime Manners and Health* (Coronet, 1957), *Appreciating Our Parents* (Coronet, 1957), *The Griper* (Centron, 1954), and *Habit Patterns* (McGraw-Hill, 1954). Taken collectively, these films stressed the importance of conforming to social and familial standards, including manners related to grooming, fashion, speech patterns, and taste. As Ken Smith has pointed out, though, "social guidance films would not have existed had America been like *Leave It to Beaver*. Instead, they thrived in a nation traumatized by war, fearful of communist witch-hunters, terrified of nuclear annihilation, and rocked by fears of generational rebellion. School boards bought films that showed well-mannered teenagers because, in the eyes of adults, teenagers weren't well mannered or well-groomed or respectful or polite. Mental hygiene films were popular because they showed life not as it was but as their adult creators wanted it to be."[44] In many ways then, the structure and order that the Lorens represented perfectly embodied this supposed ideal combination of modern domestic technology, suburban living, and the nuclear family seen on classroom projectors and family room television sets. *The Twilight Zone,* however, shows that these ideals could actually constitute a nightmare, rather than an aspirational dream.

In many ways, Jana raises concerns that would be at the heart of *The Feminine Mystique.* Just as Jana expressed frustration over how predictable her family members' lives were, Friedan lamented how those who suffered from "the problem that has no name" were victims of a "deadly dailyness." One woman she interviewed explained, "I can take the real problems; it's the endless boring days that make me desperate." And in a way that incriminates William Loren, Friedan asked why "any social scientist, with godlike manipulative superiority, take[s] it upon himself—or herself—to protect women from the pains of growing up? Protectiveness has often muffled the sound of doors closing against women; it has often cloaked a very real prejudice, even when it is offered in the name of science."[45] William Loren's calling up "science" and "development" for a defense of his lifestyle and treatment of Jana illustrates how women were especially vulnerable in a kind of prearranged suburban living arrangement. Mirra Komarovsky, one of the first sociologists to research and critically appraise gender roles, claimed the effect of sheltering women frequently leads to "a generalized dependency which will then be transferred to the husband and . . . enable her all the more readily to accept the role of wife in a family which still has many patriarchal features."[46] To put it simply, women were being subordinated in the name of science and safety.

For Friedan and many other feminists, the perpetual and cyclical subjugation of women happens in part by "permitting girls to evade tests of reality, and real commitments, in school and the world." Consequently, this evasion and inexperience "arrests their development at an infantile level, short of personal identity, with an inevitably weak core of self." In Friedan's estimation, the suburban house is, in reality, a "trap," and for women to escape it, "they must . . . exercise their human freedom, and to recapture their sense of self. They must refuse to be nameless, depersonalized, manipulated and live their own lives again according to a self-chosen purpose."[47] Though not a house-wife, Jana shows clear signs of suffering from "the problem that has no name," as she pleads for a break from routine and a chance to experience the outside world. In a similar fashion, the Loren household also reflects Mumford's observation that a suburb, in effect, operates as "an asylum for the preservation of illusion" and is "not merely a child-centered environment" but represents "a childish view of the world, in which reality [is] sacrificed to the pleasure principle."[48] Although suburban environments granted children safety and security, Jana clearly desires to grow into adulthood and be tested by the complex realities she is protected from. She wants more than just her physiological needs met; she desires to feel a part of society and thereby approach something akin to self-actualization.

Jana not only exemplifies many of the grievances given voice by Friedan and other sixties feminists, she also captures the disillusionment of many young adults at the time. Less than two years after this episode aired, the Students for a Democratic Society decried the excesses of materialism, tech-nology, and comfort in postwar America. The authors of the Port Huron Statement announced, "Loneliness, estrangement, isolation describe the vast distance between man and man today. These dominant tendencies cannot be overcome by better personnel management, nor by improved gadgets, but only when a love of man overcomes the idolatrous worship of things by man." They argued that instead of "power and personal uniqueness" being "rooted in possession, privilege, or circumstance," they should instead be based on "love, reflectiveness, reason, and creativity." In this vein, students called for a democracy where individuals can participate in the "social decisions deter-mining the quality and direction" of one's life and "that society be organized to encourage independence . . . and provide the media for their common par-ticipation."[49] For Friedan, the Students for a Democratic Society, and Jana, all the comforts and amenities offered by modern technology, coupled with the seclusion from social problems granted by suburban housing, formed the basis of many of society's problems, not the solutions.

The episode's final sequence, culminating in the revelation that Jana is a robot, emphasizes the lengths to which one might have to go to uphold postwar suburban ideals. When his daughter begins to express her own will, William offers a compromise, but he ultimately compromises his very daugh-ter so his comfortable, predictable, vacuum-sealed home can continue with-out inconvenience. The episode's conclusion casts doubt on the idea that comfortable suburban homes are child-centered, portraying them, rather, as representations of a childish view of the world. As Jana increasingly exerts her independence and need for socialization and self-actualization, her father stresses the more basic and childlike desires of security and routine. While teenagers were encouraged by television content and instructional films to be more structured and habitual in their daily lives, *The Twilight Zone* shows how such patterned thinking and behavior can lead to the creation of beings who either resemble robots, or actually are robots.

"The Lateness of the Hour" also illustrates the ways teenage rebelliousness and the discontentment of housewives were commonly handled, namely through attempts to reprogram the individual rather than change the environment. Suburban malaise and rebellion were viewed not typically as symptoms of an inability to have legitimate needs met but instead as problems originating within the individual. Instructional films and popular television programming emphasized that happiness was achieved by fitting into existing familial, social, and educational structures, rather than exploring how those same structures might preclude someone from having their needs, other than the most basic, fulfilled in real life. As Friedan decried, "for years, psychiatrists have tried to 'cure' their patients' conflicts by fitting them to the culture. But adjustment to a culture which does not permit the realization of one's entire being is not a cure at all."[50] When she summarized the most common approach to suburban discontent during the postwar period, historian Elaine Tyler May explained how for a suffering woman, "treatment was geared toward improving her mental state through drugs to help her better adapt to her situation. Rather than help her to alter the conditions that caused her emotional problems, the psychiatrist changed her tranquilizers."[51] As unfulfilled housewives and disturbed teenagers expressed frustration with being relegated permanently to the bottom of Maslow's pyramid, both the suburban environment and the nuclear family were above suspicion more often than not.

Mumford, Friedan, and Serling all emphasized that nuclear family life in the suburbs, while not necessarily anathema, was certainly not the ultimate earthly paradise it was almost universally purported to be. Just as personal anguish and social injustices were not necessarily resolved there, familial and individual happiness could not be guaranteed, either. But for Americans who were repeatedly told that buying more for their home and families was the most effective cure for extended bouts of suburban ennui, alternative solutions and ways of thinking could not emerge very easily. In this context, social commentators offered different formulas for achieving human happiness and fulfillment by pointing out how the increasingly empty physical spaces of American cities, once filled by working- and middle-class Americans, was partially reproduced by a spiritual emptiness in postwar suburbs. Within this Cold War climate and culture, which aggressively promoted consumer capitalism and portrayed modern domesticity as the ultimate fulfillment of the American Dream, Nikita Khrushchev irreverently asked Richard Nixon, "Don't you have a machine that puts food into the mouth and pushes it down? Many things you've shown us are interesting but they are not needed in life. . . . They are merely gadgets."[52] Because criticism of American policy and practice likely came from someone like Khrushchev among mainstream coverage, pundits frequently, and with very little effort, associated social criticism with un-Americanism or even communism and responded with defensive emotional appeals praising the inherent virtues of consumer capitalism.

In this complicated context, which was fraught with obstacles to those desiring to express constructive forms of dissent, social critics such as Serling, Friedan, and Mumford sought to psychologically and socially empower postwar Americans to think differently. By pointing out some of the crucial needs that modern gadgetry and domesticity could not fulfill, social commentators pushed against marketing messages that attempted to convince the public they would find ultimate fulfillment via consumption. While suburbs granted millions of Americans, especially those traumatized by war or weary of city life, a safer, more peaceful place to grow old and raise a family, these critics reminded Americans that the suburbs were also more likely to stymie social awareness, self-actualization, and self-transcendence rather than help to facilitate them. And while millions of Americans took up suburban residence to escape racial tensions, poverty, crime, noise, and pollution, they needed to also bear in mind that these problems would not disappear just because they were no longer in view.

As Kenneth Jackson and Arlene Skolnick, among many others, have shown, the mass migration to the suburbs actually exacerbated a lot of these problems in the long run, particularly in urban centers where working- and middle-class Americans once resided. And while some activists criticized Betty Friedan's brand of feminism for its lack of consideration to working-class women, Friedan's goal was not to tackle working-class problems but to shake middle-class suburban women (and men) out of their homes and into the broader world where racial, sexual, and economic disparities abounded. In fact, most working-class women were already keenly aware of these issues. But before women and men could find meaning and purpose beyond their middle-class trappings and privileges, Friedan sought to explain to her readers that those comforts could not ever truly fulfill them, even though that message was being repeated ad nauseam. In trying to walk a narrow social tightrope, she was careful to point out how the "problem that had no name" was not an individual problem but a social one. By remaining in middle-class, suburban America without experiencing anything else, Friedan made a convincing case that middle-class Americans were causing harm to themselves, their children, and their fellow citizens. Even though a nuclear family in the suburbs seemed the epitome of the American Dream, Lewis Mumford outlined the dangers of such a lifestyle: "Each of them living apart, is a stranger to the fate of all the rest—his children and his private friends constitute to him the whole of mankind; as for the rest of his fellow-citizens . . . he sees them not; he touches them, but he feels them not; he exists in himself and for himself alone; and if his kindred still remain to him, he may be said at any rate to have lost his country."[53] It was up to Americans to not simply exchange civic responsibility for private comfort and apathetically close themselves off from their fellow citizens. Doing so would place them forever in *The Twilight Zone*.

By encouraging viewers to question their prosaic habits, thinking, and actions, Serling's *Twilight Zone* sought to remind his audience that purchasing and pursuing white ideals of beauty and comfort did not necessarily bring happiness or lead to self-fulfillment. Instead, the comforts and luxuries afforded to people as a result of developments in science and technology frequently meant that people were in danger of becoming like inanimate tools—machine-like and bereft of spirit, sensitivity, and emotion—just like the devices that increasingly surround them. And just as nuclear bombs brought a kind of security to the nation, the security and comfort afforded to Americans through consumerism and suburbanization came with notable risks to humanity. This is revealed in "Number 12 Looks Just Like You," as pressures to conform to certain beauty standards lead to Marilyn sacrificing her real self, including not just her physical appearance but her intellect, emotions, and memories. It is also illustrated in "The Lateness of the Hour" as Jana, who seems to be living the American Dream, with every imaginable comfort she could ever want, finds it torturous to remain closed off from an outside world that is more unpredictable, diverse, and interesting than her sheltered and repressive existence. And while it was remarkable in many ways that this line of critical thought could be found on television, even if it was metaphorical, Serling's *Twilight Zone* carried another dilemma for postwar Americans— passively consuming social criticism in commodified form was not enough in itself. Indeed, ingesting criticism merely as just another commodity to be consumed without further thought or action could be as dangerously ineffectual as defining individual power solely in terms of the ability to purchase consumer goods. One of the biggest challenges faced by those living in postwar America was now before them: for their minds, personalities, and senses of self to not fall victim to the planned obsolescence of the marketplace and thereby permanently place them in *The Twilight Zone.*

Conclusion

"These Things Cannot Be Confined to *The Twilight Zone*"

The Twilight Zone demonstrated how postwar television writers, including Rod Serling, Richard Matheson, Charles Beaumont, and George Clayton Johnson, could provocatively capture social issues despite the limitations placed on them by sponsors and networks. The wide range of issues and topics explored in Serling's series illustrates the ways television content could dramatically depict ideas within contemporary print culture and the public sphere alike. While some episodes captured critiques and ideas found in previously published works of social criticism, the series also creatively stood on its own. It showed how writers working within the medium of television could also capture anxieties and perils before they had been fully formulated and popularized in print form. Television shows carried the potential for making social criticism more palpable, imaginative, and accessible to postwar Americans; just as television was influenced by print culture and political debate, TV affected the worlds of print and public dialogue.

Overall, *The Twilight Zone* showed viewers how the haunted American Dream can perilously disconnect us from ourselves and each other. The addictive promises of pleasure, power, security, and independence through consumption could often leave buyers feeling empty. In this way, instead of postwar consumerism being the pathway to self-actualization, it could more easily lead us to self-alienation. If we could go back to some of these nightmares, what would some alternative dreams possibly look like? For Christie in "Living Doll," perhaps the dream would have less to do with a doll than with a safe home environment with loving parents and companions. For Marilyn in "Number 12 Looks Just Like You," it might have less to do with attaining artificial beauty standards than with having relationships where she could discuss her own emotions, memories, and ideas. In "A Stop at Willoughby," it might mean Gart has a job that provided him with more professional support and allowed him more free time to pursue his own interests. For those caught in Cold War paranoia amid the monsters on Maple Street, perhaps learning to trust and cooperate with the neighbors was more vital than distrusting their every idiosyncrasy. And instead of supporting programs for the sake of political and national prestige, Americans could be better off by supporting programs that prioritized their collective health and well-being. For veterans who fought in World War II and survived it, it might be slowly learning to grieve and release the torments of survivor guilt that haunted traumatized combatants. For those swept up in the exciting promises of technological changes like Whipple, it might mean finding ways to ensure new tech will benefit workers and their families, not simply leave them behind to increase profit margins. And for Jana in "The Lateness of the Hour," maybe the dream should not just promise security and predictability but instead empower her to break out of the confines of an oppressive home life and engage with the larger world. Maybe facing himself, his own pain, and insecurities, while learning to lean on those around him, would have given Peter Vollmer in "He's Alive" the strength he so desperately sought in a deranged, fraudulent, and racist ideology. Perhaps the dream should ultimately be less about achieving something external and more about seeing oneself and one's fellow humans more authentically.

The Twilight Zone was certainly not alone in its attempts to provide and provoke critical thought on television, as several other postwar programs demonstrated this back-and-forth relationship between social criticism and television. Among these shows, *Bewitched* (1964–1972), was one of the most successful and highly rated. While Betty Friedan and women's liberationists sharply criticized popular depictions of women, *Bewitched* served as an example of a television show trying to upend the very tropes the medium helped to popularize. Starring Elizabeth Montgomery as Samantha and Dick York as Darrin, the series centered on the couple's young married life. While Darrin has an ordinary white collar job as an ad executive, in the very first episode, Samantha is revealed to be a witch. Each ensuing episode largely centers on her struggle to conceal her real self and supernatural abilities from the world. Samantha still uses her power, however, and quite often it is to subvert inequality, privilege, and various forms of oppression. For example, she messes up the appearance and clothing of arrogant and privileged characters to undermine them, and she turns an overly flirtatious man into a dog.

She also exploits her witchcraft to finish the tedious and restricting chores of a housewife, including cleaning the kitchen. When her overworked husband cannot go on vacation with her, she even uses her powers to split him in two—one half to take on vacation and the other to stay at work.[1] The many ways she uses her powers speaks to her consistent desire to overcome the social inequalities, limitations, demands, and pressures that plague the mortal world. However, that she must constantly limit her use of those abilities and always conceal her true identity speaks to the actual limitations and obstacles faced by many American viewers at the time, particularly women and sexual and racial minorities.[2]

In a similar vein, *The Addams Family* (1964–1966) brought quirky and humorous satire of American family life to television. The series was based on Charles Addams's cartoons, originally published in the *New Yorker* in the 1930s, but it carried a new relevance in the context of postwar America. Featuring a cast of unusual and eccentric characters, including Morticia, Gomez, Lurch, Uncle Fester, Pugsley, and Wednesday, the series centers on the bizarre home life of the Addamses. The unusual home décor, including several pieces of mounted taxidermy, gothic furniture, and a Baroque-era harpsichord, indicates this is not the Cleavers' household or even zip code. The show constantly and playfully subverts audience expectations—Morticia's house plants, for example, feature an odd array of carnivorous specimens. She performs routine maintenance by trimming the flowers from her rose plants, preserving the thorns. Morticia and Gomez are disturbed by the truancy officer's demands that their children must go to school, just as they grow increasingly concerned about their son's "unusual" behaviors, including wanting to play sports and have a dog.

Meanwhile, the history of another program, *The Smothers Brothers Comedy Hour* (1967–1969), served as another reminder of the limits of postwar television. Despite airing at the same time as *Bonanza*, the *Smothers Brothers* was a runaway success, particularly with younger audiences. A variety show, the program featured a blend of comedic acts and musical guests, including Pete Seeger, George Harrison, Buffalo Springfield, Joan Baez, Ray Charles, and Jefferson Airplane. The program became increasingly controversial, however, with its inclusion of political satire, particularly aimed at the Vietnam War and the 1968 presidential election. Perhaps most famous of all, Pat Paulsen ran a presidential campaign as part of the show's biting political satire. The program's deadly mixture of being both popular and subversive proved more than enough to cause alarm to President Lyndon B. Johnson. He began calling

William S. Paley, the CEO of CBS, urging him to remove political content from the program. Ultimately Paley gave in, canceling the show in 1969.[3] If *The Twilight Zone, Bewitched,* and *The Addams Family* demonstrated how to creatively subvert the status quo on television, *The Smothers Brothers* reminded audiences of the medium's limitations.[4]

Serling's career following *The Twilight Zone* included a variety of different projects for both television and film. He wrote the screenplay for *Seven Days in May* (1964); attempted a short-lived western entitled *The Loner* (1965–1966); contributed to *The Planet of the Apes* (1968); wrote several specials for television, such as *A Carol for Another Christmas* (1964) and *Eyes* (1969); and was perhaps most recognized for his hosting *The Night Gallery* (1970–1973). Although Serling contributed to a couple of episodes, he lacked creative control of *The Night Gallery,* having been hired by Universal for his popular image. He soon found the show full of formulaic horror and cheap thrills, conspicuously lacking the incisive social element he had injected into *The Twilight Zone.* "I'm staying on as announcer. . . . It's not mine at all. It's another species of formula series drama," he once remarked. After fighting so long against sponsors' dominant control of the medium, he also was hired for several TV advertisements. He narrated a Proctor & Gamble ad for floor wax and offered his celebrity status to Crest, Anacin, and Z-Best rustproofing.[5] While in his later years he seemed to be compromising his strongly held beliefs, this was partially because he had, regrettably, sold CBS the rights to *The Twilight Zone* following the show's last season. The show airs today on the Syfy channel, where it has a dedicated New Year's marathon, and it has made the leap to streaming, with Netflix, Hulu, and Paramount+ having carried the series. Serling, who proved prophetic in so many ways, failed to see the longevity of his creative output.

Regardless of these late struggles, Serling remained interested in democracy and social issues. In his later years, he found a new outlet on college campuses. In 1967, he began to teach writing classes at Ithaca College, where he remained a faculty member until his death in 1975. Thus, while his platform for social criticism had largely vanished from popular media, he regained it to some extent in the classroom. He not only taught courses but frequently made appearances at universities throughout the nation, including UCLA in 1966 and 1971 and in 1970, USC, where he gave the commencement address. These invitations to teach and speak during the height of many social movements in the United States demonstrate *The Twilight Zone's* enduring impact.

And while the phrase *The Twilight Zone* has entered into our vernacular, indicating something eerily fantastic or odd, this common usage seems to miss the point. For it was not the illusory or fantastical that served as the show's true foundation, but the perilously real particularities and prejudices that make up our actual world—the hazardous, oppressive, mind-numbing elements that we too often accept without question. These features were never exclusive to *The Twilight Zone* and never will be. By making "reality" seem stranger and more grotesque to relatively insulated Americans, Serling sought to call attention to the fact that their reality is arbitrarily constructed. Whether Americans choose, somewhat subconsciously, to cede to marketers, politicians, pundits, and actors, all responsibility and power in defining reality, without actively contributing themselves, still remains to be seen.

In a related sense, Serling also exemplified a trend that became increasingly apparent during the postwar period—the commodification of cultural dissent. While Gil Scott-Heron declared, "The Revolution Will Not Be Televised," manufacturers and marketers figured out ways to do just this, repackaging elements of the counterculture and selling them right back to "nonconforming" Americans, thereby ensuring their conformity. As Thomas Frank has recently explained, "The anointed cultural opponents of capitalism are now capitalism's ideologues." Instead of advertisers putting forth an image of conformity, tradition, and conservative values, they have, like Nike did in 1994 with William S. Burroughs, invited their once ardent critics to boost their hip factor and expand their markets to the most marginal would-be social rebels. From Burger King, one learns, "Sometimes you gotta break the rules," while Levi's lets the jean-wearing public know, "There's no one way to do it."[6] If imitation is the sincerest form of flattery, then American marketers have deluged the counterculture with an endless torrent of it. Consequently, the sponsored world has effectively declawed its once outspoken critics and offered them an open-ended invitation to join it. The world of consumerism now actively pursues the unorthodox, marginalized, and nonconforming members of the world in order to come up with fresh, new ideas, a phenomenon explored in the PBS documentaries *Merchants of Cool* and *Generation Like.*[7] Meanwhile, numerous *The Twilight Zone* characters have been transformed just like Dan Hollis was by Anthony in "It's a Good Life": they are literally now toys.

For some, this inclusion of the counterculture in the marketplace provides evidence of the democratization and inclusivity of consumer capitalism. Although racially and culturally inclusive imagery is increasingly found in ads, products, slogans, and industries, they remain largely that—images.

Whether the imagery comes from MLK, the Beat writers, the Black Panthers, social activists, or punk rockers, their truly subversive ideas are effectively removed. Consumers everywhere can now enjoy noncontroversial and intellectually dull versions of some of the most probing minds in American history. The social critics, poets, and singers of the postwar era have been manipulated and decontextualized to suit the whims of marketing campaigns. Even though William Burroughs reassures us in his Nike ad that "the purpose of technology is not to confuse the brain," there is indeed something confusing about all of this. In the same vein, why Crest once wanted to feature Serling, a world-renowned chain-smoker, to be its spokesman is a bit perplexing. But apart from simple ironies like these, there is something far more troubling at work: these figures' genuine intellectual thought has vanished before the public's eye as a direct result of being "incorporated." While the more frequent appearance of countercultural voices and critics in ads may make companies seem more eclectic, hip, and smart, they have quite possibly fooled us—if we believe that they, as companies, or the United States, as a society, genuinely embody the principles of those voices.

The revolution, in fact, is not just being televised, it is being outright promoted. For example, ZzzQuil tells one on MLK Day, "Today is the day for dreaming."[8] This irony seems almost too much to bear: a murdered civil rights leader is used to promote sleeping aids. Similarly, Popchips reminded chip eaters everywhere that MLK was a "poptomist" and featured his words, "The time is always right to do what is right," probably the vaguest and most malleable statement from MLK they could find.[9] Consumers are not encouraged consider how King worked tirelessly against poverty, economic inequality, racial violence, voter suppression, and American wars that killed millions of people. Even more recently, MLK has been wildly misappropriated in the fight against teaching Critical Race Theory or even talking about systemic racism in the interest of "colorblindness." Ibram X. Kendi has referred to it as the "second assassination of Martin Luther King Jr." and explained how "King's nightmare of racism is being presented as his dream."[10]

Nina Simone has also recently been given a second career thanks to Ford. She posthumously promoted the automobile manufacturer's 2017 line with her song "I Wish I Knew How It Would Feel to Be Free," in an advertisement along with footage of people being stuck in traffic and a poor cat that cannot get its head out of a box. Her once powerful appeal to justice, "I wish I could break all the chains holding me," now relates to simple inconveniences, like putting on pants. The fight for racial equality has been mindlessly equated with inconvenient work commutes and wearing shirts that are perhaps a little too tight to take off. While Simone worked tirelessly to promote racial equality and justice in the postwar United States, Ford reassuringly explained: "No one likes being stuck. That's why Ford is developing new ways to help you through life—faster, easier, better. Today and tomorrow we're going further so you can."

While marketing approaches and images have changed since *The Twilight Zone,* one element has remained constant—the final, simplistic, solution. Just as appliance manufacturers ensured parents that a piece of modern technology could free them to be more attentive to their families, the purchases of certain clothing items, beverages, cars, and cologne still offer guarantees of freedom. Similarly, consumer purchases are supposedly the most authentic means of confirming one's status as a self-actualized social rebel. Instead of being empowered to think critically, act collectively, and seek to resist and regulate sources of corruption that permeate society, one can, among other things, indulge in a midnight snack. Rather than think outside the proverbial box, those who are genuinely hungry for change can instead simply "think outside the bun" by placing an order at a conveniently located Taco Bell drive-thru. Being a nonconforming rebel has never been so easy.

During his years as a television writer, Serling asked, "How can you put out a meaningful drama when every fifteen minutes proceedings are interrupted by twelve dancing rabbits with toilet paper?" The question is now "How can you promote critical thought, meaningful action, and intellectual stimulation when proceedings are now interrupted by civil rights activists promoting Ford Motor vehicles?" In other words, how can one argue for the continual need to support and fight for one's rights and those of the others, when the voices of such social causes have been domesticated and mischaracterized so profoundly? Marketers have taken the work and thought of social critics and turned them into a cozy image or warm feeling. But Americans are in serious danger of amnesia if they cede all control and historical memory to marketers whose primary interest remains improving *their* images, boosting *their* sales, and making consumers "feel something." Restoring singers, activists, and writers to their proper context, focusing on their unique work and ideas, rather than image, is clearly a vital need. If America's history is to be maintained and not endlessly vandalized by marketing and political campaigns, then a more concerted effort is required.

This implies a need not to simply offer historical actors some kind of vague reverence but to constructively and creatively maintain the connection of strugglers *with* their struggle, as well as our own. It has been my attempt here to show that innovative thinkers and writers, are in fact "stuck" by the very marketing that promises liberation, and consequently, so are we. Along with these historical actors, it is clear that we too, need to exist beyond the "dimension of sight and sound," but be once again allowed to dwell with others, living and deceased, in the "dimension of mind." By reconnecting *The Twilight Zone* to the rich intellectual world in which it emerged, I have sought to do the opposite of marketers—emphasize the significant and durable ideas, rather than the overly recognizable images.

The continual cultural significance of *The Twilight Zone*, however, is represented through not merely the marketing and commodification of the show's recognizable images and characters but the persistent need for social criticism within popular media. The most obvious example is the 2019 *The Twilight Zone* reboot, hosted by Jordan Peele, which revived the original program but also, in some ways, Serling's pre–*Twilight Zone* career. The first episode, "The Comedian," has the same title and subject matter as one of Serling's Emmy-award-winning 1950s teleplays. Serling's 1957 work, starring Mickey Rooney, told the story of a viciously ambitious comedian who abused anyone and everyone around him. Similarly, the 2019 episode follows a fledgling comedian, Samir Wassan, played by Kumail Nanjiani, whose jokes about the Second Amendment and political issues consistently fall flat with audiences. After Samir realizes he can get more laughs by incorporating more personal matter, such as making fun of people from his past and present life, his career quickly takes off. His skyrocketing success, however, does not come for free, as he realizes that everyone he incorporates into his routine vanishes, never to be heard from or seen again. Very soon, his dog, his girlfriend's nephew, former classmates, and current coworkers disappear. Undeterred, Samir continues using different people in his comedy, even taking vengeance against unruly audience members by making fun of them and ensuring their disappearance. The point is clear enough—he will use and destroy anyone to advance his career and fame. When his ex-girlfriend shows up at the club where he is performing and calls him out for his abusive tactics, he makes his last joke about himself, thereby ensuring his own disappearance. Peele closes the episode: "Samir Wassan learned the hard way that sometimes getting everything you want means losing everything you love. And after finally finding himself on the verge of becoming somebody, he chose instead to once again be a nobody. In the end, Samir's final encore is a show you can only buy a ticket to . . . in *The Twilight Zone*." This episode, like so many in the original series, dramatizes the wages of success and achieving one's version of the American Dream. The new series carried the legacy, exploring such themes such as post-traumatic stress disorder, immigration, consumer culture, and misogyny.

However, one of the series' most powerful episodes returns to the one of the major reasons for the creation of *The Twilight Zone*: racial prejudice and injustice. The episode, "Replay," features a plot device from "A Most Unusual Camera," in the original series (S1, e3; S2, e10). While "A Most Unusual Camera" told the story of a camera that could foresee the future, "Replay," incorporates a camcorder that can turn back time, making it possible to alter the past. The episode features an African American family, Nina Harrison, played by Sanaa Lathan, and her son Dorian Harrison, played by Damson Idris. Dorian is accompanied by his mom as he is off to start college at Tennyson University, a historically Black university. The episode ultimately revolves around their repeated encounters with a racist police officer, Officer Lesky, who continually finds reasons to suspect them of wrongdoing. Each time they encounter him, first for speeding on a highway, later on for a noise complaint at a hotel, the exchanges escalate dramatically: the cop uses a taser on Dorian in one instance and slams his face against a glass picture frame in another. Each time, however, Nina uses the camcorder to turn back the clock, giving them another chance to reach their destination without having to encounter racial profiling and police brutality. Having rewound the tape one more time, Nina sees the officer in the diner and offers to buy him a slice of apple pie as a gesture of appreciation for his service. Her plan to gain the officer's trust, however, backfires as he soon suspects she stole her car, and he demands to see the vehicle title. As Dorian reaches for his cell phone to show the officer a photo of the car's title, Lesky fires a round into Dorian's chest. Dorian and Nina seemingly cannot escape violent run-ins with the same racist officer, no matter how many times Nina rewinds the tape.

Finally, taking a different route, Nina and Dorian visit Nina's estranged brother. With his help, Nina and Dorian find an underground tunnel that leads to Tennyson University. When they emerge on the surface, though, the officer pulls up and begins questioning them again. While Nina holds the camera, Officer Lesky says, "You think you can intimidate me with a camcorder? Don't you watch the news?" Nina replies, "You've crossed the line. Harassing us, abusing authority. You've been profiling us, targeting us, following us, shooting us, killing us. Not anymore. Now we cross the line. My son will cross that gate. Right now, right here. My son will go to college. So back the fuck up!" She finally adds, "I see it now, Officer Lasky. You're the one who's really afraid." The episode concludes with Peele's closing narration: "Nina Harrison found that only by embracing her past could she protect her son's future. And it was love, not magic, that kept evil at bay. But for some evils, there are no magical, permanent solutions, and the future remains uncertain even here in *The Twilight Zone*." The fact this episode aired amid a string of killings, whose victims were Trayvon Martin, Michael Brown, Sandra Bland, Alton Sterling, and many others, demonstrates the desperate need for popular media to continue to expose and address rampant social injustice.

While Serling would undoubtedly be troubled by the great number of injustices still being perpetrated in American society, he would be glad to see that there still are television writers who share his social consciousness and concern. Writer and producer Charlie Brooker's creative output, including *How TV Ruined Your Life,* which focuses on the suppression of reality on television, and *Black Mirror,* centering on technology's impact on modern life, are clear descendants of Serling's series. And in 2016, Ithaca College created the Rod Serling Award for Advancing Social Justice through Popular Media. The annual award was first given to David Simon, whose best-known work includes *The Wire* and *Treme,* dramatic explorations of urban life in Baltimore and New Orleans. In its second year, the award went to Kenya Barris, whose show *black-ish* has included commentary on police shootings, complicated aspects of raising Black children in America, and the continual struggle for racial equality. It remains clear that there is a need and a demand among public audiences for popular media to broach controversial subject matter so that they might not be entertained to death, but to think and thereby more meaningfully connect to their real world.

While twenty-first century Americans continue to experience various aspects of the American Nightmare, there remains a profound need for writers and sponsors, in the words of Theodor Adorno, to "let suffering speak." If Americans desire to live in a representative democracy, there is no question that one of the essential requirements for doing so is having more representative media that reflects the diverse experiences of being an American. As Serling told USC graduates in 1970, "It's simply a national acknowledgement that in any kind of priority, the needs of human beings must come first. Poverty is here and now. Hunger is here and now. Racial tension is here and now. Pollution is here and now. These are the things that scream for a response. And if we don't listen to that scream—and if we don't respond to it—we may well wind up sitting amidst our own rubble, looking for the truck that hit us—or the bomb that pulverized us. Get the license number of whatever it was that destroyed the dream. And I think we will find that the vehicle was registered in our own name." For Adorno, Serling, and the large number of postwar critics, articulating anguish was an essential requirement for revealing truth and helping to mitigate injustice. TV and popular media, however, still operate, in the words of Serling's opening narration, in the "middle ground between light and shadow" and "between the pit of man's fears and the summit of knowledge." And as news programs are increasingly formatted as entertainment outlets, it is arguably even more imperative now than ever for creative writers to cast light on socially destructive shadows and expose real suffering.

In the present day, these issues have only become more complicated with the increasing amounts of mass media constantly before our eyes and penetrating our minds. But with all that we are supposedly looking at, we are *not* looking at even more. As Serling expressed, "the moment you begin to censor the writer—and history bears this out in the ugliest of fashions—so begins a process of decay in the body politic that ultimately leads to disaster. . . . It has forever been thus: So long as men write what they think, then all of the other freedoms—all of them—may remain intact. And it is then that writing becomes a weapon of truth, an article of faith, an act of courage."[11] During his short lifetime, Serling found a creative way to express important social concerns, but that he had to do so in such a concealed way exposes how sponsorship, financial backing, and wealth powerfully affect one's ability to do so. Thus, *The Twilight Zone* revealed the underlying conflicts between democracy and capitalism and the limitations of a commodity attempting to critique commodification. Contemporary organizations, including the Algorithmic Justice League and the Center for Humane Technology, have shown how our carefully curated, individualized, and atomized experiences with online media today present these challenges anew. Layers of algorithmic complexity and "disinformation for profit" business models continue to innovate and proliferate and threaten our relationships with ourselves, each other, and the truth.

But *The Twilight Zone* also exemplified some of the limited ways popular media can be a signpost, directing its audience toward larger social issues, as well as a broader, deeper world of social criticism and intellectual thought. By censoring, obfuscating, burying, or ignoring a variety of social issues, Americans continue to place limits on living in truth. Only by exposing and looking at our nation and world honestly can we sustain constructive national conversations and minimize social problems and suffering. As Serling once stated, "there is nothing in the dark that isn't there when the lights are on." Postwar social critics helped to ensure the lights not only stayed on but perhaps even shone a bit brighter in some places. Far from doing a disservice to the nation, social commentary serves the national interest by perpetually holding it accountable. James Baldwin expressed in his 1955 work, *Notes of a Native Son,* "I love America more than any other country in this world, and, exactly for this reason, I insist on the right to criticize her perpetually." In this sense, it is the thoughtful critics, not the cheering section, that may prove most valuable in sustaining a nation's health and well-being. Whether that same nation can learn to love its critics back and be willing to look at its own shadow is a question that most assuredly cannot be confined to *The Twilight Zone.*

Acknowledgments

I first came across *The Twilight Zone* as a teenager, watching an annual Syfy Channel New Year's Eve marathon. I was enthralled—there was just something different about this show. What made the series stand apart was how it creatively played with the human imagination and, at the same time, exuded something deeply serious, critical, and dramatic. From Bernard Herrmann's opening bars of tense, mystifying orchestral music to Rod Serling's no-nonsense opening narrations, one thing was clear—what we were about to watch was not just for fun or for some fleeting sense of amusement. And I loved that. I loved that the show took itself seriously—that it took the screenwriting, music, casting, and production seriously. In doing so, it took viewers seriously, too—it took *you* and *me* seriously. The viewers' time was not to be wasted or taken for granted. Our time was, and still is, precious.

From my initiation to the show in my young adult years, I never could have predicted that the series would form the basis of an academic project that has spanned nearly a decade. Many people have shared their precious time and lives with me and made this project possible. I am deeply grateful to all of you. Chuck Shindo supported my idea from the very beginning and has been an invaluable guide along each step of the way. You are an amazing mentor and friend, Chuck, thank you. I am thankful for the number of amazing historians who have also helped me get here, particularly Aaron Sheehan-Dean, Nancy Isenberg, Alecia Long, Mike Smith, and Ronald Berger for their vital support and help throughout my academic journey. I am grateful for my colleagues Andy Wollard, Mark Ehlers, Zach Isenhower, Jeff Crawford, Jay Awtrey, Tom Barber, Lindsay Silver Hollembaek, Garrett McKinnon, and Justin Overman for providing such supportive academic camaraderie. Thank you, friends. I also thank the Wisconsin Historical Society for providing such an amazing space and staff while I poured through its collections and the Rod Serling Papers. I also want to especially thank Natalie O'Neal, Erin Holman, and Tara Dugan at the University Press of Kentucky for their tremendous support, constructive criticism, and time. And finally, I am especially grateful to my partner, Elizabeth, who has been with me throughout all the highs and lows of this project and who has provided an almost unimaginable amount of support and love. Thank you all for making this possible.

Notes

Introduction

1. Ernest Dichter, *The Strategy of Desire,* (Garden City, NY: Doubleday, 1960), 92–93.

2. Dichter, *Strategy of Desire,* 109.

3. Lawrence B. Glickman's *Buying Power: A History of Consumer Activism in America* (Chicago: University of Chicago, 2009) offers a lively account of consumer movements from the nation's founding up to the twenty-first century.

4. Louis Hyman's *Debtor Nation: The History of America in Red Ink* (Princeton, NJ: Princeton University, 2011) details how credit was responsible for both postwar affluence and its decline, creating borrowing habits that would affect the stagflation of the 1970s.

5. Andrew J. Falk, *Upstaging the Cold War American Dissent and Cultural Diplomacy, 1940–1960* (Amherst: University of Massachusetts Press, 2011) 132, 152.

6. Erik Barnouw, *Tube of Plenty: The Evolution of American Television,* 2nd rev. ed. (New York: Oxford University Press, 1990), 167, 163.

7. Falk, *Upstaging the Cold War,* 127.

8. Barnouw, *Tube of Plenty,* 166, 163.

9. Quoted in Gordon Sander, *The Rise and Twilight of TV's Last Angry Man* (New York: Dutton, 1992), 135.

10. Barnouw, *Tube of Plenty,* 163.

11. Alan Nadel, *Television in Black-and-White America: Race and National Identity* (Lawrence: University Press of Kansas, 2005), 7.

12. Adilifu Nama, *Black Space: Imagining Race in Science Fiction Film* (Austin: University of Texas Press, 2008), 10.

13. Ralph Ellison, *Invisible Man* (New York: Random House, 1952), 3–4.

14. Richard Dyer, "White," *Screen* 29, Fall 1994, 44.

15. Malcolm X, "The Ballot or the Bullet," speech delivered at King Solomon Baptist Church in Detroit, Michigan, April 12, 1964, available online at Jamie McCallum's Political Society course website, Middlebury College, accessed November 11,

2022, https://sites.middlebury.edu/soan365/files/2013/02/Malcolm-X-The-Ballot-or-the-Bullet.pdf.

16. William Bradford Huie, "The Shocking Story of Approved Killing in Mississippi," *Look*, January 24, 1956, 46–54.

17. Timothy B. Tyson, *The Blood of Emmett Till* (New York: Simon & Schuster, 2017), 6–7.

18. Alex Traub, "1955 Arrest Warrant in Emmett Till Case Is Found in Court Basement," *New York Times*, June 30, 2022.

19. Rod Serling, *Patterns: Four Television Plays with the Author's Personal Commentaries* (New York: Simon & Schuster, 1957), 20–23.

20. Interview with Rod Serling, *The Mike Wallace Interview* (September 22, 1959; New York: American Broadcasting Company, 1959), available online as "The Mike Wallace Interview featuring Rod Serling (1959)," YouTube video, 36:14, posted by Wilma Valencia, December 18, 2017, https://www.youtube.com/watch?v=KBmcvVwK6XY.

21. Abraham S. Burack, *Television Plays for Writers* (Boston: Writer, 1957), 355–56.

22. Sander, *Serling*, xvii.

23. "Definition of Addiction," American Society of Addiction Medicine website, 2019, asam.org/quality-care/definition-of-addiction.

24. George Lipsitz, *The Possessive Investment in Whiteness: How White People Profit from Identity Politics* (Philadelphia: Temple University Press, 2018), vii–viii.

25. James Baldwin, "Letter to My Nephew," *Progressive Magazine*, December 1962.

26. Quoted in Anne Serling, *As I Knew Him: My Dad, Rod Serling* (New York: Citadel, 2013), 161.

27. Marshall McLuhan, *Understanding Media: The Extensions of Man* (New York: McGraw Hill, 1964), 32.

28. Newton Minow, "Television and the Public Interest," speech delivered May 9, 1961, National Association of Broadcasters, Washington, DC, available at *American Rhetoric: Online Speech Bank*, https://www.americanrhetoric.com/speeches/newtonminow.htm.

29. Minnow, "Television and the Public Interest."

30. Evan Brier, *A Novel Marketplace: Mass Culture, the Book Trade, and Postwar American Fiction* (Philadelphia: University of Pennsylvania Press, 2010).

31. Jon Kraszewski, *The New Entrepreneurs: An Institutional History of Television Anthology Writers* (Middletown, CT: Wesleyan University Press, 2010), 173.

32. Barry Keith Grant, The Twilight Zone (Detroit: Wayne State University Press, 2020), 17.

33. Martin Grams Jr., The Twilight Zone: *Unlocking the Door to a Television Classic* (Churchville, MD: OTR Publishing, 2008); Steven Jay Rubin, The Twilight

Zone *Encyclopedia* (Chicago: Chicago Review Press, 2018); Mark Dawidziak, *Everything I Need to Know I Learned in* The Twilight Zone: *A Fifth Dimension Guide to Life* (New York: Thomas Dunne Books, 2017); Marc Scott Zicree, The Twilight Zone *Companion*, 2nd ed. (Los Angeles: Silman-James Press, 1992).

34. Nicholas Parisi, *Rod Serling: His Life, Work, and Imagination* (Jackson: University Press of Mississippi, 2018); Serling, *As I Knew Him*; Sander, *Rise and Twilight of TV's Last Angry Man*.

35. Nadel, *Television in Black-and-White America*.

36. Lawrence R. Samuel, *Brought to You By: Postwar Advertising and the American Dream* (Austin: University of Texas Press, 2001), 84.

37. Stephanie Coontz, *The Way We Never Were: American Families and the Nostalgia Trap* (New York: Basic Books, 1992), 9.

38. Thomas Doherty, *Cold War, Cool Medium: Television, McCarthyism, and American Culture* (New York: Columbia University Press, 2003).

39. Lynn Spigel, *Make Room for TV: Television and the Family Ideal in Post-war America* (Chicago: University of Chicago Press, 1992).

40. Susan J. Douglas, *Where the Girls Are: Growing Up Female with the Mass Media* (New York: Three Rivers Press, 1995).

41. Robert M. Entman and Andrew Rojecki, *The Black Image in the White Mind: Media and Race in America* (Chicago: University of Chicago Press, 2000).

42. Taylor Nygaard and Jorie Lagerwey, *Horrible White People: Gender, Genre, and Television's Precarious Whiteness* (New York: New York University Press, 2020).

43. Lawrence R. Samuel, *Freud on Madison Avenue: Motivation Research and Subliminal Advertising in America* (Philadelphia: University of Pennsylvania Press, 2010), 11.

44. Sigmund Freud, *The Interpretation of Dreams*, trans. James Strachey (New York: Basic Books, 1955), 149.

45. *Advertising and Selling*, September 8, 1926, 27.

46. Carl Jung, *Man and His Symbols* (New York: Dell, 1964), 34.

47. Roland Marchand, *Advertising the American Dream: Making Way for Modernity, 1920–1940* (Berkeley: University of California Press, 1985), xvii.

48. Jung, *Man and His Symbols*, 73.

1. A Haunting Hatred

1. "I Am the Night—Color Me Black," in *As Timeless as Infinity: The Complete Twilight Zone Scripts of Rod Serling*, ed. Tony Albarella, 10 vols. (Colorado Springs: Gauntlet, 2005), 2:501–4

2. Rod Serling, interview, *Los Angeles Times*, June 25, 1967.

3. Rod Serling, speech, August 1, 1968, Ithaca, NY, Rod Serling Papers, 1943–1971, Wisconsin Historical Society, Madison.

4. Frederick J. Simonelli, *American Fuehrer: George Lincoln Rockwell and the American Nazi Party* (Champaign: University of Illinois Press, 1999), 2, 21–23.

5. Sergei Aleksandrovich Nilus, *Protocols of the Meetings of the Zionist Men of Wisdom* (Boston: Small, Maynard, & Company, 1920), 67.

6. Philip Graves, "Proof that the Jewish Protocols Were Forged," *New York Times,* September 4, 1921.

7. Adolf Hitler, *Mein Kampf* (1925; repr., New York: Houghton-Mifflin, 1998), 307

8. "Ford's Anti-Semitism," interview with Hasia Diner, *American Experience,* PBS, accessed October 3, 2022, https://www.pbs.org/wgbh/americanexperience /features/henryford-antisemitism/.

9. "A Hoax of Hate: The Protocols of the Learned Elders of Zion," *Backgrounder,* Anti-Defamation League, January 5, 2013, https://www.adl.org /resources/backgrounders/a-hoax-of-hate-the-protocols-of-the-learned-elders-of-zion

10. James Q. Whitman, *Hitler's American Model: The United States and the Making of Nazi Race Law* (Princeton, NJ: Princeton University Press, 2018), 37

11. Hitler, *Mein Kampf,* 149–50, 64

12. Simonelli, *American Fuehrer,* 23.

13. FBI File #9–39854, "American Nazi Party," 17, available at *FBI Records: The Vault,* Freedom of Information Act website, accessed November 12, 2022, https://vault.fbi.gov/American%20Nazi%20Party%20

14. Simonelli, *American Fuehrer,* 21–23

15. Quoted in Whitman, *Hitler's American Model,* 116.

16. Ronald Takaki, *A Different Mirror: A History of Multicultural America* (New York: Back Bay Books, 2008), 286–87.

17. Erika Lee, *The Making of Asian-America: A History* (New York: Simon & Schuster, 2016), 134–35.

18. The Immigration Act of 1924 (The Johnson-Reed Act), Pub. L. No. 68-139, 43 Stat. 153 (1924).

19. Hitler, *Mein Kampf,* 438–39.

20. Whitman, *Hitler's American Model,* 29–30.

21. Madison Grant, *The Passing of the Great Race; or, The Racial Basis of European History* (New York: Scribner & Sons, 1916), 263

22. Ruth C. Engs, *The Eugenics Movement: An Encyclopedia* (Westport, CT: Greenwood, 2005), 102.

23. David Scott FitzGerald and David Cook-Martin, *Culling the Masses: The Democratic Origins of Racist Immigration Policy in the Americas* (Cambridge, MA: Harvard University Press, 2014), 115.

24. Adolf Hitler, "Address to the Reichstag," January 30, 1939, available at the Internet Archive, https://archive.org/details/AdolfHitlersSpeechDeliveredBefore TheGermanReichstagOnJanuary30th1939/page/n5/mode/2up?view=theater.

25. For additional background on the second Ku Klux Klan, refer to Linda Gordon's *The Second Coming of the KKK: The Ku Klux Klan of the 1920s and the American Political Tradition* (New York: Liveright, 2017)

26. *New York Times*, February 27, 1939.

27. Ben Macin, "Anti-Semitism: A Shield," *Social Justice*, December 5, 1938, 3.

28. Charles Coughlin, *The Golden Hour of the Little Flower*, radio broadcast, November 20, 1938, Royal Oak, MI.

29. Charles Coughlin, "Background of Persecution," *Social Justice*, December 5, 1938, 7.

30. Thomas Doherty, "The Deplatforming of Father Coughlin," *Slate Magazine*, January 21, 2021, https://slate.com/technology/2021/01/father-coughlin-deplatforming-radio-social-media.html.

31. Steven J. Simmons, *The Fairness Doctrine and the Media* (Berkeley: University of California Press, 1978), 60.

32. William Kovarik, "When Radio Stations Stopped a Public Figure from Spreading Dangerous Lies," *Smithsonian Magazine*, January 19, 2021, https://www.smithsonianmag.com/history/time-private-us-media-companies-stepped-silence-falsehoods-and-incitements-major-public-figure-1938-180976771/.

33. Herbert Kier, "Volk, Rasse und Stat," *National Socialist Handbook for Law and Legislation* (Summer 1934): 27–28.

34. Richard J. Evans, *The Third Reich in Power* (New York: Penguin, 2005), 544.

35. Phyl Newbeck, "*Loving v. Virginia* (1967)," *Encyclopedia Virginia*, Virginia Humanities, December 2020, https://encyclopediavirginia.org/entries/loving-v-virginia-1967/#:~:text=In%20Loving%20v.,violation%20of%20the%20 Fourteenth%20Amendment.

36. Richard M. Dalfiume, "The Forgotten Years of the Negro Revolution," *Journal of American History* 55, no. 1 (June 1968): 90–106.

37. James Q. Thompson, "Should I Sacrifice to Live 'Half American?'" *Pittsburgh Courier*, January 31, 1942.

38. Langston Hughes, "Beaumont to Detroit: 1943," *Common Ground* (Fall 1943): 104.

39. Dalfiume, "Forgotten Years of the Negro Revolution."

40. David Onkst, "First a Negro . . . Incidentally a Veteran: Black World War Two Veterans and the G. I. Bill of Rights in the Deep South, 1944–1948," *Journal of Social History*, 31, no. 3 (Spring 1998): 517–43.

41. Hilary Herbold, "Never a Level Playing Field: Blacks and the GI Bill," *Journal of Blacks in Higher Education* 6 (Winter 1994):104–8.

42. "Ex-Marine Slain for Moving Jim Crow Sign," *Chicago Defender,* February 23, 1946.

43. Susan Lederer, *Flesh and Blood: Organ Transplantation and Blood Transfusion in Twentieth Century America* (New York: Oxford University Press, 2008).

44. Governor George C. Wallace, 1963 inaugural address, Alabama Department of Archives and History, Montgomery, available online at Alabama Media Group website, http://media.al.com/spotnews/other/George%20Wallace%20 1963%20Inauguration%20Speech.pdf

45. Gene Santoro, *Myself When I Am Real: The Life and Music of Charles Mingus* (New York: Oxford University Press, 2001), 154.

46. Adam Chandler, "How the Civil Rights Era Made and Broke Nina Simone," *Atlantic,* June 27, 2015.

47. Quoted in Mark Boulton, "Sending the Extremists to the Cornfield: Rod Serling's Crusade against Conservatism," *Journal of Popular Culture* 47, no. 6 (December 2014): 1226.

48. Rick Perlstein, "Exclusive: Lee Atwater's Infamous 1981 Interview on the Southern Strategy," *Nation,* November 13, 2012, https://www.thenation.com /article/archive/exclusive-lee-atwaters-infamous-1981-interview-southern-strategy/.

49. Simonelli, *American Fuehrer,* 2–3.

50. Ruth Benedict, *Race and Racism,* (London: Routledge & Sons, 1942), 137, 138–39.

51. Martin Luther King Jr., "The American Dream," speech delivered at Ebenezer Baptist Church, Atlanta, Georgia, July 4, 1965.

52. Simonelli, *American Fuehrer,* 137–39.

53. A. M. Rosenthal and Arthur Gelb, *One More Victim: The Life and Death of a Jewish Nazi* (New York: New American Library, 1968), 88.

54. Simonelli, *American Fuehrer,* 145.

55. James Baldwin, "The Uses of the Blues," in *The Cross of Redemption: Uncollected Writings,* ed. Randall Kenan (New York: Pantheon, 2010), 84.

56. Hannah Arendt, *The Origins of Totalitarianism* (New York: World, 1951), 475–76.

57. Arendt, *Origins of Totalitarianism,* 474.

58. For a more recent discussion of this topic, see Heather McGee's *The Sum of Us: What Racism Costs Everyone and How We Can Prosper Together* (London: One World, 2021) and Jonathan Metzl's *Dying of Whiteness: How the Politics of Racial Resentment Is Killing America's Heartland* (New York: Basic Books, 2019)

59. Arendt, *Origins of Totalitarianism,* 315.

60. Baldwin quoted in Eddie S. Glaude, *Begin Again: James Baldwin's America and Its Urgent Lessons for Our Own* (New York: Crown, 2020), 91

61. George Schuyler, "The Negro Struggle" *Pittsburgh Courier,* December 21, 1940.

62. Abraham Foxman, introduction to Hitler, *Mein Kampf,* xxi.

2. Fighting a War, Combating a Myth

1. "Rod Serling: The Facts of Life," interview by Linda Brevelle, *Writer's Digest,* March 1976, available at the Rod Serling Memorial Foundation website: https://rodserling.com/rod-serlings-final-interview/.

2. Theodore J. Hull, "The World War II Army Enlistment Records File and Access to Archival Databases," *Prologue* 38, no. 1 (Spring 2006), https://www .archives.gov/publications/prologue/2006/spring/aad-ww2.html

3. Gordon F. Sander, *Serling: The Rise and Twilight of TV's Last Angry Man* (Ithaca, NY: Cornell University Press, 2012), 36.

4. Elaine Scarry, *The Body in Pain: The Making and Unmaking of the World* (New York: Oxford University Press, 1987), 60.

5. Paul Fussell, *Wartime: Understanding and Behavior in the Second World War* (New York: Oxford University Press, 1990), 267–68.

6. Rod Serling, speech, August 1, 1968, Ithaca, NY, Rod Serling Papers, 1943–1971, Wisconsin Historical Society, Madison.

7. John Lamberton Harper, *The Cold War* (New York: Oxford University Press, 2011), 17–18.

8. Eugene B. Sledge, *With the Old Breed: At Peleliu and Okinawa* (New York: Oxford University Press, 1981) 34.

9. E. M. Flanagan, *The Angels: A History of the 11th Airborne Division* (Novato, CA: Presidio Press, 1989), 171.

10. For a more extensive discussion on masculinity and warfare, refer to Chaim F. Shatan, "Happiness Is a Warm Gun: Militarized Mourning and Ceremonial Vengeance," *Vietnam Generation* 1, no. 3 (1989): 127–51. For a deeper discussion of masculinity and television, refer to Rebecca Feasey's *Masculinity and Popular Television* (Edinburgh: Edinburgh University Press, 2008).

11. Flanagan, *Angels,* 199.

12. *Leatherneck,* March 1945, 37.

13. John W. Dower, *War without Mercy: Race and Power in the Pacific War* (New York: Pantheon Books, 1986), 11.

14. Sledge, *With the Old Breed,* 152.

15. Sledge, *With the Old Breed,* 148

16. Anthony Coulis, "When Marines Wondered," in *The Purple Testament: Life Stories by Disabled War Veterans,* ed. Don M. Wolfe (Harrisburg, PA: Stackpole Sons, 1946), 191–92.

17. Quoted in James Patterson's *Grand Expectations: The United States, 1945–1974* (New York: Oxford University Press, 1996), 23, 24.

18. Lizabeth Cohen, *A Consumer's Republic: The Politics of Mass Consumption in Postwar America* (New York: Vintage, 2003), 167–69.

19. Dower, *War without Mercy,* 12.

20. Sledge, *With the Old Breed,* 60.

21. Rod Serling, speech, August 1, 1968, Ithaca, NY.

22. Rod Serling, Lecture #2, East Lansing Michigan, May 1971, on *Rod Serling Speaks* (New York: Master Classics Records, 2008).

23. Rod Serling, "One of the Wounded," *The Loner* (New York: Columbia Broadcasting System, October 15, 1965).

24. For more on this topic, see Allen Bérubé, *Coming Out Under Fire: The History of Gay Men and Women in World War Two* (New York: Free Press, 1990).

25. Harry Stack Sullivan, "Mental Hygiene and National Defense: A Year of Selective Service Psychiatry," *Mental Hygiene* 26, no. 1 (1942): 7–14.

26. William C. Menninger, "Psychiatric Experiences in the War, 1941–1946," *American Journal of Psychiatry* 103 (May 1947): 577–86.

27. Roy R. Grinker and John P. Spiegel, *War Neuroses* (Philadelphia: Blakiston, 1945), 115

28. Grinker and Spiegel, *War Neuroses,* 65, 66.

29. Grinker and Spiegel, *War Neuroses,* vii–viii.

30. Quoted in George Seldes, *Witness to a Century: Encounters with the Noted, Notorious, and the Three SOBs* (New York: Ballantine, 1987), 1.

31. Alan Axelrod, *Patton: A Biography* (London: Palgrave Macmillan, 2006), 117.

32. Anonymous, "Death and Drama," in *The Purple Testament,* 185–87.

33. Roy R. Grinker and John P. Spiegel, *Men under Stress* (Philadelphia: Blakiston, 1945), 456, 444, 460.

34. Grinker and Spiegel, *War Neuroses,* 4–5.

35. Sledge, *With the Old Breed,* 269

36. Grinker and Spiegel, *Men under Stress,* 304.

37. Grinker and Spiegel, *Men under Stress,* 280, 449.

38. Leo Kocher, "511th Casualties & Medals," *Photos, TAPS, KIA's (WWII and Korea), Articles, History links, etc. of & for My 11th Airborne Friends,* accessed October 4, 2022, https://users.owt.com/leodonna/511thMedals.htm.

39. Sander, *Serling,* 45.

40. Sander, *Serling.*

41. Grinker and Spiegel, *Men under Stress,* 281.

42. Ellen Dwyer, "Psychiatry and Race during World War II," *Journal of the History of Medicine and Allied Sciences* 61, no. 2 (2006): 117–43

43. Herbert X. Spiegel, "Preventive Psychiatry with Combat Troops," *American Journal of Psychiatry* 101, no. 3 (1944): 310–15.

44. Albert J. Glass, "Mental Health Programs in the Armed Forces," in *Child and Adolescent Psychiatry, Sociocultural and Community Psychiatry,* ed. Gerald Caplan, vol. 2 of *American Handbook of Psychiatry* (New York: Basic, 1972), 995.

45. Grinker and Spiegel, *War Neuroses,* 91

46. Normal Q. Brill and Gilbert W. Beebe, *A Follow-up Study of War Neuroses* (Washington, DC: Veterans Administration, 1955).

47. Grinker and Spiegel, *Men under Stress,* 288

48. Sledge, *With the Old Breed,* 270

49. Daniel A. McDonald, "Out of Uniform: A Strange New World," in Wolfe, *The Purple Testament,* 261–62.

3. Cold War Space and Technology

1. Derek De Solla Price, *Science since Babylon* (New Haven: Yale University Press, 1961), 129–30.

2. David Noble, *Progress without People: New Technology, Unemployment, and the Message of Resistance* (Toronto: Between the Lines Books, 1995), 71.

3. Audra J. Wolfe, *Competing with the Soviets: Science, Technology, and the State in Cold War America* (Baltimore: Johns Hopkins University Press, 2013), 5, 53.

4. "Crisis in Education," *Life,* March 24, 1958, 26–37.

5. Philip Wylie, *Generation of Vipers* (New York: Farrar & Rinehart, 1942), 225.

6. For a detailed exploration of this topic, refer to David Meerman Scott and Richard Jurek, *Marketing the Moon: The Selling of the Apollo Lunar Program* (Cambridge, MA: MIT Press, 2014).

7. Dewitt Douglas Kilgore, *Astrofuturism: Science, Race, and Visions of Utopia in Space* (Philadelphia: University of Pennsylvania Press, 2003), 1.

8. David Weinstein, *The Forgotten Network: DuMont and the Birth of American Television* (Philadelphia: Temple University Press, 2004), 75.

9. *Galaxy Science Fiction* No. 1, October 1950, back cover.

10. "Man in Space," *Disneyland,* directed by Ward Kimball (American Broadcasting Company, March 9, 1955).

11. Jim Korkis, "Man in Space," *USA Today,* December 28, 2011.

12. Alan Nadel, *Television in Black-and-White America: Race and National Identity* (Lawrence: University Press of Kansas, 2005), 84.

13. John F. Kennedy, Democratic National Convention acceptance speech, Memorial Coliseum, Los Angeles, July 15, 1960, available at John F. Kennedy Presidential Library and Museum website, https://www.jfklibrary.org/learn

/about-jfk/historic-speeches/acceptance-of-democratic-nomination-for-president.

14. For more information on this topic, see Michael Beschloss, *The Crisis Years: Kennedy and Khrushchev, 1960–1963* (New York: HarperCollins, 1991); and Seymour Harris, *Economics of the Kennedy Years, and a Look Ahead* (New York: Harper & Row, 1964).

15. John F. Kennedy, speech delivered before a joint session of Congress, May 25, 1961, available at John F. Kennedy Presidential Library and Museum website, https://www.jfklibrary.org/learn/about-jfk/historic-speeches/address-to-joint-session-of-congress-may-25-1961.

16. Report to the President-Elect of the Ad-Hoc Committee on Space, 16–17, January 10, 1961, available at the NASA History Office website, https://www.hq.nasa.gov/office/pao/History/report61.html.

17. For more information on this topic refer to Walter A. McDougall, *The Heavens and the Earth: A Political History of the Space Age* (New York: Basic Books, 1985).

18. John F. Kennedy, address at Rice University on the Nation's Space Effort, September 12, 1962, available at the John F. Kennedy Presidential Library and Museum website, https://www.jfklibrary.org/learn/about-jfk/historic-speeches/address-at-rice-university-on-the-nations-space-effort.

19. James Patterson, *Grand Expectations: The United States, 1945–1974* (New York: Oxford University Press, 1996), 468.

20. Amitai Etzioni, *The Moon-Doggle: Domestic and International Implications of the Space Race* (Garden City, NY: Doubleday, 1964), 14–15.

21. Quoted in Etzioni's *Moon-Doggle*, 8–9.

22. Etzioni, *Moon-Doggle*, 114.

23. Paul D. Lowman Jr., "Our First Lunar Program: What Did We Get from Apollo?" *Godard Space Flight Center*, NASA, October 17, 2007, http://www.nasa.gov/centers/goddard/news/series/moon/first_lunar_program.html.

24. Kennedy, address before a joint session of Congress.

25. Etzioni, *Moon-Doggle*, 158.

26. David Potter, *People of Plenty: Economic Abundance and the American Character* (Chicago: University of Chicago Press, 1954), 123–24, 160.

27. Wallace Reid, "A Marine on the Cost of War," in *The Purple Testament: Life Stories by Disabled War Veterans*, ed. Don M. Wolfe (Harrisburg, PA: Stackpole Sons, 1946), 305–6.

28. Gil Scott-Heron, "Whitey on the Moon," *A New Black Poet—Small Talk at 125th and Lenox* (New York: Flying Dutchman/RCA, 1970).

29. Kurt Vonnegut, *Player Piano* (New York: Charles Scribner's Sons, 1952), 347.

30. Statement of D. J. Davis, vice president of Ford Motor Company, in *Automation and Technological Change: Report of the Joint Committee on the Economic Report to the Congress of the United States* (Washington, DC: GPO, 1956). 58.

31. *Electronics*, April 17, 1980, 153.

32. Franklin Delano Roosevelt, to Vannevar Bush, Office of Scientific and Research Development, November 17, 1944, available in *The Scientific War Work of Linus C. Pauling*, at Special Collections & Archives Research Center, Oregon State University, http://scarc.library.oregonstate.edu/coll/pauling/war/corr/sci13 .006.4-roosevelt-bush-19441117.html.

33. Vannevar Bush, *Science: The Endless Frontier* (Washington, DC: GPO, 1945).

34. Edwin Mansfield, *The Economics of Technological Change* (New York: Norton, 1968), 56.

35. Stephen Meyer, "An Economic 'Frankenstein': UAW Workers' Response to Automation at the Ford Brook Park Plant in the 1950s," *Automobile in American Life and Society*, University of Michigan–Dearborn and Benson Ford Research Center, 2004–2010, http://www.autolife.umd.umich.edu/Labor/L_Casestudy/L_ casestudy4.htm.

36. Thomas J. Sugrue, "From Motor City to Motor Metropolis: How the Automobile Industry Reshaped Urban America," *Automobile in American Life and Society*, http://www.autolife.umd.umich.edu/Race/R_Overview/R_Overview5 .htm.

37. Meyer, "Economic Frankenstein."

38. Statement of James B. Carey, Secretary-Treasurer, CIO, and President, International Union of Electrical Workers, in *Automation and Technological Change*, 224, 230–31.

39. Statement of James B. Carey, 231.

40. Patterson, *Grand Expectations*, 467.

41. Dorothy Sue Cobble, *The Other Women's Movement: Workplace Justice and Social Rights in Modern America* (Princeton, NJ: Princeton University Press, 2005), 12–13.

42. Myra Wolfgang, testimony before the US Senate, ERA Hearings, May 6, 1970, 52–55, available at Moore, OK, Public Schools website, https://www .mooreschools.com/cms/lib/OK01000367/Centricity/Domain/2094/Equal%20 Rights%20Amendment.pdf

43. Statement of Howard Coughlin, president, Office Employees International Union, AFL, in *Automation and Technological Change*, 217.

44. Meyer, "Economic Frankenstein," 63–90.

45. Karl Marx, *Capital*: vol. 1, *A Critique of Political Economy* (New York: Modern Library, 1906), 470.

46. Dick Greenwood, "Starvin' in Paradise with the New Technology," in Noble, *Progress without People*, 151.

47. Wylie, *Generation of Vipers,* 223.

48. Students for a Democratic Society, Port Huron Statement, August 1962, available in the *American Yawp Reader,* https://www.americanyawp.com /reader/27-the-sixties/the-port-huron-statement-1962/.

4. Duck, Cover, and Accuse

1. Quoted in Paul Boyer, *By the Bomb's Early Light: American Thought and Culture at the Dawn of the Atomic Age* (Chapel Hill: University of North Carolina Press, 1994), 7.

2. Quoted in Boyer, *By the Bomb's Early Light,* 7.

3. John F. Kennedy, "Radio and Television Report to the American People on the Berlin Crisis," July 25, 1961, available at John F. Kennedy Presidential Library and Museum website, https://www.jfklibrary.org/archives/other-resources/john-f-kennedy-speeches/berlin-crisis-19610725.

4. "Bob Crane Interviews Rod Serling, Executive Producer, Writer, Actor, and Host," *The Bob Crane Show* (Los Angeles, CA: KNX-CBS Radio, December 11, 1961).

5. Quoted in Walter Goodman, "The Truth about Fallout Shelters," *Redbook,* January 1962, 74.

6. Gerard Piel, "The Illusion of Civil Defense," *Bulletin of the Atomic Scientists* 17, no. 2 (February 1962): 7–8.

7. Bentley Glass, "The Biology of Nuclear War," in *The Fallen Sky: Medical Consequences of Thermonuclear War,* ed. Saul Aronow (New York: Hill & Wang, 1963), 104.

8. Quoted in Joseph Roddy, "The Big March for Peace," *Look,* July 3, 1962, 14.

9. House Subcommittee, Civil Defense—Fallout Shelter Program, 3059 (1963).

10. "A New Urgency, Big Things to Do—and What You Must Learn," *Life,* September 15, 1961, 96–97.

11. "A Message to You from the President," *Life,* September 15, 1961, 95–107.

12. Rogers S. Cannell, *Live: A Handbook of Survival in Nuclear Attack* (Englewood Cliffs, NJ: Prentice Hall, 1962).

13. "Coffins or Shields?" *Time,* February 2, 1962, 15.

14. House Subcommittee, *Civil Defense* 47, (1960), 47.

15. Curtis LeMay in House Subcommittee, *Civil Defense* (1960), 156–57.

16. P. Herbert Leiderman and Jack H. Mendelson, "Some Psychiatric Considerations in Planning for Defense Shelters," in Aronow, *Fallen Sky,* 52.

17. Erich Fromm and Michael Maccoby, "The Case against Shelters," in *No Place to Hide: Fact and Fiction about Fallout Shelters,* ed. Seymour Melman (New York: Grove Press, 1962), 78.

18. "Civil Defense: The Sheltered Life," *Time,* October 20, 1961, 21.

19. Robert B. Meyner, "Bomb Shelters Will Not Save Us!" *Coronet* 48, no. 5 (September 1960): 68.

20. James Patterson, *Grand Expectations: The United States, 1945–1974* (New York: Oxford University Press, 1996), 179–80.

21. Daniel J. Tichenor, *Dividing Lines: The Politics of Immigration Control in America* (Princeton, NJ: Princeton University Press, 2002), 195

22. *Los Angeles Times,* August 1, 1961

23. Quoted in Spencer R. Weart, *Nuclear Fear* (Cambridge, MA: Harvard University Press, 1988), 256.

24. Bernard Brodie, *Strategy in the Missile Age* (Princeton, NJ: Princeton University Press, 1959), 212–13.

25. Kenneth D. Rose, *One Nation Underground: The Fallout Shelter in American Culture* (New York: New York University Press, 2001), 206.

26. Langston Hughes, "Radioactive Red Caps," *The Best of Simple* (New York: Hill & Wang, 1997), 211.

27. "Gun Thy Neighbor?" *Time,* August 18, 1961, 58

28. L. C. McHugh, "Ethics at the Shelter Doorway," *America,* September 30, 1961, 824–26.

29. Rose, *One Nation Underground,* 202.

30. Herbert Marcuse, *One-Dimensional Man: Studies in the Ideology of Advanced Industrial Society,* 2nd ed. (Boston: Beacon, 1991), 17.

31. House Subcommittee No. 3 of the Committee on Armed Service, *Civil Defense—Fallout Shelter Program,* 88th Cong., 1st Sess., 3040 (1963).

32. J. Edgar Hoover, speech before the House Committee on Un-American Activities, March 26, 1947, available at *Voices of Democracy: The U.S. Oratory Project,* University of Maryland, College Park, https://voicesofdemocracy.umd .edu/hoover-speech-before-the-house-committee-speech-text/

33. Internal Security Act, 1950, Veto Message from the President of the United States, September 22, 1950, in Cong. Rec,, 81st Cong., 2nd sess., 15629–32 (1950).

34. James F. O'Neil, "How You Can Fight Communism," *American Legion Magazine,* August 1948, 43, 16–17.

35. J. Edgar Hoover, testimony, House Committee on Un-American Activities, Hearings on H. R. 1884 and H. R. 2122, 80th Cong., 1st Sess., March 26, 1947.

36. Ellen Schrecker, *Many Are the Crimes: McCarthyism in America* (Princeton, NJ: Princeton University Press, 1999), 274–75, 284–85

37. Hoover, speech before the House Committee on Un-American Activities.

38. Truman, Speech on the Veto of the McCarran Internal Security Act, September 22, 1950, available at *The American Presidency Project,* University of California, Santa Barbara, https://www.presidency.ucsb.edu/node/230264.

39. David Halberstam, *The Fifties* (New York: Random House, 1993), 59.

40. Mickey Spillane, *One Lonely Night,* vol. 2 of *The Mike Hammer Collection* (New York: New American Library, 2001), 169.

41. Halberstam, *Fifties,* 54

42. Schrecker, *Many Are the Crimes,* 243.

43. Resolution on Expulsion of the UERMWA and Withdrawal of Certificate of Affiliation, Report to the 11th Constitutional Convention of the Congress of Industrial Organizations by the Committee on Resolutions, November 1949, Walter P Reuther Papers, UAW President's Office, box 62, folder 15, Archives of Labor History and Urban Affairs, Wayne State University, Detroit.

44. George Kennan, *Memoirs: 1950–1963* (Boston: Pantheon, 1972), 228.

45. William O. Douglas, "The Black Silence of Fear," *New York Times Magazine,* January 13, 1952.

46. Ellen Schrecker, "Comments on John Earl Haynes, 'The Cold War Debate Continues: A Traditionalist View of Historical Writing on Domestic Communism and Anti-Communism,'" *Journal of Cold War Studies* 2, no. 1 (Winter 2000): 76–115.

5. Cold War Childhood

1. Elaine Tyler May, *Homeward Bound: American Families in the Cold War Era* (New York: Basic Books, 2008), 26, 153.

2. "Woman in the House," *Father Knows Best,* dir. William D. Russell (New York: Columbia Broadcasting System, 1955).

3. Grace Hechinger and Fred M. Hechinger, *Teen-Age Tyranny* (Greenwich, CT: Fawcett Crest, 1962), 127.

4. This episode was written by Serling but based on Jerome Bixby's short story "It's a Good Life," which appeared in *Star Science Fiction Stories,* no. 2, ed. Frederik Pohl (New York: Ballantine, 1953), 66–85.

5. Theodor W. Adorno et al., *The Authoritarian Personality* (New York: Harper & Brothers, 1950), 346–58, 357.

6. Lena Sadler and William Sadler, *The Mother and Her Child* (Chicago: A. C. McClurg & Co., 1916), 101–2.

7. John B. Watson, *The Psychological Care of the Infant and Child* (New York: Harper, 1928), 81–82.

8. Martha Wolfenstein, "The Emergence of Fun Morality," *Journal of Social Issues* 7, no. 4 (Fall 1951): 15.

9. Benjamin Spock, *The Common Sense Book of Baby and Child Care*, 2nd ed. (New York: Duell, Sloan, & Pearce, 1957), 1–2.

10. Thomas Maier, *Dr. Spock* (New York: Basic Books, 2003), 321, 323.

11. Spock, *Common Sense Book of Baby and Child Care*, 254, 258.

12. William Graebner, "The Unstable World of Benjamin Spock," *Journal of American History* 67, no 3 (December 1980): 612–13.

13. David Riesman, *The Lonely Crowd: A Study of the Changing American Character*, rev. ed. (New Haven: Yale University Press, 2001) 19–22.

14. Hannah Arendt, *The Origins of Totalitarianism* (New York: World, 1951), 474.

15. Graebner, "Unstable World of Benjamin Spock," 269.

16. Gerald H. J. Pearson, *Psychoanalysis and the Education of the Child* (New York: W. W. Norton, 1954), 81.

17. Edgar Z. Friedenberg, *The Vanishing Adolescent* (New York: Dell, 1959), 37.

18. Erik Erikson, *Childhood and Society* (New York: W. W. Norton, 1963), 406–7.

19. Spock, *Common Sense Book of Baby and Child Care*, 4.

20. Spock, *Common Sense Book of Baby and Child Care*, 6.

21. US Department of Commerce, *National Income and Product Accounts, 1959–1988* (Washington, DC: GPO, 1992), 2:70, 75; US Department of Commerce, *Statistical Abstract of the United States* (Washington, DC: GPO, 1995), 491.

22. "Mattel, Inc. History," *International Directory of Company Histories*, vol. 61 (St. James, MO: St. James Press, 2000).

23. Gary Cross, *Kids' Stuff: Toys and the Changing World of American Childhood* (Cambridge, MA: Harvard University Press, 1997), 162–71.

24. Gilbert quoted in Hechinger and Hechinger, *Teen-Age Tyranny*, 147–48

25. "Vintage Chatty Cathy Toy Doll TV Commercial 1960's," YouTube video, 1:05, posted by "Vintage TV Commercials," November 3, 2008, https: //www .youtube.com/watch? v=f-sYQ8_2v_Q.

26. *New Orleans (LA) Times Picayune*, October 24, 1963.

27. Vance Packard, *The Waste Makers* (New York: Ig Publishing, 2011), 152, 153.

28. For further information on this topic, refer to Louis Hyman, *Debtor Nation: The History of America in Red Ink* (Princeton, NJ: Princeton University Press, 2011).

29. Charles Dicken, "Should the Credit Department Be Self-Supporting?" *Credit Management Year Book 1958–1959* (New York: National Retail Dry Goods Association, 1958), 92. None that I could find

30. Sigmund Freud, *Introductory Lectures on Psycho-Analysis*, trans. Joan Riviere (London: Allen & Unwin, 1922), 251, 332, 321

31. Freud, *Introductory Lectures*, 309, 321.

6. White-Collar Weariness

1. James Patterson, *Grand Expectations: The United States, 1945–1974* (New York: Oxford University Press, 1997), 323.

2. Sloan Wilson, *The Man in the Gray Flannel Suit* (New York: Simon & Schuster, 1955), 300.

3. C. Wright Mills, *White Collar: The American Middle Classes* (New York: Oxford University Press, 1951), xv.

4. David Potter, *People of Plenty: Economic Abundance and the American Character* (Chicago: University of Chicago Press, 1954), 105.

5. William Whyte, *The Organization Man* (1956; repr., Philadelphia: University of Pennsylvania Press, 2002), 397–98.

6. David Riesman, *The Lonely Crowd: A Study of the Changing American Character,* rev. ed. (New Haven: Yale University Press, 2001), 15.

7. Riesman, *Lonely Crowd,* 25.

8. David Potter, "American Women and the American Character," *Stetson University Bulletin* 62, no. 1 (January 1962): 1–6.

9. James Gilbert, *Men in the Middle: Searching for Masculinity in the 1950s* (Chicago: University of Chicago Press, 2005), 45.

10. Potter, *People of Plenty,* 72.

11. Andras Angyal, "Evasion of Growth," *American Journal of Psychiatry* 110, no. 5 (November 1953): 358–61.

12. Betty Friedan, *The Feminine Mystique,* fiftieth anniversary ed. (New York: W. W. Norton, 2013), 372.

13. Mrs. [Dorothy] Dale Carnegie, "How to Help Your Husband Get Ahead," *Coronet,* January 1954, 65.

14. R. E. Dumas Milner, "Before I Hire Your Husband, I Want to Meet You!" *Good Housekeeping,* January 1956, 52.

15. Whyte, *Organization Man,* 147.

16. Stephanie Coontz's *The Way We Never Were: American Families and the Nostalgia Trap* (New York: Basic Books, 1992) explores this topic further and discusses the many ways women have been historically held responsible to counteract the dehumanizing forces of capitalism.

17. Friedan, *Feminine Mystique,* 366.

18. Vance Packard, *The Waste Makers* (New York: Ig Publishing, 2011), 222.

19. Andrea Tone, *The Age of Anxiety: A History of America's Turbulent Affair with Tranquilizers* (New York: Basic Books, 2008), 159.

20. Roche Laboratories, *Aspects of Anxiety,* 2nd ed. (Philadelphia: Lippincott, 1968), 88.

21. Whyte, *Organization Man,* 404.

22. Louis Cheskin, *Why People Buy: Motivation Research and Its Successful Application* (New York: Liveright, 1959), 99.

23. Friedan, *Feminine Mystique,* 249.

24. Cheskin, *Why People Buy,* 51.

25. Vance Packard, *The Hidden Persuaders,* reissue ed. (New York: Ig Publishing, 2007), 240.

26. Ernest Dichter, *The Strategy of Desire* (1960; repr., Eastford, CT: Martino Fine Books, 2012), 263.

27. Packard, *Waste Makers,* 73, 118.

28. Dichter, *Strategy of Desire,* 173.

29. Packard, *Waste Makers,* 120.

30. Friedan, *Feminine Mystique,* 264.

31. Mills, *White Collar,* 182.

32. Mills, *White Collar,* 184.

33. Quoted in Mills, *White Collar,* 228.

34. Cited in James Gilbert, *A Cycle of Outrage: America's Reaction to the Juvenile Delinquent in the 1950s* (New York: Oxford University Press, 1988), 75.

35. Mills, *White Collar,* 237.

7. Consuming Conformity

1. Lizabeth Cohen, *A Consumer's Republic: The Politics of Mass Consumption in Postwar America* (New York: Random House, 2003), 119.

2. Brett Harvey, *The Fifties: A Women's Oral History* (New York: HarperCollins, 1993), 110.

3. Vance Packard, *The Hidden Persuaders,* reissue ed. (New York: Ig Publishing, 2007).

4. Kendis Rochlen, "Movie Ulcer Crowd Goes for New 'Tranquil Pill,'" *Los Angeles Mirror-News,* February 8, 1956.

5. Andrea Tone, *The Age of Anxiety: A History of America's Turbulent Affair with Tranquilizers* (New York: Basic Books, 2008), 59.

6. "Report on Tranquilizing Drugs by the Committee on Public Health of the New York Academy of Medicine, " *Bulletin of Academy of Medicine* vol. 71 no. 11 (April 1957): 282–89.

7. "Academy Endorses Sleeping Pill Curb, " *New York Times,* July 9, 1947.

8. Tone, *Age of Anxiety,* 172–73.

9. E. Franklin Frazier, *Black Bourgeoisie* (New York: Free Press, 1957), 189–90.

10. The Boston Women's Health Book Collective, *Our Bodies, Ourselves: A Book by and for Women,* 2nd ed. (New York: Simon & Schuster, 1973) 24.

11. Tone, *Age of Anxiety,* 189

12. Phyllis Chesler, *Women and Madness* (Garden City, NY: Doubleday, 1972), 287.

13. Boston Women's Health Book Collective, *Our Bodies, Ourselves*, 13.

14. R. C. Murphy, "Reverend Peale's Panacea," *Nation*, May 7, 1955, 398–400.

15. Allan V. Horwitz and Jerome C. Wakefield, *The Loss of Sadness: How Psychiatry Transformed Normal Sorrow into Depressive Disorder* (New York: Oxford University Press, 2012), 89.

16. Boston Women's Health Book Collective, *Our Bodies, Ourselves*, 22.

17. Jacqueline Susann, *Valley of the Dolls* (New York: Bantam, 1966), 254.

18. Horwitz and Wakefield, *Loss of Sadness*, 75–79.

19. Horwitz and Wakefield, *Loss of Sadness*, 75–79, 89, 103.

20. Herbert Marcuse, *One-Dimensional Man: Studies in the Ideology of Advanced Industrial Society*, 2nd ed. (Boston: Beacon, 1991), 5.

21. Thomas Whiteside, "Getting There First with Tranquility," *New Yorker*, May 3, 1958, 104.

22. Harvey J. Sachs to *Ms.* Magazine Corporation, December 10, 1975, carton 3, folder 66, Letters to *Ms.* Magazine, Schlesinger Library, Radcliffe Institute, Harvard University Cambridge, MA.

23. Tone, *Age of Anxiety,* 103.

24. *Our Bodies, Ourselves*, 24.

25. Tanisha C. Ford, "Black Is Beautiful," *Aperture* no. 228 (Fall 2017), 46–53.

26. Sigmund Freud, *New Introductory Lectures on Psychoanalysis*, trans. W. J. H. Sprott (New York: Martino, 1933) 170.

27. Betty Friedan, *The Feminine Mystique*, fiftieth anniversary ed. (New York: W. W. Norton, 2013), 120.

28. Ernest Jones, *The Life and Work of Sigmund Freud*, 3 vols. (New York: Basic Books, 1953), 1:176.

29. Freud, *New Introductory Lectures on Psychoanalysis*, 184.

30. Richard Hofstadter, *Anti-Intellectualism in American Life* (New York: Alfred Knopf, 1963), 7.

31. Friedan, *Feminine Mystique*, 138, 431, 436 440

32. Marcuse, *One-Dimensional Man*, 5.

33. Lewis Mumford, *The City in History: Its Origins, Its Transformations, and Its Prospects* (New York: Harcourt, 1961), 487.

34. Michael Harrington, *The Other America: Poverty in the United States* (New York: Simon & Schuster, 1962), xxvi, 1–2.

35. Jane Jacobs, *The Death and Life of Great American Cities* (New York: Random House, 1961), 17, 36

36. Jacobs, *Death and Life of Great American Cities*, 20, 30, 31–32, 46.

37. National Advisory Commission on Civil Disorders, *The Kerner Report* (Princeton, NJ: Princeton University Press, 2016), 2, 83.

38. Mumford, *City in History,* 512.

39. Abraham H. Maslow, "A Theory of Human Motivation," *Psychological Review* 50 (1943): 370–96.

40. Abraham H. Maslow, "The Farther Reaches of Human Nature," *Journal of Transpersonal Psychology* 1, no. 1 (1969): 1–9

41. Maslow, "Theory of Human Motivation," 380.

42. Mumford, *City in History,* 494.

43. Friedan, *Feminine Mystique,* 464.

44. Ken Smith, *Mental Hygiene: Classroom Films, 1940–1970* (New York: Blast Books, 1999), 25.

45. Friedan, *Feminine Mystique,* 377, 141.

46. Mirra Komarovsky, "Functional Analysis of Sex Roles, " *American Sociological Review,* vol. 15, no.4 (August 1950): 508–16.

47. Friedan, *Feminine Mystique,* 347, 372

48. Mumford, *City in History,* 494.

49. Students for a Democratic Society, Port Huron Statement, August 1962, available in the *American Yawp Reader,* https://www.americanyawp.com/reader /27-the-sixties/the-port-huron-statement-1962/.

50. Friedan, *Feminine Mystique,* 374.

51. Elaine Tyler May, *Homeward Bound: American Families in the Cold War Era* (New York: Basic Books, 1988), 215.

52. Nikita Khrushchev, Kitchen Debate, Moscow, July 24, 1959, available at the Freedom of Information Act Electronic Reading Room, CIA website, https://www.cia.gov/readingroom/docs/1959-07-24.pdf.

53. Mumford, *City in History,* 513.

Conclusion

1. "Divided He Falls," *Bewitched* (New York: American Broadcasting Corporation, May 5, 1966).

2. For a more extensive analysis of *Bewitched,* see Susan Douglas's *Where the Girls Are: Growing Up Female with the Mass Media* (New York: Three Rivers Press, 1995), 123–39.

3. David Bianculli, *Dangerously Funny: The Uncensored Story of* The Smothers Brothers Comedy Hour (New York: Touchstone, 2009).

4. For a more extensive analysis of *The Smothers Brothers Comedy Hour,* refer to Aniko Bodroghkozy, *Groove Tube: Sixties Television and the Youth Rebellion* (Durham, NC: Duke University Press, 2001), 123–64.

5. Gordon Sander, *Serling: The Rise and Twilight of Television's Last Angry Man* (New York: Dutton, 1992), 213, 209.

6. Thomas Frank, "Why Johnny Can't Dissent," in *Commodify Your Dissent: Salvos from The Baffler*, ed. Thomas Frank and Matt Weiland (New York: W. W. Norton, 1997) 35, 41.

7. Rachel Dretzin and Barak Goodman, prods., *The Merchants of Cool*, FRONTLINE (Alexandria, VA: PBS Home Video, 2003); and Frank Koughan and Douglas Rushkoff, prods., *Generation Like, FRONTLINE* (Arlington, VA: PBS Home Video, 2014).

8. ZzzQuil (@ZzzQuil), "Today is the day for dreaming. Happy MLK Day," Twitter, January 20, 2014, 7:28 a.m., https://twitter.com/zzzquil/status/425273661260849153

9. Popchips (@popchips), "Eternal poptimist," Twitter, January 20, 2014, 10:00 a.m., https://twitter.com/popchips/status/425311806333419520.

10. Ibram X. Kendi, "The Second Assassination of Martin Luther King Jr.," *Atlantic*, October 14, 2021, https://www.theatlantic.com/ideas/archive/2021/10/martin-luther-king-critical-race-theory/620367/.

11. Rod Serling, "The Challenge of the Mass Media to the 20th Century Writer," January 15, 1968, quoted in Anne Serling, *As I Knew Him: My Dad, Rod Serling* (New York: Citadel, 2013), 165.

Bibliography

Primary Sources

Adorno, Theodor W., Else Frenkel-Brunswik, Daniel Levinson, and Nevitt Sanford. *The Authoritarian Personality.* New York: Harper & Brothers, 1950.

Angyal, Andras. "Evasion of Growth." *American Journal of Psychiatry* 110, no. 5 (November 1953): 358–61.

Arendt, Hannah. *The Origins of Totalitarianism.* New York: World, 1951.

Automation and Technological Change: Report of the Joint Committee on the Economic Report to the Congress of the United States. Washington, DC: GPO, 1956.

Aronow, Saul, ed. *The Fallen Sky: Medical Consequences of Thermonuclear War.* New York: Hill & Wang, 1963.

Baldwin, James. *The Cross of Redemption: Uncollected Writings.* Edited by Randall Kenan. New York: Pantheon, 2010.

Benedict, Ruth. *Race and Racism.* London: Routledge, 1942.

Bixby, Jerome. "It's a Good Life." *Star Science Fiction Stories,* no. 2. Edited by Frederik Pohl, 66–85. New York: Ballantine, 1953,

The Boston Women's Health Book Collective. *Our Bodies, Ourselves: A Book by and for Women.* 2nd ed. New York: Simon & Schuster, 1973.

Brill, Normal Q and Gilbert W. Beebe. *A Follow-up Study of War Neuroses.* Washington, DC: Veterans Administration, 1955.

Brodie, Bernard. *Strategy in the Missile Age.* Princeton, NJ: Princeton University Press, 1959.

Burack, Abraham S. *Television Plays for Writers.* Boston: Writer, 1957.

Bush, Vannevar. *Science: The Endless Frontier.* Washington, DC: GPO, 1945.

Cannell, Rogers S. *Live: A Handbook of Survival in Nuclear Attack.* Englewood Cliffs, NJ: Prentice Hall, 1962.

Cheskin, Louis. *Why People Buy: Motivation Research and Its Successful Application.* New York: Liveright, 1959.

Chesler, Phyllis. *Women and Madness.* Garden City, NY: Doubleday, 1972.

Dichter, Ernest. *The Strategy of Desire.* 1960. Reprint, Eastford, CT: Martino Fine Books, 2012.

Dicken, Charles. "Should the Credit Department Be Self-Supporting?" In *Credit Management Year Book 1958–1959*, 92. New York: National Retail Dry Goods Association, 1958.

Ellison, Ralph. *The Invisible Man*. New York: Random House, 1952.

Erikson, Erik. *Childhood and Society*. New York: W. W. Norton, 1963.

Etzioni, Amitai. *The Moon-Doggle: Domestic and International Implications of the Space Race*. Garden City, NY: Doubleday, 1964.

Frazier, E. Franklin. *Black Bourgeoisie*. New York: Free Press, 1957.

Friedan, Betty. *The Feminine Mystique*. Fiftieth anniversary ed. New York: W. W. Norton, 2013.

Friedenberg, Edgar Z. *The Vanishing Adolescent*. New York: Dell, 1959.

Freud, Sigmund. *The Interpretation of Dreams*. Translated by James Strachey. New York: Basic Books, 1955.

———. *Introductory Lectures on Psycho-Analysis*. Translated by Joan Riviere. London: Allen & Unwin, 1922.

———. *New Introductory Lectures on Psychoanalysis*. Translated by W. J. H. Sprott. New York: Martino, 1933.

Fromm, Erich. *Escape from Freedom*. New York: Holt, Reinhart, & Winston, 1941.

Fromm, Erich, and Michael Maccoby. "The Case against Shelters." In *No Place to Hide: Fact and Fiction about Fallout Shelters*. Edited by Seymour Melman, 78. New York: Grove Press, 1962.

Grant, Madison. *The Passing of the Great Race or The Racial Basis of European History*. New York: Scribner & Sons, 1916.

Grinker, Roy R. and John P. Spiegel. *Men under Stress*. Philadelphia: Blakiston, 1945.

———. *War Neuroses*. Philadelphia: Blakiston, 1945.

Harrington, Michael. *The Other America: Poverty in the United States*. New York: Scribner, 1962.

Hechinger, Grace, and Fred M. Hechinger. *Teen-Age Tyranny*. Greenwich, CT: Fawcett Crest, 1962.

Hitler, Adolf. *Mein Kampf*. 1925. Reprint, New York: Houghton-Mifflin, 1998.

Hofstadter, Richard. *Anti-Intellectualism in American Life*. New York: Alfred Knopf, 1963.

Horney, Karen. *The Neurotic Personality of Our Time*. New York: W. W. Norton, 1936.

Hughes, Langston. *The Best of Simple*. 1961. Reprint, New York: Hill & Wang, 1997.

Jacobs, Jane. *The Death and Life of Great American Cities*. New York: Random House, 1961.

Jung, Carl. *Man and His Symbols*. New York: Dell, 1964.

Kennan, George. *Memoirs: 1950–1963*. Boston: Pantheon, 1972.

Kier, Herbert. "Volk, Rasse und Stat." *National Socialist Handbook for Law and Legislation* (Summer 1934): 27–38.

Komarovsky, Mirra. "Functional Analysis of Sex Roles." *American Sociological Review* 15, no. 4 (August 1950): 508–16.

Kostelanetz, Richard. *Beyond Left and Right: Radical Thought for Our Times*. New York: William Morrow, 1968.

McLuhan, Marshall. *Understanding Media: The Extensions of Man*. New York: McGraw Hill, 1964.

Mansfield, Edwin. *The Economics of Technological Change*. New York: Norton, 1968.

Marcuse, Herbert. *One-Dimensional Man: Studies in the Ideology of Advanced Industrial Society*. 2nd ed. Boston: Beacon, 1991.

Marx, Karl. *Capital*. Vol. 1, *A Critique of Political Economy*. New York: Modern Library, 1906.

Maslow, Abraham. H. "The Farther Reaches of Human Nature." *Journal of Transpersonal Psychology* 1, no. 1 (1969): 1–9.

———. "A Theory of Human Motivation." *Psychological Review* 50 (1943): 370–96.

Menninger, William C. "Psychiatric Experiences in the War, 1941–1946." *American Journal of Psychiatry* 103 (May 1947): 577–86.

Meyner, Robert B. "Bomb Shelters Will Not Save Us!" *Coronet* 48, no. 5 (September 1960): 62–69.

Mills, C. Wright. *White Collar: The American Middle Classes*. New York: Oxford University Press, 1951.

Mumford, Lewis. *The City in History: Its Origins, Its Transformations, and Its Prospects*. New York: Harcourt, 1961.

National Advisory Commission on Civil Disorders. *The Kerner Report*. Princeton, NJ: Princeton University Press, 2016.

Nilus, Sergei Aleksandrovich. *Protocols of the Meetings of the Zionist Men of Wisdom*. Boston: Small, Maynard, & Company, 1920.

O'Neil, James F. "How You Can Fight Communism." *American Legion Magazine*, August 1948, 16–17.

Packard, Vance. *The Hidden Persuaders*. Reissue ed. New York: Ig Publishing, 2007.

———. *The Naked Society*. New York: David McKay, 1964.

———. *The Waste Makers*. New York: Ig Publishing, 2011.

Peale, Norman Vincent. *The Power of Positive Thinking*. New York: Prentice-Hall, 1956.

Pearson, Gerald H. J. *Psychoanalysis and the Education of the Child*. New York: W. W. Norton, 1954.

Piel, Gerard. "The Illusion of Civil Defense." *Bulletin of the Atomic Scientists* 17, no. 2 (February 1962): 7–8.

Potter, David. *People of Plenty: Economic Abundance and the American Character.* Chicago: University of Chicago Press, 1954.

Price, Derek De Solla. *Science since Babylon.* New Haven: Yale University Press, 1961.

"Report on Tranquilizing Drugs by the Committee on Public Health of the New York Academy of Medicine." *Bulletin of Academy of Medicine* 70, no. 11 (April 1957): 282–89.

Riesman, David. *The Lonely Crowd: A Study of the Changing American Character.* New Haven: Yale University Press, 2001.

Roche Laboratories. *Aspects of Anxiety.* 2nd ed. Philadelphia: Lippincott, 1968.

Rosenthal, A. M. and Arthur Gelb. *One More Victim: The Life and Death of a Jewish Nazi.* New York: New American Library, 1968.

Sadler, Lena, and William Sadler. *The Mother and Her Child.* Chicago: A. C. McClurg & Co, 1916.

Serling, Rod. *As Timeless as Infinity: The Complete Twilight Zone Scripts of Rod Serling.* Edited by Tony Albarella. Colorado Springs: Gauntlet, 2011.

———. "The Facts of Life." Interview by Linda Brevelle, *Writer's Digest,* March 1976, available at the Rod Serling Memorial Foundation website: https://rodserling.com/rod-serlings-final-interview/.

———. *Patterns: Four Television Plays with the Author's Personal Commentaries.* New York: Simon & Schuster, 1957.

Sledge, Eugene B. *With the Old Breed: At Peleliu and Okinawa.* New York: Oxford University Press, 1981.

Spillane, Mickey. *One Lonely Night.* Vol. 2 of *The Mike Hammer Collection,* New York: New American Library, 2001.

Spock, Benjamin. *The Common Sense Book of Baby and Child Care.* New York: Duell, Sloan, & Pearce, 1946.

Spock, Benjamin. *The Common Sense Book of Baby and Child Care.* 2nd ed. New York: Duell, Sloan, & Pearce, 1957.

Sullivan, Harry Stack. "Mental Hygiene and National Defense: A Year of Selective Service Psychiatry." *Mental Hygiene* 26 no. 1 (1942): 7–14.

Susann, Jacqueline. *Valley of the Dolls.* New York: Bantam, 1966.

Vonnegut, Kurt. *Palm Sunday: An Autobiographical Collage.* New York: Delacorte Press, 1981.

Vonnegut, Kurt. *Player Piano.* New York: Charles Scribner's Sons, 1952.

Watson, John B. *The Psychological Care of the Infant and Child.* New York: Harper, 1928.

Whyte, William. *The Organization Man.* 1956. Reprint, Philadelphia: University of Pennsylvania Press, 2002.

Wilson, Sloan. *The Man in the Gray Flannel Suit.* New York: Simon & Schuster, 1955.

Wolfe, Don M., ed. *The Purple Testament: Life Stories by Disabled War Veterans.* Harrisburg, PA: Stackpole Sons, 1946.

Wolfenstein, Martha. "The Emergence of Fun Morality." *Journal of Social Issues* 7, no. 4 (Fall 1951): 15–25.

Wylie, Philip. *Generation of Vipers.* New York: Farrar & Rinehart, 1942.

Secondary Sources

Barnouw, Eric. *Tube of Plenty: The Evolution of American Television.* 2nd rev. ed. New York: Oxford University Press, 1975.

Bérubé, Allen. *Coming Out Under Fire: The History of Gay Men and Women in World War Two.* New York: Free Press, 1990.

Beschloss, Michael. *The Crisis Years: Kennedy and Khrushchev, 1960–1963.* New York: HarperCollins, 1991.

Bianculli, David. *Dangerously Funny: The Uncensored Story of* The Smothers Brothers Comedy Hour. New York: Touchstone, 2009.

Bodroghkozy, Aniko. *Groove Tube: Sixties Television and the Youth Rebellion.* Durham, NC: Duke University Press, 2001.

Boulton, Mark. "Sending the Extremists to the Cornfield: Rod Serling's Crusade against Conservatism." *Journal of Popular Culture* 47, no. 6 (December 2014): 1226–44.

Boyer, Paul. *By the Bomb's Early Light: American Thought and Culture at the Dawn of the Atomic Age.* Chapel Hill: University of North Carolina Press, 1994.

Brier, Evan. *A Novel Marketplace: Mass Culture, the Book Trade, and Postwar American Fiction.* Philadelphia: University of Pennsylvania Press, 2010.

Cobble, Dorothy Sue. *The Other Women's Movement: Workplace Justice and Social Rights in Modern America.* Princeton, NJ: Princeton University Press, 2005.

Cohen, Lizabeth. *A Consumer's Republic: The Politics of Mass Consumption in Postwar America.* New York: Vintage, 2003.

Coontz, Stephanie. *The Way We Never Were: American Families and the Nostalgia Trap.* New York: Basic Books, 1992.

Cross, Gary. *Kids' Stuff: Toys and the Changing World of American Childhood.* Cambridge, MA: Harvard University Press, 1997.

Dalfiume, Richard M. "The Forgotten Years of the Negro Revolution." *Journal of American History* 55, no. 1 (June 1968): 90–106.

Dawidziak, Mark. *Everything I Need to Know I Learned in* The Twilight Zone: A Fifth-Dimension Guide to Life. New York: Thomas Dunne Books, 2017.

Doherty, Thomas. *Cold War, Cool Medium: Television, McCarthyism, and American Culture.* New York: Columbia University Press, 2003.

Douglas, Susan J. *Where the Girls Are: Growing Up Female with the Mass Media.* New York: Three Rivers Press, 1995.

Dower, John W. *War without Mercy: Race and Power in the Pacific War.* New York: Pantheon, 1986.

Dwyer, Ellen. "Psychiatry and Race during World War II." *Journal of the History of Medicine and Allied Sciences* 61, no. 2 (2006): 117–43.

Engs, Ruth C. *The Eugenics Movement: An Encyclopedia.* Westport, CT: Greenwood, 2005.

Entman, Robert M. and Andrew Rojecki. *The Black Image in the White Mind: Media and Race in America.* Chicago: University of Chicago Press, 2000.

Evans, Richard J. *The Third Reich in Power.* New York: Penguin, 2005.

Falk, Andrew J. *Upstaging the Cold War American Dissent and Cultural Diplomacy, 1940–1960.* Amherst: University of Massachusetts Press, 2011.

Feasey, Rebecca. *Masculinity and Popular Television.* Edinburgh: Edinburgh University Press, 2008.

FitzGerald, David Scott, and David Cook-Martin. *Culling the Masses: The Democratic Origins of Racist Immigration Policy in the Americas.* Cambridge, MA: Harvard University Press, 2014.

Flanagan, E. M. *The Angels: A History of the 11th Airborne Division.* Novato, CA: Presidio Press, 1989.

Fussell, Paul. *Wartime: Understanding and Behavior in the Second World War.* New York: Oxford University Press, 1990.

Gilbert, James. *A Cycle of Outrage: America's Reaction to the Juvenile Delinquent in the 1950s.* New York: Oxford University Press, 1988.

———. *Men in the Middle: Searching for Masculinity in the 1950s.* Chicago: University of Chicago Press, 2005.

Gitlin, Todd. *The Whole World is Watching: Mass Media in the Making and Unmaking of the New Left.* Berkeley: University of California Press, 2003.

Glaude, Eddie S. *Begin Again: James Baldwin's America and Its Urgent Lessons for Our Own.* New York: Crown, 2020.

Glickman, Lawrence B. *Buying Power: A History of Consumer Activism in America.* Chicago: University of Chicago Press, 2009.

Gordon, Linda. *The Second Coming of the KKK: The Ku Klux Klan of the 1920s and the American Political Tradition.* New York: Liveright, 2017.

Graebner, William. "The Unstable World of Benjamin Spock." *Journal of American History* 67, no 3 (December 1980): 612–13.

Grams, Martin Jr. The Twilight Zone: *Unlocking the Door to a Television Classic.* Churchville, MD: OTR Publishing, 2008.

Grant, Barry Keith. *The Twilight Zone.* Detroit: Wayne State University Press, 2020.

Halberstam, David. *The Fifties.* New York: Random House, 1993.

Haralovich, Mary Beth and Lauren Rabinovitz. *Television, History, and American Culture: Feminist Critical Essays.* Durham, NC: Duke University Press, 1999.

Harper, John Lamberton. *The Cold War.* New York: Oxford University Press, 2011.

Harris, Seymour. *Economics of the Kennedy Years, and a Look Ahead.* New York: Harper & Row, 1964.

Harvey, Brett. *The Fifties: A Women's Oral History.* New York: HarperCollins, 1993.

Herbold, Hilary. "Never a Level Playing Field: Blacks and the GI Bill." *Journal of Blacks in Higher Education* 6 (Winter 1994): 104–8.

Herman, Edward S. and Noam Chomsky. *Manufacturing Consent: The Political Economy of the Mass Media.* New York: Pantheon, 1988.

Horwitz, Allan V. and Jerome C. Wakefield. *The Loss of Sadness: How Psychiatry Transformed Normal Sorrow into Depressive Disorder.* New York: Oxford University Press, 2012.

Hyman, Louis. *Debtor Nation: The History of America in Red Ink.* Princeton, NJ: Princeton University Press, 2011.

Jones, Ernest. *The Life and Work of Sigmund Freud,* 3 vols. New York: Basic Books, 1953.

Kilgore, Dewitt Douglas. *Astrofuturism: Science, Race, and Visions of Utopia in Space.* Philadelphia: University of Pennsylvania Press, 2003.

Kraszewski, Jon. *The New Entrepreneurs: An Institutional History of Television Anthology Writers.* Middletown, CT: Wesleyan University Press, 2010.

Lederer, Susan. *Flesh and Blood: Organ Transplantation and Blood Transfusion in Twentieth Century America.* New York: Oxford University Press, 2008.

Lee, Erika. *The Making of Asian-America: A History.* New York: Simon & Schuster, 2016.

Lipsitz, George. *The Possessive Investment in Whiteness: How White People Profit from Identity Politics.* Philadelphia: Temple University Press, 2018.

Lotz, Amanda D. *Cable Guys: Television and Masculinities in the 21st Century.* New York: New York University Press, 2014.

McDougall, Walter A. *The Heavens and the Earth: A Political History of the Space Age.* New York: Basic Books, 1985.

McGee, Heather. *The Sum of Us: What Racism Costs Everyone and How We Can Prosper Together.* London: One World, 2021.

Marchand, Roland. *Advertising the American Dream: Making Way for Modernity, 1920–1940.* Berkeley: University of California Press, 1985.

May, Elaine Tyler. *Homeward Bound: American Families in the Cold War Era.* New York: Basic Books, 1988.

Metzl, Jonathan. *Dying of Whiteness: How the Politics of Racial Resentment Is Killing America's Heartland.* New York: Basic Books, 2019.

Nadel, Alan. *Television in Black-and-White America: Race and National Identity.* Lawrence: University Press of Kansas, 2005.

Nama, Adilifu. *Black Space: Imagining Race in Science Fiction Film.* Austin: University of Texas Press, 2008.

Nygaard, Taylor, and Jorie Lagerwey. *Horrible White People: Gender, Genre, and Television's Precarious Whiteness.* New York: New York University Press, 2020.

Noble, David. *Progress without People: New Technology, Unemployment, and the Message of Resistance.* Toronto: Between the Lines Books, 1995.

Onkst, David. "First a Negro . . . Incidentally a Veteran: Black World War Two Veterans and the G. I. Bill of Rights in the Deep South, 1944–1948," *Journal of Social History* 31, no. 3. (Spring 1998): 517–43.

Parisi, Nicholas. *Rod Serling: His Life, Work, and Imagination.* Jackson: University Press of Mississippi, 2018.

Patterson, James. *Grand Expectations: The United States, 1945–1974.* New York: Oxford University Press, 1996.

Rose, Kenneth D. *One Nation Underground: The Fallout Shelter in American Culture.* New York: New York University Press, 2001.

Rubin, Steven Jay. The Twilight Zone *Encyclopedia.* Chicago: Chicago Review Press, 2018.

Samuel, Lawrence R. *Brought to You By: Postwar Television and the American Dream.* Austin: University of Texas Press, 2001.

———. *Freud on Madison Avenue: Motivation Research and Subliminal Advertising in America.* Philadelphia: University of Pennsylvania Press, 2010.

Sander, Gordon. *The Rise and Twilight of TV's Last Angry Man.* New York: Dutton, 1992.

Scarry, Elaine. *The Body in Pain: The Making and Unmaking of the World.* New York: Oxford University Press, 1987.

Schrecker, Ellen. "Comments on John Earl Haynes, 'The Cold War Debate Continues: A Traditionalist View of Historical Writing on Domestic Communism and Anti-Communism.'" *Journal of Cold War Studies* 2, no. 1 (Winter 2000): 76–115.

———. *Many Are the Crimes: McCarthyism in America.* Princeton, NJ: Princeton University Press, 1999.

Scott, David Meerman, and Richard Jurek. *Marketing the Moon: The Selling of the Apollo Lunar Program.* Cambridge, MA: MIT Press, 2014.

Seed, David. *American Science Fiction and the Cold War: Literature and Film.* Chicago: Fitzroy Dearborn, 1999.

Seldes, George. *Witness to a Century: Encounters with the Noted, Notorious, and the Three SOBs.* New York: Ballantine, 1987.

Serling, Anne. *As I Knew Him: My Dad, Rod Serling.* New York: Citadel, 2013.

Shatan, Chaim F. "Happiness Is a Warm Gun: Militarized Mourning and Ceremonial Vengeance." *Vietnam Generation* 1, no. 3 (1989): 127–51.

Simmons, Steven J. *The Fairness Doctrine and the Media.* Berkeley: University of California Press, 1978.

Simonelli, Frederick J. *American Fuehrer: George Lincoln Rockwell and the American Nazi Party.* Champaign: University of Illinois Press, 1999.

Spigel, Lynn. *Make Room for TV: Television and the Family Ideal in Postwar America.* Chicago: University of Chicago Press, 1992.

Smith, Ken. *Mental Hygiene: Classroom Films, 1940–1970.* New York: Blast Books, 1999.

Santoro, Gene. *Myself When I Am Real: The Life and Music of Charles Mingus.* New York: Oxford University Press, 2001.

Takaki, Ronald. *A Different Mirror: A History of Multicultural America.* New York: Back Bay Books, 2008.

Tichenor, Daniel J. *Dividing Lines: The Politics of Immigration Control in America.* Princeton, NJ: Princeton University Press, 2002.

Tone, Andrea. *The Age of Anxiety: A History of America's Turbulent Affair with Tranquilizers.* New York: Basic Books, 2008.

Tyson, Timothy B. *The Blood of Emmett Till.* New York: Simon & Schuster, 2017.

Weart, Spencer R. *Nuclear Fear.* Cambridge, MA: Harvard University Press, 1988.

Weinstein, David. *The Forgotten Network: DuMont and the Birth of American Television.* Philadelphia: Temple University Press, 2004.

Whitman, James Q. *Hitler's American Model: The United States and the Making of Nazi Race Law.* Princeton, NJ: Princeton University Press, 2018.

Wolfe, Audra J. *Competing with the Soviets: Science, Technology, and the State in Cold War America.* Baltimore: Johns Hopkins University Press, 2013.

Zicree, Marc Scott. The Twilight Zone *Companion,* 2nd ed. Los Angeles: Silman-James Press, 1992.

Index

Index